Shadow
of the
Antichrist

IVAN FOSTER

AMBASSADOR
Belfast • Greenville

Shadow of the Antichrist
Copyright © 1996 Ivan Foster
This edition 1996

ISBN 1 898787 85 9

Published by

AMBASSADOR PRODUCTIONS, LTD.
Providence House
16 Hillview Avenue,
Belfast, BT5 6JR

Emerald House
1 Chick Springs Road, Suite 206
Greenville, South Carolina, 29609

Dedicated to the memory of my father-in-law

CHARLES ALEXANDER BEATTIE, 1908 - 1963

H e had a testimony among his fellow believers as a man of prayer and extensive and penetrating Biblical knowledge. He was a foundation member and later an elder and treasurer in the Gospel Tabernacle, Ballymena, founded by the late Pastor James Kyle Paisley, after his separation from the Baptist Union of Great Britain and Ireland in November1933.

Charles Beattie went to be with Christ on 11th January 1963, aged 54. He was a man I was never privileged to meet, yet the on-going answers to his prayers have benefited and prospered me, my wife Ann, his grandchildren and his great-grandchildren.

The character of Charles Beattie may be gauged from a reference to him in a sermon preached by Pastor Paisley at a Sovereign Grace Advent Testimony meeting in Highgate Road Chapel in London in April 1947. The sermon was later published as an article entitled: **'Reasons why the Great Tribulation must precede the Church's translation.'**

In the article, there is a section which reads: "-There is a young farmer in the church at Ballymena who studies the Scriptures even in the fields at his work. One day he came to me and began to talk about the Coming of the Lord. He said, 'I believe that the tribulation and the manifestation of the Antichrist must precede the Coming of the Lord.'

He asked me to explain to him Revelation 20:4 and 5: 'And I saw thrones, and they sat upon them, and judgment was given unto them: and I saw the souls of them that were beheaded for the witness of Jesus, and for the word of God, and which had not worshipped the beast, neither his image, neither had received his mark upon their foreheads, or in their hands; and they lived and reigned with Christ a thousand years. But the rest of the dead lived not again until the thousand years were finished. *This is the first resurrection.*' Who will take part in the first resurrection, he desired to know. He pointed out that these were those who lived during the reign of the Antichrist and had refused his mark and were martyred for the witness of Jesus and the Word of God. These souls were raised at the first resurrection. Therefore he said Christ could not come until the end of the tribulation and the end of the reign of the Antichrist. It is evident that the Holy Spirit gave this young man illumination as he studied the Scriptures."

That man was Charlie Beattie.

Acknowledgements

In putting my name to this book, I am made to recognise just how much of it belongs to others. I am conscious of how much of what I have put down in these pages has its origins in the expressed thoughts of those, under whose ministry it has been my privilege to sit, or whose writings have profited and guided me. Sadly, it is most likely true that my treatment of the teaching given me has dulled its edge and clouded its beauty. But we hope that it is not so.

I owe much to many a lengthy discussion I had with Dr. John Douglas, my esteemed brother-in-law, back in the days following my conversion. I had the thirst of the new convert and those discussions laid the foundation of my own investigations into the revelation given us in the Bible of those things that the Lord would have us know about the future.

From February 1985 to February 1986 I preached a series of expository messages on the book of the Revelation. I was encouraged to embark on such a study by listening to some tapes of a series of sermons preached by Dr. Alan Cairns in Ballymoney Free Presbyterian Church. It was in listening to those tapes that I realised that such a book as the Revelation contained much that was eminently practical, and its study would provide rich spiritual food for the child of God. I also learned that those portions, that were considered as obscure by many Christians, were not really so at all. It was thus I was prompted to embark on my own pulpit expositions to my congregation in Kilskeery. Some eight years later, I repeated those studies in a simplified form in the morning assemblies of our Christian school in Kilskeery. I gladly acknowledge the help that Dr. Cairn's sermon tapes provided.

I am grateful for the helpful observations and suggestions of my good friend, Mr. Stephen Toms, Secretary of the Sovereign Grace Advent Testimony. From the time that I first mentioned to him that I was considering this project he has encouraged me to proceed.

This publication owes much to the labours and the knowledge of my wife, Ann. She had the privilege of learning the truths contained in this exposition at her father's knee and under the ministry of Pastor Paisley. I would like to think that those times of sweet fellowship she had with her father around God's Word were continued, in some measure at least, in our own times of spiritual fellowship over the last thirty years. I am indebted to her for her many helpful suggestions which, undoubtedly, will have improved the publication. Her patient correcting of the manuscript put the finishing touches to it. If there is a smoothness to the syntax, the credit is hers alone.

To the reader I urge one word of counsel. Read this book with your Bible open at the relevant passage in the book of the Revelation. Follow the example of the Bereans in Acts 17:11. *These were more noble than those in Thessalonica, in that they received the word with all readiness of mind, and searched the scriptures daily, whether those things were so.* May you grow in grace and in the knowledge of our Lord Jesus Christ.

This is only a small labour but I must acknowledge the mercy of my Saviour, the Lord Jesus Christ. Without His grace, this witness for Him could not have been accomplished.

I thank Christ Jesus our Lord, who hath enabled me,
1 Timothy 1:12.

Contents

THE TERRITORIES OF ANTICHRIST

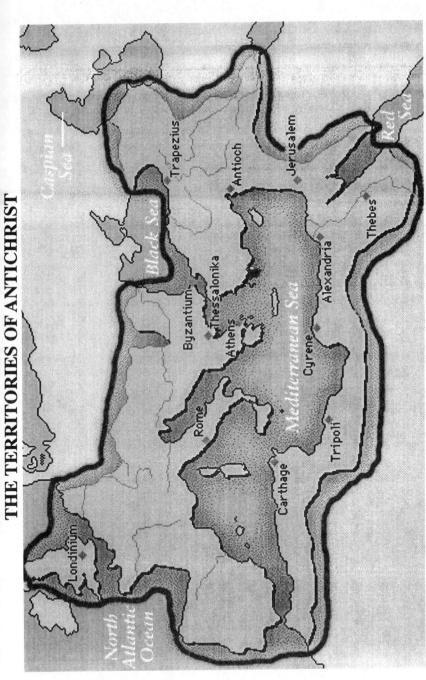

A map of the Ancient Roman Empire, on which the author has emphasised the border, shows the territory over which Antichrist will reign.
(Courtesy of Microsoft Encarta)

Stretching from the border between Scotland and England, in the north, to the Red Sea in the south east, and over to the Euphrates River in the north east, the borders of the Roman Empire excluded Germany which at present is a very important member of the European Community. When the Antichrist's kingdom is consolidated, it will be confined to those territories which comprised the Roman Empire at its zenith. It can be seen that great changes have yet to take place with regard to the present allegiances of those nations which will make up Antichrist's kingdom.

The past and ongoing attempts to force Northern Ireland out of the United Kingdom, and the agitation to have Scotland secede from the United Kingdom are interesting developments in the light of the borders of the old Roman Empire.

Every believer should observe carefully the ebbing and flowing of political alliances and the gradual emergence of a political entity within the confines of the old boundaries of Rome.

The preface of the book
CHAPTER 1:1-3

The Revelation of Jesus Christ, which God gave unto him, to shew unto his servants things which must shortly come to pass; and he sent and signified it by his angel unto his servant John: who bare record of the word of God, and of the testimony of Jesus Christ, and of all things that he saw. Blessed is he that readeth, and they that hear the words of this prophecy, and keep those things which are written therein: for the time is at hand.

The full title of the last book of the Bible is given in its first verse: *the Revelation of Jesus Christ, which God gave unto him, to shew unto his servants things which must shortly come to pass.* Being the last book of the canon of Holy Scripture, it is of special significance. It is the closing word of Christ to His church. It stands in contrast, in many ways, to the first book of the Bible.

In the book of Genesis, you have the creation of the first earth; the entrance of sin and man lost.

In the book of the Revelation, you have the creation of the new earth; the final overthrow of sin and the elect saved.

The first three verses form a fitting and an instructive introduction to the book.

I.   THE FOCAL POINT OF THE BOOK.

This book has been given us by Christ. It is, primarily, *the Revelation of Jesus Christ.* It is His revelation to His people. But it is also a

revelation about Christ.   Peter said, *To him give all the prophets witness, that through his name whosoever believeth in him shall receive
remission of sins*, Acts 10:43.   Though speaking retrospectively of the
prophets who had gone before, Peter's words apply just as surely to
John's prophecies in this book.   The book of the Revelation speaks
much of Christ.   Many view this book as a book about future events and
personalities.   It is true that it reveals things that must shortly come to
pass, but those future things are revealed in relation to Christ.   Thus in
1:7, we have the first of a number of references in which Christ is the
centre of the world's attention as He comes again in glory.   In 1:13, it is
Christ in the midst of the candlesticks.   Again in 4:2 and 5:6, it is Christ
in the midst of heaven's throne.   In chapter 19, He is seen at the head of
the armies of heaven as He comes to destroy Antichrist. In chapter 21:23,
He is the light of the Holy Jerusalem.

I repeat, this book centres upon Christ.   Indeed, it tells us things
about Christ that are only touched upon in other books.   This gives us
all the more reason to study this book.   Christ is the One we should be
looking for when we read its pages.   While He is not the exclusive
subject of the book, I think it may justifiably be said that every subject
and person, dealt with in this book, are set forth in the light of God's
glorious purpose in Christ.

This book being full of Christ, it explains why the devil opposes its
study.   Many have been deceived into thinking that this book should not
be studied, since it is so mystical and obscure that only the most advanced
Christians may benefit from it.   If we look for Christ in this book we
shall find much of Him to the blessing of our souls and we shall also
preserve ourselves from adopting wild notions and theories about some
of the passages that do require careful study.

As a suggestion, look for the PERSON of Christ to be revealed in
this book.

In the very first chapter, there is a detailed description of the glorified Christ walking in the midst of the seven golden candlesticks.   Since
we shall look at that portion in greater detail later, suffice it to say that
such a description is unique in the New Testament.

Again, you will find the POWER of Christ revealed in this book.

Much of the New Testament is taken up with the gospel narrative of
Christ in His humility, walking amongst men.   Here we see Him in the

heavens, robed with glory and power and coming to claim His heritage, promised from all eternity by the Father.

Also, the POSITION of Christ is revealed.

It is so easy to forget, in the midst of the increasingly rebellious deeds and God-defying attitudes of men in the world generally and in our terror-stricken land in particular, that Christ is upon the throne of this world's affairs. A study of this book will leave us refreshed in soul and peaceful in our minds. It provides us with a visit to God's throne room, there to behold the sovereign power of Jehovah at work in the midst of earth's kingdoms.

II. THE CLARITY OF THE BOOK.

It is intended that this book should be a revelation. The Greek word *apokalupsis*, translated by our English word *revelation*, appears for the first time in our New Testament in Luke 2:32. *A light to lighten the Gentiles, and the glory of thy people Israel.* Here it is translated by the word *lighten*, that which sheds light and reveals. It is the purpose of God in giving His people this book that they may be enlightened by it, not confused and misled. What an enemy to zeal and progress ignorance among God's people is! Hosea was aware of this. *My people are destroyed for lack of knowledge*, Hosea 4:6. Would Noah ever have built his ark if he had been ignorant of what the future held? Would Pharaoh ever have built his granaries, had he been ignorant of the famine that was coming? Likewise, much of the apathy and listlessness and, much worse, the worldliness and compromise among God's people can be put down to ignorance concerning what lies ahead of this world.

We have no excuse for such ignorance. So said Paul to the first century Christians. *But of the times and the seasons, brethren, ye have no need that I write unto you. For yourselves know perfectly that the day of the Lord so cometh as a thief in the night. For when they shall say, Peace and safety; then sudden destruction cometh upon them, as travail upon a woman with child; and they shall not escape. But ye, brethren, are not in darkness, that that day should overtake you as a thief,* 1 Thessalonians 5:1-4. Men read the sky in order to make preparation for foul weather. How important it is to read the Bible in order to be prepared for evil times that are repeatedly referred to in the New

Testament by the inspired writers! These prophetical passages are written for our learning: *they are written for our admonition, upon whom the ends of the world are come*, 1 Corinthians 10:11.

The thought of revealing is seen also in the word *shew*. If we look at the first occurrence of the word *shew* (deiknuo), it will give us a clear understanding of its meaning. *Again, the devil taketh him up into an exceeding high mountain, and sheweth him all the kingdoms of the world, and the glory of them*, Matthew 4:8. The meaning is plain. The devil wished Christ to see the kingdoms of this world and their glory. He thought he could thus entice Christ to fall down and worship him by offering the kingdoms to Him. God would have us see plainly that which He reveals in this book.

The word *signify* (semaino) further endorses this truth. It means to *indicate or to make known*. The first use of it demonstrates this. *And I, if I be lifted up from the earth, will draw all men unto me. This he said, signifying what death he should die*, John 12:32-33. If there was one truth the Saviour wished His disciples to understand, it was that of His death. Let it be clear in every Christian's mind that Christ intended this book to be a source of enlightenment and instruction to His church. Through these three words, *revelation, shew* and *signifed,* found in the opening verse, we have a three-fold witness to this intention.

The revelation was to be made known to his servants (*doulos*). This further highlights the practical nature of this book. It is not a book for speculators or vainglorious scholars seeking abstract knowledge or for mere dabblers in prophecy. It is not a book filled with so much mystical symbolism that its interpretation is a matter of guesswork and speculation. No! It is for the *doulos*, the bondslaves of Christ. Here is information for the Saviour's workmen. Is this not a day for such information? It is surely evident from the confused and disordered state of many professing Christians and many denominations, that they stand in immediate need of a clear revelation of God's will for these days of apostasy. Here then is the book for us all.

How relevant this book is! It reveals things which must shortly come to pass for *the time is at hand*. Each passing year since John wrote this book has made it all the more relevant. Living as we do, within the confines of a lifespan of some seventy years, a century is to us a much longer period than it is to Him with Whom *one day is as a thousand years, and a thousand years as one day,* 2 Peter 3:8. These phrases are not intended to suggest that John or the early church generally expected the return of Christ to take place within their lifetime. Rather, it refers to the duration of the intervening period of time before the prophecies begin to be fulfilled, as it was perceived by the Lord. To Him the time was at hand.

The phrase, *must shortly come to pass,* is to be interpreted as a reference, not to the nearness of the events, but to the shortness of the time taken for the events to occur once they begin. The words of Christ, in Matthew 24:15-22, bear out this interpretation. There Christ warns of the swiftness with which events will take place, when once the abomination of desolation is displayed in the temple in Jerusalem. He urges immediate flight for the believers in Jerusalem with no delaying, not even for the packing of a few items of clothing. So great is going to be the persecution unleashed by this event that there would be little hope of the survival of any of the elect, if God did not shorten those days. Christ has promised, however, that for *the elect's sake those days shall be shortened,* verse 22. It is not a matter of the days having less hours but rather of events happening swiftly and coming to a climax in a short time.

In a special way, I believe the book of the Revelation is a means whereby God's people may put their hands upon that weapon that is so much needed today. That weapon was wielded very successfully by the Issacharites in the days of David. *And of the children of Issachar, which were men that had understanding of the times, to know what Israel ought to do,* 1 Chronicles 12:32. The knowledge these men possessed did much to confirm David upon his throne and so establish his kingdom. Such knowledge is needed today. Daniel sought to understand those revelations that were given to him regarding the last times. He was refused such knowledge for it was not for his day. God operates the *need to know* rule. If you do not need to know a matter, then you will not be given knowledge of that matter. So Daniel's plea was rejected. *And I heard, but I understood not: then said I, O my Lord, what shall be the end of these things? And he said, Go thy way, Daniel: for the words are closed up and sealed till the time of the end. Many shall be purified, and made white, and tried; but the wicked shall do wickedly: and none of the wicked shall understand; but the wise shall understand,* Daniel

12:8-10. There is a need today for the discretion of Joseph, who in his day guided Pharaoh aright. In reply to Joseph's advice for Pharaoh to seek out a man discreet and wise, Pharaoh said, *Forasmuch as God hath shewed thee all this, there is none so discreet and wise as thou art,* Genesis 41:39. The word *discreet* is the same Hebrew word as is translated *understand* in Daniel 12:10. As we face the perilous times spoken of by Paul, we surely need such wisdom and understanding of the times.

III.   THE NATURE OF THE BOOK.

There is a threefold description of the book given in verses 2 and 3.

1. It is referred to as the Word of God, verse 2. Let us handle it accordingly. The doctrine of the inspiration of the Holy Scriptures is much attacked today. It is overtly attacked by those who are openly the enemies of Christ. Though they occupy, in many instances, positions within the professing church of Christ and adorn themselves with titles that betoken allegiance to Christ, yet they utter words that indicate that they are enemies of God and His Truth. As it was said of Jacob, so it might be said of them: *The voice is Jacob's voice, but the hands are the hands of Esau,* Genesis 27:22. The bitter words spoken against the Bible by many clerics belie their pretended servitude to Christ.

But there are many covert attacks upon this doctrine. The most notable takes place under the guise of improving the Authorised or King James translation of the Holy Scriptures. One of the latest such improvement is to be found in the New International Version of the Scriptures. It has gained much favour among many evangelicals. They speak loudly of it being an improvement upon the Authorised version. That is not so. Rather, it is an attack upon God's Word in exactly the same vein as that which is mounted by more notorious translations such as the New English Bible and the Good News Bible. The attack is carried out more cautiously and more subtly but it has the same evil intent, irrespective of its endorsement by many who truly love the Lord.

That which was given to John was the Word of God. That which John passed on to the churches was the Word of God. That which we have miraculously preserved for us in our Authorised Version is the Word of God. What was said of the Old Testament, *For the prophecy came not in old time by the will of man: but holy men of God spake as they were moved by the Holy Ghost,* 2 Peter 1:21, may rightly be said of this book. John wrote that which was given him of God.

2. It is referred to as the testimony of Jesus Christ. This is a message from *the faithful and true witness* to His people to tell them of things that must shortly come to pass. Many have found the contents of this book too fantastic to be taken literally. For me, it is sufficient for the Lord Jesus to say it, for me to believe it, no matter how fantastic human logic may claim it to be. It is unbelief that has fathered various notions and lines of interpretation in order to avoid the simple acceptance of what is said in this book as literal, where such a literal interpretation does not conflict with that established and universally accepted rule of biblical interpretation, which requires us to distinguish between parabolic language and literal language, the metaphorical or allegorical and the literal.

You have the chain of revelation in these verses. God the Father gave the revelation to His Son and He, by the inspiration of the Holy Spirit, gave it to John, who in turn distributed it to the churches.

3. The faithfulness of the record is given. John says that ALL he saw he wrote, verse 2. This is a full, a faithful and a finished account of what Christ gave to John.

As John wrote, so ought preachers to preach. We must not allow prejudice or the fear of man to cause us to waver in our allegiance to the whole counsel of God. As it says in Proverbs 11:26, regarding withholding corn, *he that withholdeth corn, the people shall curse him.* How much more will the people from whom the bread of life has been withheld not rise to curse such faithless preaching on that day.

IV. THE BENEFITS DERIVED FROM READING THIS BOOK.

There is a blessing awaiting the reader at the beginning of this book. *Blessed is he that readeth, and they that hear the words of this prophecy, and keep those things which are written therein,* verse 3. The book also closes with a blessing, for in the last chapter it says, *Behold, I come quickly: blessed is he that keepeth the sayings of the prophecy of this book,* 22:7. This book is bound by blessings. It carries a guarantee of blessing. This is an exclusive feature of this book. While a blessing is generally promised to the reader of the Bible, this is the only book in the Bible which carries such a specific promise to that end.

Please notice how we obtain the blessing here promised.

READ. It is our privilege to study privately the words of God closely and to meditate upon them, to read so as to have them speak to us. *When thou goest, it shall lead thee; when thou sleepest, it shall keep thee; and when thou awakest, it shall talk with thee,* Proverbs 6:22. We really have begun to read God's word when it starts talking to us.

HEAR. This is a reference to the public hearing of God's word. The singular *he* is changed to the plural *they*. Reading is primarily a private affair while hearing is something done in the company of other believers. Is there not a word here for preachers? The Lord intended this book to be preached! There are some preachers who believe it to be a display of superior grace to proclaim ignorance of the prophetic scriptures. They speak of them as having little or no importance. They seem to show no concern at being ignorant of what God means by them and deem the pursuit of an understanding as some form of fanaticism that is to be avoided. What little honour would be given to a man who openly professed little knowledge of the Scripture's teaching on the atonement or of pardon for sins or the deity of the Lord Jesus Christ! It is no excuse to say that there is much confusion about prophecy and that there are many conflicting views and theories on the subject. That may well be so, but the variety of views on all the cardinal doctrines of the Word of God is much more profuse than the number of views on the doctrine of the last things. It is the minister's duty to *study to show himself approved unto God*. It belongs to the lazy schoolboy to complain that he found his homework too hard and therefore did not attempt it. It ought not to be the attitude of the man of God.

KEEP. The word means to *attend to diligently, to guard*. This shows the value of this book. It is to be treasured. The word is used of the action of those guarding a prison. (See Matthew 28:4 - *keepers*, and Acts 24:23 - *keep*.)

Those who thus read, hear and keep the truths of this book are assured of a blessing. Is it not the case that those who read, hear and keep God's word shall get to Heaven? Here is the way whereby God converts sinners. He addresses the sinner through His word. He who hears what God has to say and heeds it, shall be saved.

The greeting of the apostle

CHAPTER 1:4-8

John to the seven churches which are in Asia: Grace be unto you, and peace, from him which is, and which was, and which is to come; and from the seven Spirits which are before his throne; and from Jesus Christ, who is the faithful witness, and the first begotten of the dead, and the prince of the kings of the earth. Unto him that loved us, and washed us from our sins in his own blood, and hath made us kings and priests unto God and his Father; to him be glory and dominion for ever and ever. Amen.
Behold, he cometh with clouds; and every eye shall see him, and they also which pierced him: and all kindreds of the earth shall wail because of him. Even so, Amen. I am Alpha and Omega, the beginning and the ending, saith the Lord, which is, and which was, and which is to come, the Almighty.

T hese words serve to remind us that we are looking at an epistle sent, first and foremost, to the seven churches in Asia. Being an epistle, it opens with the commonly used apostolic greeting. (Cp Romans 1:7, 1 Cor 1:3, 2 Cor 1:2, Gal 1:3 etc.)

I.   THE DESIRE OF THE APOSTLE'S HEART.

Grace and peace. These are two most valuable blessings. It is what the apostles desired most for the churches, as we note in the opening greetings at the commencement of nearly all of the New Testament's epistles. How highly we ought to value grace and peace! How earnestly we ought to seek after God's grace! God's free unmerited favour is the concise definition of grace. To abide in the place of God's favour is something to be greatly coveted. We should be prepared to jettison anything and everything in order to enjoy it continually. *Let them curse, but bless thou*, Psalm 109:28. We ought to be ready to bear all that man may heap upon us in order to retain God's blessing. Where there is grace, there is peace, *the peace of God which passeth all understanding*. How rich is the man, the woman, the church, in which the peace of God reigns. To have peace in our soul, in our conscience, with our neighbour, and above all with God, is to be blessed indeed.

Grace and peace. Note that the two go together. We can never know God's peace without the experience of God's grace. Graceless hearts and lives know nothing of true peace. *There is no peace, saith my God, to the wicked*, Isaiah 57:21.

II. THE SOURCE OF ALL BLESSING.

The Triune Jehovah - Father, Son and Holy Spirit - is the source.

From him which is, and which was, and which is to come. Here is the name of the Eternal and Unchangeable God, the 'I AM' of Exodus 3:13-14. *And Moses said unto God, Behold, when I come unto the children of Israel, and shall say unto them, The God of your fathers hath sent me unto you; and they shall say to me, What is his name? what shall I say unto them? And God said unto Moses, I AM THAT I AM: and he said, Thus shalt thou say unto the children of Israel, I AM hath sent me unto you.*

The seven Spirits which are before his throne. This is a title of the Holy Spirit. It refers to His seven-fold perfection, seven being the number in Scripture that is associated with perfection and fullness. In Isaiah 11:2, The Holy Spirit is described as *the **spirit of the LORD** . . . . the **spirit of wisdom and understanding**, the **spirit of counsel and might**, the **spirit of knowledge** and **of the fear of the LORD**.* Here is His seven-fold mode of operation. On Christ the fullness of the Holy Spirit rested.

From Jesus Christ, who is the faithful witness, and the first begotten of the dead, and the prince of the kings of the earth. Is there not a mention here of the three offices that our Saviour fills? He is our Prophet - *the faithful witness*. He is our Priest - *the first begotten of the dead*. He is our King - *the prince of the kings of the earth*. The Shorter Catechism gives us a splendid statement of this truth. 'Christ, as our Redeemer, executeth the offices of a prophet, of a priest, and of a king, both in his estate of humiliation and exaltation.'

'Christ executeth the office of a prophet, in revealing to us, by his word and Spirit, the will of God for our salvation.'

'Christ executeth the office of a priest, in his once offering up of himself a sacrifice to satisfy divine justice, and reconcile us to God; and in making continual intercession for us.'

'Christ executeth the office of a king, in subduing us to himself, in ruling and defending us, and in restraining and conquering all his and our enemies.' (Answers to questions 23-26.)

Here then is the source of all our blessings. They come from the FATHER, conveyed to us by the HOLY SPIRIT through the LORD JESUS, our mediator.

III. THE SONG OF THE SAINTS.

There is a natural sequence of thought to be observed in John moving from a reference to Christ and His death and resurrection to a song of praise. This is the first of a number of songs in this book. Though the book deals much with judgment, there is much singing. The night of the judgment of God in Egypt was also a night of deliverance and singing for Israel, Exodus 15:1. Was not the night of the Saviour's betrayal also a night of singing? Matthew 36:30. Was not the night of the sufferings of Paul and Silas also a night of singing? Acts 16:25. We need not lose our song in the midst of the tribulations of this world. Strange to relate, the roaring of the flames of the martyr fires was often accompanied by the voice of the singing victim, as the sufferer's soul was carried upward in praise and song before it was borne upward to God, when released by the flames from its earthly tabernacle. May God be pleased to give His people a song in these dark days.

Note what it was that prompted the song. The song is *unto him that loved us, and washed us from our sins in his own blood, and hath made us kings and priests unto God and his Father*, verses 5-6. It was the thought of the Saviour's love, His shedding of His blood to cleanse us and His fashioning of us into kings and priests unto God. When we think of what we were, what was required for our redemption and to what heights we have been lifted, who can refrain from singing? Does not a silent church indicate that there is little preaching of and little meditation upon these glorious truths? All praise be to our Saviour, for the work of our redemption from guilt to glory was His alone.

See what Christ by His grace has made us: *kings and priests*. Note the order. We are to be priests to serve the Lord by offering the sacrifices of praise, 1 Peter 2:5. But we can only be priests, mighty in prayer and intercession, after we have become kings who rule and reign in the power of Christ. A powerless church is a prayerless church. It is a church that knows little of the victory that is in Christ.

See what it is we should sing. *To Him be glory and dominion for ever and ever. Amen,* verse 6. Those whose hearts rightly praise the Saviour are those who desire His honour and His glory to be manifested among men.

IV. THE SPLENDOUR OF THE SAVIOUR'S COMING.

John's soul is carried upward and forward and he sees by faith the return of Christ. Is this not the direction that our souls will take when we worship the Lord in Spirit and in truth? The spiritually-elevated soul will ever be conscious of that glorious event, the return of Christ. Is not indifference to His return a mark of carnality? A lively, industrious, conscientious church is one that ever contemplates the Saviour's promised return. *While the bridegroom tarried, they all slumbered and slept,* Matthew 25:5. Let us not sleep in indifference but toil and sing in anticipation of His return. *And that, knowing the time, that now it is high time to awake out of sleep: for now is our salvation nearer than when we believed. The night is far spent, the day is at hand: let us therefore cast off the works of darkness, and let us put on the armour of light. Let us walk honestly, as in the day; not in rioting and drunkenness, not in chambering and wantonness, not in strife and envying. But put ye on the Lord Jesus Christ, and make not provision for the flesh, to fulfil the lusts thereof,* Romans 13:11-14. *Therefore let us not sleep, as do others; but let us watch and be sober. For they that sleep sleep in the night; and they that be drunken are drunken in the night. But let us, who are of the day, be sober, putting on the breastplate of faith and love; and for an helmet, the hope of salvation. For God hath not appointed us to wrath, but to obtain salvation by our Lord Jesus Christ, who died for us, that, whether we wake or sleep, we should live together with him,* 1 Thessalonians 5:6-10.

Notice in these words of John in verse 7:-

1. The coming of Christ is central to the creed of the saints. *He cometh with clouds.* The Lord Jesus is coming again. That is the expectation of the church. He has clearly stated that He will return. *In my Father's house are many mansions: if it were not so, I would have told you. I go to prepare a place for you. And if I go and prepare a place for you, I will come again, and receive you unto myself; that where I am, there ye may be also,* John 14:2-3. This promise was emphasised upon His ascension. *And while they looked stedfastly toward heaven as he went up, behold, two men stood by them in white apparel; which also said, Ye men of Galilee, why stand ye gazing up into heaven? this same Jesus, which is taken up from you into heaven, shall so come in like manner as ye have seen him go into heaven,* Acts 1:10-11. As His ascension was marked by clouds so shall His return. Nahum tells us that *the LORD hath his way in the whirlwind and in the storm, and the clouds are the dust of his feet,* Nahum 1:3. The heavens shall be set astir when the Lord comes again.

2. The coming of Christ shall be manifest. Every eye will see Him coming. The first to see Him will be those who look for Him, whose eyes and thoughts never stray from the expectation of His return.

The unbelieving world will also see Him. Those who will have given allegiance to Antichrist and thereby denied and denounced Jehovah will see Him to their utter consternation.

Special reference is given to Israel. The appellation used is not one of the many names of endearment bestowed by the Lord upon His ancient people. No, rather it is that title of shame: *they also which pierced him.* That is their title today. That awful sin stands yet against their name. Though popes and parliaments and councils may decree pardon and mouth forgiveness, the crime stands unforgiven in heaven.

3. The coming of Christ will initiate mourning. The word *wail* means *to cut down.* It is a sorrow so acute that it causes fainting. The word appears in Matthew 21:8 and is used of the people cutting down branches and spreading them in the path of Christ as He entered Jerusalem. The return of Christ will cut down the proud hearts of unbelievers and lay them in the dust before Christ. *And then shall appear the sign of the Son of man in heaven: and then shall all the tribes of the earth mourn, and they shall see the Son of man coming in the clouds of heaven with power and great glory,* Matthew 24:30. Earth's day of despising Christ and mocking of His message of mercy will end and the Day of the Lord will begin. A fuller picture of the despair of the Christ-rejecting worshipper of Antichrist is given in chapter 6:12-17.

Reference to the coming of Christ prompts a longing within the heart of the believer. *Even so, Amen.* The coming of the Saviour and the consequent overthrow of evil is longed for by the true people of God. Every reference to His return will bring a fervent 'Amen' from the child of God as it did with John.

V. THE SIGNATURE OF THE KING.

This section ends with the signature of the Lord Jesus. *I am Alpha and Omega, the beginning and the ending, saith the Lord, which is, and which was, and which is to come, the Almighty.* It is a declaration of His deity.

The title He uses incorporates that used of Jehovah in the Old Testament. *Who hath wrought and done it, calling the generations from the beginning? I the LORD* (Jehovah), *the first, and with the last; I am he,* Isaiah 41:4. *Thus saith the LORD the King of Israel, and his redeemer the LORD of hosts; I am the first, and I am the last; and beside me there is no God, Isaiah 44:6. Hearken unto me, O Jacob and Israel, my called; I am he; I am the first, I also am the last,* Isaiah 48:12.

It is also the title used of the Father in verse 4 - *Him which is, and which was, and which is to come.* The Lord Jesus and the Father are equal in power and glory as stated in the Westminster Confession of Faith. 'The Son of God, the second person in the Trinity, being very and eternal God, of one substance, and equal with the Father . . . . . ', Chapter VIII Paragraph 2. This bears out what the Saviour said in John 10:30: *I and my Father are one.* The highest possible view of Christ will be engendered by a study of this book.

Christic in the midst of the churches

CHAPTER 1:9-20

I John, who also am your brother, and companion in tribulation, and in the kingdom and patience of Jesus Christ, was in the isle that is called Patmos, for the word of God, and for the testimony of Jesus Christ. I was in the Spirit on the Lord's day, and heard behind me a great voice, as of a trumpet, saying, I am Alpha and Omega, the first and the last: and, What thou seest, write in a book, and send it unto the seven churches which are in Asia; unto Ephesus, and unto Smyrna, and unto Pergamos, and unto Thyatira, and unto Sardis, and unto Philadelphia, and unto Laodicea. And I turned to see the voice that spake with me. And being turned, I saw seven golden candlesticks; and in the midst of the seven candlesticks one like unto the Son of man, clothed with a garment down to the foot, and girt about the paps with a golden girdle. His head and his hairs were white like wool, as white as snow; and his eyes were as a flame of fire; and his feet like unto fine brass, as if they burned in a furnace; and his voice as the sound of many waters. And he had in his right hand seven stars: and out of his mouth went a sharp twoedged sword: and his countenance was as the sun shineth in his strength. And when I saw him, I fell at his feet as dead. And he laid his right hand upon me, saying unto me, Fear not; I am the first and the last: I am he that liveth, and was dead; and, behold, I am alive for evermore, Amen; and have the keys of hell and of death. Write the things which thou hast seen, and the things which are, and the things which shall be hereafter; the mystery of the seven stars which thou sawest in my right hand, and the seven golden candlesticks. The seven stars are the angels of the seven churches: and the seven candlesticks which thou sawest are the seven churches.

No one is ever the poorer for serving Christ, no matter what reproach may be heaped upon one's head. Here John, the exiled apostle of Christ, is honoured and blessed with a glorious vision of Christ.

I.   THE PLACE WHERE THE VISION WAS GIVEN.

The isle that is called Patmos, verse 9. This a small island in the Aegean Sea some 6-8 miles long and about 1 mile broad. It has a circumference of approximately 15 miles. It was most likely uninhabited in the day of John's banishment. John may have been separated from his congregation but he was not separated from his Saviour. How often Christ has hallowed the prison cell or the lonely place of exile to those who suffer for His cause! Heaven came down on Patmos during John's exile or should we say that John visited heaven from Patmos. The worst tortures that evil men have sought to devise against the saints of God have been made by the Saviour to be but stepping stones to glory for the afflicted believer.

II.   THE PERSON TO WHOM THE VISION WAS GIVEN.

1. His identity. The writer again introduces himself. This use of his name by John stands in contrast to his concealing of his name in his gospel. There he never named himself but rather referred to himself as *that disciple* or *that disciple whom Jesus loved*. See John 13:23, 18:15, 20:2, 21:20. The use of his name in the gospel may have been misinterpreted as boastful when linked to the special status that was claimed for the writer, regarding the love that Christ had for him, while, in the book before us, the use of the name of the writer is required as a matter of authenticity and authority.

2. His affinity. Many years before, the Saviour had indicated to John and his brother James, that they would drink of the cup of suffering, Matthew 20:20-23. James had been slain by Herod, Acts 12:1-2, and now John was exiled for the gospel's sake. He was suffering for *the word of God and the testimony of Jesus Christ*. If we suffer, then let it be for this reason. If we suffer for this reason then let us rejoice, 1 Peter 2:19, 3:14-17.

Though separated from the churches in Asia he was their *brother, and companion in tribulation, and in the kingdom and patience of Jesus Christ.* The word *companion* means *partaker.* It is used by Paul when referring to the Gentiles sharing in the riches of the gospel when they were grafted into the olive tree, Romans 11:17. John considered his tribulation but a sharing in that which was being generally suffered by the saints of God.

As the Saviour indicated to John, entrance into the kingdom of God and its honours and glories is linked with suffering and tribulation. This truth was repeated often by the writers of the New Testament. *Confirming the souls of the disciples, and exhorting them to continue in the faith, and that we must through much tribulation enter into the kingdom of God,* Acts 14:22. *And if children, then heirs; heirs of God, and joint-heirs with Christ; if so be that we suffer with him, that we may be also glorified together,* Romans 8:17. *If we suffer, we shall also reign with him: if we deny him, he also will deny us,* 2 Timothy 2:12. *Beloved, think it not strange concerning the fiery trial which is to try you, as though some strange thing happened unto you: but rejoice, inasmuch as ye are partakers of Christ's sufferings; that, when his glory shall be revealed, ye may be glad also with exceeding joy,* 2 Peter 4:12-13.

The Lord would have none of His people under any delusions regarding the trials that they will face on their pilgrimage to heaven. Such information makes trials to become thereby a means of encouragement, James 1:2-4.

3. His spirituality. *I was in the Spirit on the Lord's day*, verse 10. Being on his own did not deter John from observing the Lord's day. I remember reading one old preacher's statement to young people in which he gave them a simple test by which they could gauge their heart's affections for Christ. 'If you were alone and could do what you wish, without the slightest fear of your actions ever being known, how would you behave? Your answer will tell you the state of your heart in the sight of God.' John was alone. He had not the company of others to require him to observe the Lord's day or report on him if he did not, but nevertheless he did.

The Lord's day ought to be sanctified by Christians by endeavouring to cultivate a spirit of worship that our labours and duties on other days hinder us achieving. While all our duties ought to be carried out with a view to God's glory and a consciousness of His observation of us, on the Lord's day there is a specific requirement for us to enter into the Spirit in order rightly to undertake the duties of that day which are distinct from those of all other days. *God is a Spirit: and they that worship him must worship him in spirit and in truth*, John 4:24.

Here is a picture of first century holiness. Does it not contrast greatly with those views held by many 'fundamentalists' and 'Bible-believers' who contend that Sabbath observation is a legalistic anachronism? Such a view has infiltrated denominations, the creed of which strictly requires Sabbatarianism. The Westminster Confession of Faith teaches the observation of the Sabbath. Yet it has become a thing that is all too common for the Lord's day to be but an extension of Saturday, a day for trips to the seaside and going on holiday and visiting friends, when it ought to be, as the Confession of Faith puts it, a day 'kept holy unto the Lord, when men, after due preparing of their hearts, and ordering of their common affairs before-hand, do not only observe an holy rest all the day from their own works, words, and thoughts about their worldly employments and recreations; but also are taken up the whole time in the public and private exercises of his worship, and in the duties of necessity and mercy.' As the world returns to first century paganism, let the church return to first century Sabbatarianism.

Notice that John *heard*, then *turned* and then *saw*. Let us listen to the Word of God and it will generate a desire to know more of God. Remember, it was after Moses had listened to the voice of God on the Mount that he expressed the desire to see His glory, Exodus 33:18.

It should also be noticed that John had to turn to see Christ. We have a natural propensity to face away from God. Even the most holy of men are subject to this drawing away from God, this decline from His presence. But let us submit to the Word of God and we will be drawn to see the Lord as was John here.

III.   THE PARTICULARS OF THE VISION GIVEN.

1. Where Christ was seen. Verses 12-13. He was seen in the midst of the seven candlesticks which represented the churches in Asia, verse 20. As it was with the three suffering saints in Daniel 3:25, Christ stood with His people in this their hour of trial. History shows that Christ has never been more present with His people than in their times of trouble. The experiences of the Pauls, the Johns, the Rutherfords, the Bunyans and countless thousands of others clearly demonstrate that. There is not one Ulster Free Presbyterian, who lived through the trying days of the middle 1960s and the early 1970s in Northern Ireland, but has looked back upon those days and pined for the sense of Christ's presence amongst us that was then experienced.

2. How Christ was dressed. *Clothed with a garment down to the foot, and girt about the paps with a golden girdle*, verse 13. He was dressed in His High Priestly garments. How appropriate for Him to appear so dressed. He is the Interceder for His people. *Seeing then that we have a great high priest, that is passed into the heavens, Jesus the Son of God, let us hold fast our profession. For we have not an high priest which cannot be touched with the feeling of our infirmities; but was in all points tempted like as we are, yet without sin. Let us therefore come boldly unto the throne of grace, that we may obtain mercy, and find grace to help in time of need*, Hebrews 4:14-16. *Wherefore he is able also to save them to the uttermost that come unto God by him, seeing he ever liveth to make intercession for them*, Hebrews 7:25. When faced by trials and enduring afflictions then think on this-the Son of God pleads for you before His Father's face. What harm can come to us if that be so? It is by forgetting this that we rob ourselves of comfort and add to our miseries when faced by the devil's temptations. Would Peter have acted as he did when tried, had he but remembered the words of the Saviour spoken to him before he denied the Lord? *But I have prayed for thee, that thy faith fail not: and when thou art converted, strengthen thy brethren*, Luke 22:32.

3. How Christ is described. There is a sevenfold description of the Saviour.

His head. *His head and his hairs were white like wool, as white as snow*. The description given here is the same as that given of the Father, the Ancient of Days. *I beheld till the thrones were cast down, and the Ancient of days did sit, whose garment was white as snow, and the hair of his head like the pure wool: his throne was like the fiery flame, and his wheels as burning fire*, Daniel 7:9. The eternal equality of the Son with the Father is thus set forth yet again.

His eyes. *His eyes were as a flame of fire.* The piercing flame is used to describe His eyes, reminding us of the all-seeing observance that the Saviour exercises both within His church and over His enemies.

The LORD is in his holy temple, the LORD'S throne is in heaven: his eyes behold, his eyelids try, the children of men, Psalm 11:4. *The eyes of the LORD are in every place, beholding the evil and the good*, Proverbs 15:3. *Neither is there any creature that is not manifest in his sight: but all things are naked and opened unto the eyes of him with whom we have to do*, Hebrews 4:13.

His feet. *And his feet like unto fine brass, as if they burned in a furnace.* These are the feet that stood amidst the fire of His Father's wrath against sin, even the sin of the elect for whom the Lord Jesus came to die. These feet withstood the fire of judgment even as the brass of the altar (Exodus 27:1-8) was able to withstand the fire that consumed the sacrifices that were offered daily. The purity of Christ is symbolised by the brass. He is *the One Who did no sin, neither was guile found in his mouth*, 1 Peter 2:22. Only One Who was sinless could stand amidst the fire of wrath and not be consumed.

These burnished feet shall trample down all His and our enemies. *I saw in the night visions, and, behold, one like the Son of man came with the clouds of heaven, and came to the Ancient of days, and they brought him near before him. And there was given him dominion, and glory, and a kingdom, that all people, nations, and languages, should serve him: his dominion is an everlasting dominion, which shall not pass away, and his kingdom that which shall not be destroyed*, Daniel 7:13-14. *For he must reign, till he hath put all enemies under his feet*, 1 Corinthians 15:25. There will be an utter crushing of His enemies under those feet of brass. How much wiser to cast yourself down at His nail-pierced feet and obtain mercy now than to oppose Him until He rises to put down all rebellion. *Be wise now therefore, O ye kings: be instructed, ye judges of the earth. Serve the LORD with fear, and rejoice with trembling. Kiss the Son, lest he be angry, and ye perish from the way, when his wrath is kindled but a little. Blessed are all they that put their trust in him*, Psalm 2:10-12.

His voice. *And his voice as the sound of many waters.* What authority and power there is in that voice! *Verily, verily, I say unto you, The hour is coming, and now is, when the dead shall hear the voice of the Son of God: and they that hear shall live*, John 5:25. It is an unmistakable voice. *And when he putteth forth his own sheep, he goeth before them, and the sheep follow him: for they know his voice*, John 10:4.

Every one that is of the truth heareth my voice, John 18:37. This is the voice that halted Saul the persecutor on the road to Damascus and changed his life forever, Acts 9:4. This is a voice that cannot be opposed. Who can speak in the presence of the Niagara Falls and challenge the mighty power of that cataract? So sinful men shall be silent in the presence of Christ the Judge when He comes *to execute judgment upon all, and to convince all that are ungodly among them of all their ungodly deeds which they have ungodly committed, and of all their hard speeches which ungodly sinners have spoken against him*, Jude 15. The word *convince* means *to speak against*. They who have spoken against Christ will find Him speaking against them and silencing them in their guilt by His words on that great and terrible day of wrath. In this vision John sees Christ standing. How often Christ sat when He spoke to men during His earthly ministry! Read Matthew 5:1, 13:1-2, 15:29, 24:3 and 26:55 for examples of the Saviour sitting among men. His rising and speaking is the Lord Jesus Christ assuming the posture of a judge preparing to pass sentence. *Arise, O God, judge the earth: for thou shalt inherit all nations*, Psalm 82:8. *Therefore wait ye upon me, saith the LORD, until the day that I rise up to the prey: for my determination is to gather the nations, that I may assemble the kingdoms, to pour upon them mine indignation, even all my fierce anger: for all the earth shall be devoured with the fire of my jealousy*, Zephaniah 3:8.

His right hand. *And he had in his right hand seven stars*. Here is the Saviour's sceptre. We are told in verse 20 that the stars are the angels of the seven churches. The word for angel is *aggelos*. It means *messenger*. Angels are the messengers of God. *Aggelos* is used of John the Baptist, Matthew 11:10. The seven stars symbolise the ministers of the seven churches in Asia who are the messengers of God unto the churches.

The preacher of the Word of Christ is His chief instrument of rule amongst His people. *Obey them that have the rule over you, and submit yourselves: for they watch for your souls, as they that must give account, that they may do it with joy, and not with grief: for that is unprofitable for you*, Hebrews 13:17. The sceptre has no power of itself but it derives its power from the one who holds it. We do not believe in any mystical priestly power pertaining to the office of a minister. Rather, the minister's power is derived from his relationship to Christ. Many ministers have no power. They are like Samson. They have departed from the Lord and have forfeited His power. But those who walk with God have power, even the authority of Christ and must be obeyed in the Lord. There is a useful analogy of this truth in the sceptre of Ahasuerus the king in the book of Esther. It was by the pointing of the sceptre that the king made known his will and manifested his favour. Those who approached the king were required to acknowledge the power of the sceptre by touching it, by submitting to it, 4:11 and 5:2. Preaching is an ordinance of God. It is His power unto salvation. To despise it is to dishonour God and incur His wrath.

His mouth. *And out of his mouth went a sharp twoedged sword.* Out of the mouth of Christ goes forth a sharp two-edged sword. God has put forth His power in Creation by the word of His mouth. He has and He will again, in a universal fashion, put forth His power in judgment against His enemies by the word of His mouth. When the Word of God goes forth powerfully in mercy, the sinner who is the subject of that mercy is regenerated. *Being born again, not of corruptible seed, but of incorruptible, by the word of God, which liveth and abideth for ever*, 1 Peter 1:23. When the Word of God goes forth powerfully in judgment, then the subjects of that judgment will be cut off forever.

This sword is the sword of destruction which, according to 19:15, the world shall see when Christ returns and by which He shall smite the rebellious nations of the earth. Paul, in 2 Thessalonians 2:8, tells us that Antichrist shall be destroyed by this very weapon. *And then shall that Wicked be revealed, whom the Lord shall consume with the spirit of his mouth, and shall destroy with the brightness of his coming.*

Men shall yet feel the terrible power of the Word that they have so lightly esteemed when preached by God's servants.

His countenance. *His countenance was as the sun shineth in his strength*. The last mentioned feature is the Saviour's face. It will be the last aspect of our Saviour the redeemed will behold. *And they shall see his face; and his name shall be in their foreheads*, Revelation 22:4. Seeing Him in His beauty, they will be like Him. It will be what Moses experienced in a measure when He saw the glory of the Lord in Exodus 33:18-23. He saw only a fleeting glimpse of the glory of God and was not permitted to see His face, for no mortal man may do so and live. But in our resurrected bodies when the mortal believer shall have put on immortality, we shall be able to look upon the glorious face of the Lord and live.

We shall not only look upon His glory but we shall share in His glory. *Then shall the righteous shine forth as the sun in the kingdom of their Father*, Matthew 13:43. *Beloved, now are we the sons of God, and it doth not yet appear what we shall be: but we know that, when he shall appear, we shall be like him; for we shall see him as he is*, 1 John 3:2. The believer ought to bear some likeness to his glorious Lord even while pilgrimaging through this world. The process of sanctification is set forth in 2 Corinthians 3:18. *But we all, with open face beholding as in a glass the glory of the Lord, are changed into the same image from glory to glory, even as by the Spirit of the Lord.* Fellowship with Christ, beholding His countenance in the mirror of the word and in prayer will stamp His likeness upon us. *Who is she that looketh forth as the morning, fair as the moon, clear as the sun, and terrible as an army with banners?* Song of Solomon 6:10. Something of the shining glory of our Saviour's countenance ought to be reflected in ours even while we are still in the midst of this earth's sin. As the moon's fairness is but a reflection of the sun's glory so let our countenance be turned toward Christ and shine in this dark world with something of His brightness. After all, the whole purpose of the gospel is to call us *to the obtaining of the glory of our Lord Jesus Christ*, 2 Thessalonians 2:14.

IV. THE POWER OF THE VISION.

1. The unworthiness of the saint. *And when I saw him, I fell at his feet as dead*, verse 17. Just the sight of Christ, even when He appears on an errand of mercy, overcomes the believer, even one as strong in grace as John the apostle. How unfitted we are for heaven and the presence of God! Pride makes us consider ourselves ever ready for the presence of God and little preparation is taken before prayer or worship. Pride in self has made us complacent and presumptuous regarding coming before the Lord. We may, it is true, come with boldness, but let it be humble boldness: a strong faith in the promises of God coupled with a strong sense of our unworthiness.

2. The fearfulness of the believer. John's falling down in fear and dread serves to remind us that the believer has not been delivered entirely from sin and its accompanying sense of guilt and condemnation. It is true that the child of God is free from condemnation with regards to eternity. But with regards our day to day walk we are conscious of the sinful nature that yet abides within. There is yet a remnant of that fear that gripped Adam in the garden of Eden. *And they heard the voice of the LORD God walking in the garden in the cool of the day: and Adam and his wife hid themselves from the presence of the LORD God amongst the trees of the garden. And the LORD God called unto Adam, and said unto him, Where art thou? And he said, I heard thy voice in the garden, and I was afraid, because I was naked; and I hid myself,* Genesis 3:8-10. While we remain in the body that dread will remain, for it is the inseparable companion of our sin.

John had confidently laid his head upon the Saviour's breast many years before, while the Saviour had walked among men with His glory veiled. Now, when he sees the Saviour in His glory, John attempts no such familiarities.

3. The effect of a sight of the glorious Saviour. *And when I saw him, I fell at his feet as dead*, verse17. There is a slaying effect wrought upon the earthly element of our being. All bodily strength was taken from John by the sight of Christ. In essence, we have the work of sanctification demonstrated. Communion and close fellowship with Christ slay the fleshly appetites and desires of the flesh and free the spiritual aspirations of the new nature from the constraints that the flesh exercises upon them. Paul deals with this matter in Romans, chapter 7. He there sets forth the two warring elements within his being, the flesh and the spirit, the new and the old natures, verses 22-23. He cries aloud for deliverance asking, in verse 24, the question: *O wretched man that I am! who shall deliver me from the body of this death?* Deliverance from the dominion of the flesh there is, and that through the Lord Jesus Christ. Paul answers his own question with the triumphant and joyful announcement: *I thank God through Jesus Christ our Lord*, verse 25. Paul elaborates on this deliverance in Galatians 2:20 when he says, *I am crucified with Christ: nevertheless I live; yet not I, but Christ liveth in me: and the life which I now live in the flesh I live by the faith of the Son of God, who loved me, and gave himself for me*, Galatians 2:20. The death he speaks of is the death of the flesh and the living he speaks of is the outworking of the life of Christ in his life. Thus the flesh is slain and the spirit flourishes. This is essentially illustrated by John's falling at the feet of Christ as one dead and then being raised to experience heavenly things and to undertake the great work of recording the visions that are about to be unfolded to him.

John's experience was that of many of the prophets of old. Consider just some of the accounts given us of the men of God in times past, Ezekiel 1:28; Daniel 8:18, 10:8-9, 17; Habakkuk 3:16.

4. The tenderness of the Saviour. *He laid his right hand upon me, saying unto me, Fear not; I am the first and the last: I am he that liveth, and was dead; and, behold, I am alive for evermore, Amen; and have the keys of hell and of death*, verses 17 and 18.

Fear not. The child of God has nothing to fear from a sight of the Saviour. Where there is fear the Saviour seeks to reassure the fearful one. How often the Lord has uttered these words to His people. They were first uttered to Abram. *After these things the word of the LORD came unto Abram in a vision, saying, Fear not, Abram: I am thy shield, and thy exceeding great reward*, Genesis 15:1. These words of promise and comfort followed Abram's refusal of any reward from the king of Sodom for the rescue he had effected of them from the hands of Chedorlaomer. The Lord swiftly assures Abram that He would be his Protector and reward. Here in Revelation 1:17, we have the last occurrence of such assurance. It was admirably suited to one who was suffering for Christ in the midst of a terrible time of persecution.

The title: *the first and the last*, is similar to that which the Lord has already employed twice in verses 8 and 11 and again in verse 17. Alpha and Omega is an employment of the first and the last letter of the Greek alphabet. The title is found in 2:8 and 22:13. The Lord Jesus will have the last word on all matters. When men have done their worst, the Saviour will have the final say. While men are raging forth their bitter opposition and apparently reigning supreme in this world, just remember that the Lord Jesus is the First and the Last, the Alpha and the Omega. *Why do the heathen rage, and the people imagine a vain thing? The kings of the earth set themselves, and the rulers take counsel together, against the LORD, and against his anointed, saying, Let us break their bands asunder, and cast away their cords from us. He that sitteth in the heavens shall laugh: the Lord shall have them in derision. Then shall he speak unto them in his wrath, and vex them in his sore displeasure*, Psalm 2:1-

5. In faith let us laugh with God at man's rebellion and wait patiently for the Lord to arise and speak that last and awful word that will end man's defiance.

Christ declares Himself to be *he that liveth, and was dead; and, behold, I am alive for evermore, Amen; and have the keys of hell and of death.* At a time when many saints were being cruelly put to death, and undoubtedly John would have been feeling his separation from them in their hour of trial, the Lord reminds His servant that He is the conqueror of death. Death, in truth, holds no fear for the child of God. If David, in an age when the fullness of gospel light was not yet given to the saints, was able to say: *Yea, though I walk through the valley of the shadow of death, I will fear no evil: for thou art with me; thy rod and thy staff they comfort me,* Psalm 23:4, how much more ought we who enjoy the full revelation of God fear no evil upon death's approach. Upon those occasions when thoughts of death rise to trouble us, call to mind, dear Christian, the words of the Saviour in John 11:25 and 26: *I am the resurrection, and the life: he that believeth in me, though he were dead, yet shall he live: and whosoever liveth and believeth in me shall never die.*

V. THE PURPOSE OF THE VISION.

Write the things which thou hast seen, and the things which are, and the things which shall be hereafter, verse 19.

John must tell the things that he saw. It was for this reason that John was shown them. He was made an eyewitness and must testify before men of what he has seen. With Peter the writers of the New Testament can say: *For we have not followed cunningly devised fables, when we made known unto you the power and coming of our Lord Jesus Christ, but were eyewitnesses of his majesty,* 2 Peter 1:16. Paul likewise was privileged to see things that were for the instruction of the church. *But rise, and stand upon thy feet: for I have appeared unto thee for this purpose, to make thee a minister and a witness both of these things which thou hast seen, and of those things in the which I will appear unto thee; delivering thee from the people, and from the Gentiles, unto whom now I send thee, to open their eyes, and to turn them from darkness to light, and from the power of Satan unto God, that they may receive forgiveness of sins, and inheritance among them which are sanctified by faith that is in me,* Acts 26:16-18.

Converted, called and holy men are the vessels by which the truth of God is disseminated abroad. Their knowledge is gained from Christ. Educational institutions, run on Biblical principles, may hone and enhance the natural and God-given mental gifts of the servant of God, but the 'message' he is sent to preach must come from Christ.

The messenger must proclaim *the things that are.* There are matters that are; they are fixed; they have taken place. The moral law of God is something that is. The depravity of man is something that is. The guilt and condemnation of man is something that is. The death of Christ upon the cross of Calvary for His people is something that is. The resurrection of Christ on the third day, the first day of the week, is something that is. The ascension of Christ to His Father's right hand where He ever lives to intercede for His people is something that is. These truths must be proclaimed by the servant of God for they are essential elements of the message of God. There are things which the preacher may lay before men as having taken place, as symbolised -in the parable in Matthew 22. *Tell them which are bidden, Behold, I have prepared my dinner: my oxen and my fatlings are killed, and all things are ready: come unto the marriage,* verse 4. The work of atonement is finished and all that is required for the salvation of the sinner is in place. These are things that are.

But there are things *which shall be hereafter.* These too must be preached. The Lord Jesus was going to show them to John that he might write them down for the instruction of the church. Many despise the study of prophecy and belittle those who would endeavour to understand the words of Christ. Such an attitude is not in keeping with the import of these instructions to John. It is the Saviour's wish that the church be acquainted with the things to come which have been revealed in Scripture. Paul said when he wrote to the Thessalonians that he did not wish them to be ignorant of what the future held for the child of God, 1 Thessalonians 4:13-18. Ignorance is the field in which the devil grows his best crops. Much that is preached and written to the shame of the work of God would have received no hearing, had God's people only been instructed in the things which shall be hereafter as they ought to have been.

Sinners need to be instructed in the things which shall be hereafter. They need to be told that there are things to come. Let us follow Paul's example when he witnessed to Felix in Acts 24:25. *And as he reasoned of righteousness, temperance, and judgment to come, Felix trembled.*

Indeed, let us follow the Saviour's example for He spoke much of judgment to come and the wrath that awaits guilty sinners. The duty given to Ezekiel is the duty of every preacher. *So thou, O son of man, I have set thee a watchman unto the house of Israel; therefore thou shalt hear the word at my mouth, and warn them from me*, Ezekiel 33:7.

Christ's messages to the seven churches
CHAPTERS 2 AND 3

I t is to be noticed that before the general matters related to the prophetic earth are dealt with, Christ speaks to His people in the seven churches in Asia about their own sins. There is a following of the principle that judgment must begin at the house of God, 1 Peter 4:17. It is true to say that the sins of God's people are more heinous to God than even the wicked excesses of the unbelieving world. *If therefore the light that is in thee be darkness, how great is that darkness!* Matthew 6:23.

John had already been instructed by the Saviour to write all that he had seen and was about to see in a book and send it to the seven churches in Asia: unto Ephesus, and unto Smyrna, and unto Pergamos, and unto Thyatira, and unto Sardis, and unto Philadelphia, and unto Laodicea, 1:11. As already noted in our comments on 1:1-2, we see the chain of revelation again set down. The Father gave it to the Son; He gave it to John who writes it down. He is now instructed to pass it on to the angel or minister of the church, who in turn proclaims it to the believers in the church.

The minister is called literally an angel and symbolically a star, 1:20. We have already noted that the word *aggelos* or angel means minister or messenger. The use of the symbol of a star illustrates the work of a minister. Men may still plot their course with absolute accuracy by the stars. They are a universal guide available to all. Daniel speaks of wise teachers as *they that be wise and who shall shine as the brightness of the firmament; and they that turn many to righteousness as the stars for ever and ever*, Daniel 12:3. The Lord Jesus Christ, the Great Teacher and Prophet of His people, is termed the Star that shall come out of Jacob, Numbers 24:17. False teachers, in whom no trust can be placed, are termed *wandering stars, to whom is reserved the blackness of darkness for ever*, Jude 13.

It is the task of the minister to relay the message of God to His people. It should also be noted that since the messages are addressed to the ministers first of all, they must apply the message to their own heart. Thus what is said in 2:4: *Nevertheless I have somewhat against thee, because thou hast left thy first love*, is to be taken to heart by the minister first of all. How much more effective would be our preaching if we had our hearts first of all wrought upon by the word that we preach to our congregations. Let ministers emulate Jeremiah. *Thy words were found, and I did eat them; and thy word was unto me the joy and rejoicing of mine heart*, Jeremiah 15:16. Ezekiel was commanded in like manner to first eat the word that he was to proclaim. He found the same sweetness in his mouth as experienced by Jeremiah. *Moreover he said unto me, Son of man, eat that thou findest; eat this roll, and go speak unto the house of Israel. So I opened my mouth, and he caused me to eat that roll. And he said unto me, Son of man, cause thy belly to eat, and fill thy bowels with this roll that I give thee. Then did I eat it; and it was in my mouth as honey for sweetness. And he said unto me, Son of man, go, get thee unto the house of Israel, and speak with my words unto them*, Ezekiel 3:1-4. No man can rightly preach the message of God who has not first of all assimilated it himself.

In considering these seven letters let us first of all consider:-

I.   THE INTIMATE KNOWLEDGE OF HIS CHURCHES THAT THE LORD JESUS DISPLAYS.

The Lord Jesus is omniscient. He knows all things. *For, lo, he that formeth the mountains, and createth the wind, and declareth unto man what is his thought, that maketh the morning darkness, and treadeth upon the high places of the earth, The LORD, The God of hosts, is his name*, Amos 4:13. *The LORD is in his holy temple, the LORD'S throne is in heaven: his eyes behold, his eyelids try, the children of men,* Psalm 11:4. *But Jesus did not commit himself unto them, because he knew all men,* John 2:24. *And they prayed, and said, Thou, Lord, which knowest the hearts of all men,* Acts 1:24. The Lord Jesus especially knows all about His people. *I am the good shepherd, and know my sheep,* John 10:14.

Seven times the phrase *I know* appears in the Greek text of these two chapters and seven is the number of perfection in the Bible. In 2:9 it appears twice in our English translation, once in italics where the translators put it in to bring out the sense of the Greek, but put it in italics so that we might know that the Greek does not actually include the words so translated.

In these epistles He shows that He knew their works and labours for Him perfectly, for the phrase *I know thy works* appears seven times in 2:2, 9, 13, 19 and 3:1, 8, 15. He speaks of the *patience* that some have shown, 2:2, 3, 19 and 3:10. The word means *steadfastness.* Patience is one of the chief marks of a true believer, Luke 8:15. He commends their inability to bear with or *carry in their hands* the evil of some, 2:2. He noted, on the other hand, their readiness to suffer for Him and bear with affliction, 2:3, 13, 19; 3:8. He commends their hatred for the deeds of the Nicolaitans, a faction which sanctioned lewdness and immorality, 2:6. He was not deceived by appearances of orthodoxy and outward propriety, 3:1. He was perfectly acquainted with every nuance of feeling and attitude within the churches and commended or rebuked them accordingly.

How perfect is the knowledge of Christ regarding not just His church, but all things! *Neither is there any creature that is not manifest in his sight: but all things are naked and opened unto the eyes of him with whom we have to do,* Hebrews 4:13.

Let the believer tremble before these two simple words: *I know.* Drawn curtains and closed doors and the cloak of darkness that descends in the evening may hide much from the eyes of men, but not from Christ. Sinful men commonly believe that they can deceive God and hide their sins. *Then said he unto me, Son of man, hast thou seen what the ancients of the house of Israel do in the dark, every man in the chambers of his imagery? for they say, The LORD seeth us not; the LORD hath forsaken the earth,* Ezekiel 8:12. If ever there was a day in which this view prevailed, it is today. Men believe they can sin with impunity. The notion of the ancient sinner is commonly believed in society today. *He hath said in his heart, God hath forgotten: he hideth his face; he will never see it*, Psalm 10:11. Such a delusion is the fruit of ignorance concerning God. *Thou thoughtest that I was altogether such an one as thyself*, Psalm 50:21. Natural man can conceive of no being higher than himself. He may acknowledge the existence of such but can frame a view of such a being only within the confines of his own limited knowledge. Hence, he thinks that God cannot know all things since such an understanding is beyond his comprehension. When Bible truth ceases to be the foundation of our religion then such foolish notions prevail.

Let not the saint be deceived into such error. Be warned! Christians have succumbed to the temptation that God can be deceived and have acted as if God could not see their sin. Did not David act so when he sinned with Bathsheba? Did not Ananias and Sapphira act upon this foolish assumption when they lied to the Holy Ghost in Acts 5:3? How much wiser was Moses when he said: *Thou hast set our iniquities before thee, our secret sins in the light of thy countenance*, Psalm 90:8. Let us live in the light of the words of Solomon in Ecclesiastes 12:14: *For God shall bring every work into judgment, with every secret thing, whether it be good, or whether it be evil.*

II. THE INDIVIDUAL GREETINGS TO THE CHURCHES THAT CHRIST GIVES.

Let no Christian feel himself to be lost in the crowd. Christ deals with us as individuals and this is demonstrated in the terms He employs when greeting each church. The title that He adopts for each church is uniquely suited to each church. He sets forth that particular aspect of His person to each church which is most appropriate for them.

Unto the angel of the church of Ephesus write; These things saith he that holdeth the seven stars in his right hand, who walketh in the midst of the seven golden candlesticks, 2:1.

Christ shows Himself to be walking in the midst of the churches and holding His ministers in His right hand. Is this not a most appropriate revelation of the Saviour to be given to a church whose backsliding threatened their status? *Remember therefore from whence thou art fallen, and repent, and do the first works; or else I will come unto thee quickly, and will remove thy candlestick out of his place, except thou repent,* verse 5. Except they heeded the warning they would forfeit the privilege of His presence and the power of His right hand. Christ will not stay where He is not loved with all the heart, and with all the soul, and with all the mind. This is the Bible's definition of the first love.

And unto the angel of the church in Smyrna write; These things saith the first and the last, which was dead, and is alive, 2:8.

To a church facing persecution even unto death what could be more comforting than a reminder that their Saviour was the One Who was dead but is now alive and that for evermore?

And to the angel of the church in Pergamos write; These things saith he which hath the sharp sword with two edges, 2:12.

The sin that threatened the church at Pergamos was the presence of those who held the doctrine of Balaam. The Saviour reminds the church that Balaam had taught Balac to entice Israel into great sin through eating offerings made unto idols and committing fornication. The incident referred to is recorded in Numbers 25:1-5. There we are told of the judgment that the Lord demanded against the transgressors, namely that of decapitation. It is most likely that the execution of the guilty was carried out by the sword. Now, those guilty of the same sin in Pergamos are reminded that they too are in danger of the sword of judgment, even the sword of Christ. He had but to speak and they would feel the power of that terrible instrument of death. The sword that kept Adam and Eve from further sinning through their eating of the tree of life (Genesis 3:24) still guards against disobedience. Woe unto the believer who defies it! Let us not provoke a fight with Christ by defying His Word.

And unto the angel of the church in Thyatira write; These things saith the Son of God, who hath his eyes like unto a flame of fire, and his feet are like fine brass, 2:18.

There can be nothing hidden from the eyes of fire. Let, therefore, those in Thyatira take heed that their sinful entanglement with the evil prophetess, tolerated in their midst, was not going unnoticed. They faced being made an example of so that other churches might learn that Christ is *He which searcheth the reins and hearts: and . . . . will give unto every one of you according to your works*, verse 23.

And unto the angel of the church in Sardis write; These things saith he that hath the seven Spirits of God, and the seven stars; I know thy works, that thou hast a name that thou livest, and art dead, 3:1.

For a church that had only a name to live and was ready to die altogether, what better thing to be reminded of than that Christ has the fullness of the Holy Spirit which He can bestow upon His servants, the stars which He holds in His right hand? Is not the fullness of the Holy Spirit the need of the church today? It is tragic that particularly within Reformed churches the experience of the fullness of the Holy Spirit is derided. They are up to their elbows in the dry and dead dust of orthodoxy, their pews are emptying and their witness, such as it is, goes unheard and unheeded, and all the while they mock those who speak of the need for the Holy Spirit to fill His servants with power. It is little wonder that spurious and devilish delusions such as 'The Toronto Blessing' are so widely received. There is a vacuum of power that the devil is only too anxious to fill with his counterfeit.

There is a day-to-day experience of the Holy Ghost's fullness awaiting the believer. Paul urged upon the Ephesian church that they *be filled with the Spirit*, Ephesians 5:18. The word filled means to *fill to the brim and keep filled*. The experience of men such as George Whitefield, Jonathan Edwards, Asahel Nettleton and Charles Haddon Spurgeon is what is required by God's servants today. There is a fullness of the Holy Spirit to be experienced and no man should dare preach without that experience. Were the pulpits filled with such men, what a change would be initiated within the land!

And to the angel of the church in Philadelphia write; These things saith he that is holy, he that is true, he that hath the key of David, he that openeth, and no man shutteth; and shutteth, and no man openeth, 3:7.

When facing the power of the synagogue of Satan and its attempts to close down the work of God, what comfort to receive a message from the One Who holds the key of David, the key of the kingdom and Who can open so that no man can shut! His promise that He will build His church and the gates of hell shall not prevail against it (Matthew 16:18) is true. The door that He opens cannot be shut by Satan. The promise of Christ shall not fail so take heart all you who have little strength and who feel the power of Satan arrayed against you. *Let us hold fast the profession of our faith without wavering; (for he is faithful that promised),* Hebrews 10:23.

And unto the angel of the church of the Laodiceans write; These things saith the Amen, the faithful and true witness, the beginning of the creation of God, 3:14.

How disingenuous was the church at Laodicea! How unfaithful and how untrue it was! It was neither hot nor cold. It considered itself utterly self-sufficient and in need of nothing. To this church comes a message from the One Who is altogether genuine, the *One Who is the Amen, the Faithful and True Witness,* the One Who is the origin of all things and upon Whom all creatures depend for their continuance, Who is *upholding all things by the word of his power,* Hebrews 1:3. This deceived church must listen to the witness of Christ and recognise their utter dependence upon Him. Having prospered and grown rich in this world's goods, the Laodiceans felt no need of Christ and had by their attitude excluded Him from their fellowship.

The church in Laodicea was repeating the error of Israel in the days of Hosea. *When Ephraim spake trembling, he exalted himself in Israel; but when he offended in Baal, he died,* Hosea 13:1. When conscious of his weakness, Ephraim tremblingly held onto the Lord. Prosperity brought self-reliance and departure from the Lord. This is the tale of the church in many ages. May it not be the tale of the Free Presbyterian Church of Ulster in this generation! May the Lord keep us ever aware of our utter dependence upon Him, no matter how we may prosper and grow, for without Him we can do nothing!

III. THE IMMEDIATE PRAISE THAT CHRIST OFFERS.

Christ offers praise before He condemns for sin. Does this not show His longsuffering and mercy? He does not come to these churches full of fury but rather full of grace. His eye is especially upon those matters where they showed forth His grace in their lives. Where it is possible, He lists first of all their virtues and offers praise. In this the marks of the Servant of Jehovah are exemplified. *Behold my servant, whom I have chosen; my beloved, in whom my soul is well pleased: I will put my spirit upon him, and he shall shew judgment to the Gentiles. He shall not strive, nor cry; neither shall any man hear his voice in the streets. A bruised reed shall he not break, and smoking flax shall he not quench, till he send forth judgment unto victory*, Matthew 12:18-20. He will not break the fragile and feeble but rather strengthen and heal.

Christ does not, however, pass over sin in the feeble believer. Of this let all in authority in the church of Christ take note. It is of no help to those who have fallen into sin that we remain silent and inactive regarding their sin, simply because they are in a weakened spiritual state. Like the Great Physician that He is, the Saviour seeks to strengthen His patients by encouraging words, before He applies the scalpel of truth. Let us learn from that. Church discipline is not to be conducted in the atmosphere of a slaughter house but rather in the caring atmosphere of a hospital. *Brethren, if a man be overtaken in a fault, ye which are spiritual, restore such an one in the spirit of meekness; considering thyself, lest thou also be tempted. Bear ye one another's burdens, and so fulfil the law of Christ*, Galatians 6:1-2. Thus we see our Master practise what He would have His servants do.

IV. THE INVITING OFFER THAT CHRIST MAKES.

There is an invitation to hear.

He that hath an ear, let him hear what the Spirit saith unto the churches. This is addressed to all the churches. Not all have the ear that will hear what the Holy Spirit says. The ungodly man most certainly cannot comprehend the Spirit's utterances. *But the natural man receiveth not the things of the Spirit of God: for they are foolishness unto him: neither can he know them, because they are spiritually discerned*, 1 Corinthians 2:14. But sometimes the believer cannot hear the voice of the Spirit either. Thus the Saviour says to all the churches, *He that hath an ear, let him hear.* Believers may turn away their ears or stop their ears so that they will not hear what the Lord is saying to them. *Thus speaketh the LORD of hosts, saying, Execute true judgment, and shew mercy and compassions every man to his brother: and oppress not the widow, nor the fatherless, the stranger, nor the poor; and let none of you imagine evil against his brother in your heart. But they refused to hearken, and pulled away the shoulder, and stopped their ears, that they should not hear*, Zechariah 7:9-11. There are many today who have no ear for God's truth. They will leave the church where the word is preached and seek out a place where they hear only that which is pleasing to the flesh. They are of the same spirit as those Isaiah and Jeremiah encountered, *which say to the seers, See not; and to the prophets, Prophesy not unto us right things, speak unto us smooth things, prophesy deceits*, Isaiah 30:10. *The prophets prophesy falsely, and the priests bear rule by their means; and my people love to have it so*, Jeremiah 5:31.

There is a correspondence between the invitation and the church to which it is directed.

In Ephesus, there had been a refusing of the lie of the deceiver and to this church was offered the promise of eating of *the tree of life, which is in the midst of the paradise of God*, 2:7.

Smyrna was a church facing deadly persecution and to it was offered the promise: *he that overcometh shall not be hurt of the second death*, 2:11.

Pergamos was being tempted to join in heathen feasts and commit fornication. To Pergamos was offered the promise: *to him that overcometh will I give to eat of the hidden manna*, 2:17.

Thyatira was coming under the power of an evil woman. To those who heeded the warning sounded by the Saviour and who responded was promised: *he that overcometh, and keepeth my works unto the end, to him will I give power over the nations: and he shall rule them with a rod of iron; as the vessels of a potter shall they be broken to shivers*, 2:26-27.

In Sardis there were those who sought to retain undefiled garments. To them was promised: *he that overcometh, the same shall be clothed in white raiment; and I will not blot out his name out of the book of life, but I will confess his name before my Father, and before his angels*, 3:5.

The believers at Philadelphia were under attack from unbelieving Jews from the synagogue of Satan. To them was given a most appropriate promise: *him that overcometh will I make a pillar in the temple of my*

God, and he shall go no more out: and I will write upon him the name of my God, and the name of the city of my God, which is new Jerusalem, which cometh down out of heaven from my God: and I will write upon him my new name, 3:12.

The Laodiceans were guilty of putting Christ out of the church. To that church Christ says: *to him that overcometh will I grant to sit with me in my throne, even as I also overcame, and am set down with my Father in his throne*, 3:21.

All the churches are called to a life of overcoming. The word means simply *to get the victory*. In the light of what follows in the rest of the Revelation, it will be readily seen how essential such a spirit of victory is for those, called upon to live through that which is revealed as coming upon the world.

The throne set in heaven

T he beginning of this chapter 4 marks the beginning of the prophetic section of the book. It is the will of God that His people be instructed in the things that shall come to pass. This book demonstrates this. Such instruction was an integral part of the apostolic ministry. Paul was able to write to the Thessalonian church and remind them that he had dealt with the issue of the manifestation of the man of sin, whose destruction would come about at the return of the Lord Jesus. *Remember ye not, that, when I was yet with you, I told you these things?* 2 Thessalonians 2:5. Paul underlines the fact that his teaching of the churches included the vital subject of eschatology or the study of the last things, when he again said to the Thessalonian church: *But of the times and the seasons, brethren, ye have no need that I write unto you. For yourselves know perfectly that the day of the Lord so cometh as a thief in the night,* 1 Thessalonians 5:1-2. This book of the Revelation is a book of prophecy and it is with it that God closes the canon of Holy Scripture. We cannot preach the whole counsel of God without giving to prophecy its proper place in our message. We emphasise this truth again because there is a strong antipathy toward the study of prophetic subjects amongst many ministers. There is no question about the abuse that the study has been subjected to by sensation-seekers with their charts and predictions of when exactly the Lord will return. But then, every doctrine set forth in God's word has been subjected to perverse interpretations and falsification. Who amongst us would boldly declare that we never preach the doctrine of the atonement or the resurrection of Christ because it has been the subject of such division and controversy? We would be horrified at such a thought. In like manner, the deliberate avoidance of a close study of prophecy, which occupies a large portion of God's word, simply because it has attracted controversy, must be considered wrong.

The one who avoids the study of prophecy is required to avoid much of the teaching of the Saviour. Many of the parables have a prophetic character, particularly those of Matthew, chapter 13. The chapters 24 and 25 of Matthew are given over entirely to answering two questions that were posed by the disciples. *And as he sat upon the mount of Olives, the disciples came unto him privately, saying, Tell us, when shall these things be? and what shall be the sign of thy coming, and of the end of the world?* Matthew 24:3. Far from discouraging His disciples in their pursuit of such a topic, the Lord gives them a very detailed answer to their questions. Is it possible that a true disciple of Christ can say that a close study of the Saviour's answer is not profitable? Antipathy toward a study of prophecy is an unthinkable position to adopt when viewed in this light.

The instrument of revelation and instruction is again the voice of Christ. This is vital for us to note. There can be no seeking of instruction in future events from any other source than the Bible. It alone is the record of all that the Lord Jesus has to say to His church. John says: *And the first voice which I heard was as it were of a trumpet talking with me; which said, Come up hither, and I will shew thee things which must be hereafter*, verse 1. The voice of Christ is the beginning of all things. In the beginning of the physical creation, it was so. Genesis chapter 1 shows us that the Lord spoke and all of creation came into existence at the sound of His voice. His voice is also the beginning of all spiritual creation. *Incline your ear, and come unto me: hear, and your soul shall live; and I will make an everlasting covenant with you, even the sure mercies of David*, Isaiah 55:3.

The voice of Christ, speaking unto John, was as a trumpet. That instrument was chosen in ages past to give directions on the battle field, because of its piercing notes and ability to carry long distances with clarity. The instructions that John is about to receive and pass on to the church will be trumpet-like – clear and understandable.

The trumpet-voice gave him direction - *Come up hither.* It was the voice of tuition - *I will shew thee things which must be hereafter.* To heed that voice was to be elevated into the heavenlies. May the Lord give us an obedient heart that will readily yield to His instruction.

John says that immediately he was *in the spirit*, verse 2. This change that John experienced reminds us that none can go to heaven without a spiritual transformation. I must stress that baptism or any other rite, practised amongst professing Christians, will not bring about the transformation sinners need in order to get to heaven. There is need of a work that can be done only by the Holy Spirit. That work involves the infusing of a new nature into the sinner. It is called regeneration. It is to this that the Saviour referred when speaking to the unenlightened Pharisee, Nicodemus. He said: *Verily, verily, I say unto thee, Except a man be born again, he cannot see the kingdom of God*, John 3:3. By regeneration the sinner is given a new nature, one fashioned in a like-ness to God's nature. The convert to Christ becomes *a partaker of the divine nature, having escaped the corruption that is in the world through lust*, 2 Peter 1:4. He becomes *a new creature: old things are passed away; behold, all things are become new*, 2 Corinthians 5:17.

John was already a born-again man. What he experienced here as he was taken up to heaven was not the new birth but rather a taking of his spirit out of his body and a translating of him to heaven for a time. It was an experience that very few have ever been granted. I believe that Paul the apostle had a similar experience to which he refers when writ-ing to the Corinthian church: *It is not expedient for me doubtless to glory. I will come to visions and revelations of the Lord. I knew a man in Christ above fourteen years ago, (whether in the body, I cannot tell; or whether out of the body, I cannot tell: God knoweth;) such an one caught up to the third heaven. And I knew such a man, (whether in the body, or out of the body, I cannot tell: God knoweth;) how that he was caught up into paradise, and heard unspeakable words, which it is not lawful for a man to utter*, 2 Corinthians 12:1-4. Thus John, in a manner not easily understood by us, was caught up to heaven in the spirit, to be shown things that he was then to write down for the instruction of the church in the ages to follow.

In seeking to interpret the heavenly scenes set before us in this and the succeeding chapters, we must not place arbitrary meanings upon that depicted. Rather, following the Holy Scriptures' principle of comparing spiritual things with spiritual (1 Corinthians 2:13) we shall seek to arrive at an understanding of the meaning of the terms and the symbols used.

Upon his entrance into heaven, it is to be noted that the first thing John sees is a throne set in heaven. Here is POWER, GOVERNMENT and PERMANENCE. That throne is presently invisible to unconverted man. He sees and knows nothing of its existence. We, as believers, ought never to forget that throne that is set in heaven and the glorious rule that is exercised therefrom. We will be in greater need of a constant remembering of this throne and its sovereignty, as the dark events that are set forth later in the book of the Revelation begin to come to pass. The comfort of the saints stems from the truth that God is still on the throne, and that He will remember His own.

We shall consider this throne, since it is the focal point of this chapter.

I.   THE ONE ON THE THRONE.

And one sat on the throne. And he that sat was to look upon like a jasper and a sardine stone: and there was a rainbow round about the throne, in sight like unto an emerald, verses 2-3. A likeness to the glory of Christ can be set down only in terms of symbolism. The terms that we would use to describe one another are utterly inadequate when it comes to setting forth the likeness of the Lord. Thus we are told that the One on the throne had the likeness of a jasper and a sardine stone. This is a spiritual rather than a physical description of the Lord. We have never been given in the Bible a physical description of the Lord. I only wish that artists and would-be artists would take note of this truth and refrain from doing that which I believe is forbidden in the second commandment.

In chapter 21:11, we are told that the jasper stone was clear as crystal. It was a stone of clarity and purity. The sardine stone was a red stone. The combination of the attributes of these two brilliant and flashing gems is very instructive regarding the person of the One Who sits upon the throne.

1. He is the Holy One. The crystal brightness of the jasper and the fiery-red of the sardine combine to portray the holiness of Christ. The jasper with its flawless radiance and the sardine with its rays of fiery brilliance both speak of purity. We are told that *God is light, and in him is no darkness at all*, 1 John 1:5. Again, we are told that *our God is a consuming fire*, Hebrews 12:29. Thus the symbolism of the jasper and of the sardine combine to teach us this most fundamental of truths about our God. He is holy. His is a holiness that burns against sin and impurity. *There is none holy as the LORD: for there is none beside thee: neither is there any rock like our God*, 1 Samuel 2:2. *Let us have grace, whereby we may serve God acceptably with reverence and godly fear: for our God is a consuming fire*, Hebrews 12:28-29. This truth ought ever to dominate our everyday thoughts and the most common of our actions. It especially ought to occupy our minds as we approach the Lord in worship.

2. He is the Eternal One. These two stones are mentioned in Exodus 39:10-13, where the precious stones that were set in the breastplate of the high priest are listed. *And they set in it four rows of stones: the first row was a sardius, a topaz, and a carbuncle: this was the first row. And the second row, an emerald, a sapphire, and a diamond. And the third row, a ligure, an agate, and an amethyst. And the fourth row, a beryl, an onyx, and a jasper: they were inclosed in ouches of gold in their inclosings.* It is seen that the sardine is the first mentioned and the jasper is the last mentioned. The Saviour had declared to John, *I am the first and the last*, Revelation 1:17. That name denotes that Christ is the Eternal One. His eternality is set forth by Him being likened unto the jasper and the sardine stones.

3. He is the Son of God. *And the stones were according to the names of the children of Israel, twelve, according to their names, like the engravings of a signet, every one with his name, according to the twelve tribes*, Exodus 39:14. The first stone, the sardius, represented the firstborn of Jacob's sons, Reuben. The jasper, the last stone, represented the last-born son, Benjamin. The meaning of the two names is interesting. Reuben means 'Behold a son' and Benjamin means 'Son of my right hand.' These two names combined bring before us the Lord Jesus of Whom His Father said: *This is my beloved Son, in whom I am well pleased*, Matthew 3:17, and Who even now *sits at His Father's right hand a Prince and a Saviour*, Acts 5:31.

4. He is the Mighty Redeemer. These stones, representing as they do the first and the last of the tribes of Israel, the ancient people of God, bring before us the certainty of glory for **all** the people of God. Christ is our forerunner and His presence in heaven upon the throne is an immutable token that **all** those He represents will, in God's time, join Him there. *Wherein God, willing more abundantly to shew unto the heirs of promise the immutability of his counsel, confirmed it by an oath: that by two immutable things, in which it was impossible for God to lie, we might have a strong consolation, who have fled for refuge to lay hold upon the hope'set before us: which hope we have as an anchor of the soul, both sure and stedfast, and which entereth into that within the veil; whither the forerunner is for us entered, even Jesus, made an high priest for ever after the order of Melchisedec*, Hebrews 6:17-20. Read again, Christian, those words of our Shepherd and rejoice. *And I give unto them eternal life; and they shall never perish, neither shall any man pluck them out of my hand*, John 10:28. *I go to prepare a place for you. And if I go and prepare a place for you, I will come again, and receive you unto myself; that where I am, there ye may be also*, John 14:2-3. All the saints, from first to last, shall enter glory.

Let us continue to consider this throne in heaven by looking at that which is:-

II.   ROUND ABOUT THE THRONE.

1. The rainbow. *And there was a rainbow round about the throne, in sight like unto an emerald*, verse 3. It is a rainbow-embraced throne. The rainbow reminds us of the gracious purpose of God regarding this earth, which He proclaimed following the judgment flood in the days of Noah. *I do set my bow in the cloud, and it shall be for a token of a covenant between me and the earth. And it shall come to pass, when I bring a cloud over the earth, that the bow shall be seen in the cloud: and I will remember my covenant, which is between me and you and every living creature of all flesh; and the waters shall no more become a flood to destroy all flesh. And the bow shall be in the cloud; and I will look upon it, that I may remember the everlasting covenant between God and every living creature of all flesh that is upon the earth*, Genesis 9:13-16.

God's purpose in mercy still stands today. That bow was seen by Ezekiel in his vision of the glory of God, Ezekiel 1:28. The rainbow encircles the throne still today and its colours tint all that is decreed from the throne and nothing contrary to the covenant it symbolises will issue forth from the throne.

The predominant colour of the rainbow was emerald or green. There is one colour that predominates creation and it is the colour green. It must surely denote GRACE. *The LORD is good to all: and his tender mercies are over all his works*, Psalm 145:9. As we study this book we shall see that great and dreadful judgments shall fall upon this world from the hand of God. But even such judgments are in order to advance mercy and grace. God's judgments follow many opportunities of mercy bestowed upon the nations of men, and will be followed by unequalled manifestations of mercy in the age that is to follow our present age.

2. Twenty-four elders. The elder in church government is a representative. He is elected by the congregation of believers to rule and represent them and their needs as God gives him wisdom. When John sees twenty-four elders sitting round about the throne, is this not a gathering of the representatives of the church before the throne of God? These elders are certainly redeemed sinners for they are seen to be singing the song of redemption in chapter 5:9-10. They are clothed in white raiment and that is the garment of the saints, 3:18; 19:8. The number twenty-four is representative of the church of the Old and New Testament. The number twelve dominates the Old and the New Testament church with the twelve tribes of the old dispensation and the twelve apostles of the new dispensation. I suggest that we have a representation of all the people of God before the throne in heaven.

The wearing of the golden crowns (verse 10) suggests a victorious church. These are they who have, like Paul, *fought a good fight, . . have finished the course, . . . have kept the faith,* 2 Timothy 4:7. They have obtained the prize which awaits all who so live, *even a crown of righteousness, which the Lord, the righteous judge, shall give . . . unto all them also that love his appearing,* 2 Timothy 4:7-8.

What a glorious prospect awaits the child of God! Dear reader, will you be numbered amongst those around the throne?

Consider now that which proceeds:-

III. OUT OF THE THRONE.

And out of the throne proceeded lightnings and thunderings and voices, verse 5.

This reminds us of what we read about Mount Sinai when the Lord came down upon it to give Israel His law. *And it came to pass on the third day in the morning, that there were thunders and lightnings, and a thick cloud upon the mount, and the voice of the trumpet exceeding loud; so that all the people that was in the camp trembled*, Exodus 19:16.

God has not changed. Some may blasphemously claim that the so-called tribal deity of the Old Testament was a figment of primitive Israel's imagination, but it is not so. John witnesses the same accompaniments of power and judgment surrounding the throne in heaven as did Moses and Israel some 1500 years before at Mount Sinai. Jesus Christ is the God of Judgment as well as the loving Saviour. This world shall yet see this demonstrated. On three other occasions, John witnesses thunder and lightning. All are connected with God's wrath and judgment. In 8:5, the prayers of God's people move God to judge the world. In 11:19, lightning and thunder are seen and heard, in conjunction with the opening of the temple of God in heaven and the revealing of the ark of testament within, as the time of judgment draws near. And in 16:18, thunders and lightning accompany God's judgment upon that great city of man's latter day rebellion: Babylon.

This world shall yet learn that it should have heeded the warning of Elihu contained in the book of Job, *Because there is wrath, beware lest he take thee away with his stroke: then a great ransom cannot deliver thee*, Job 36:18.

Consider now what John saw:-

IV. BEFORE THE THRONE.

And there were seven lamps of fire burning before the throne, which are the seven Spirits of God, verse 5. We have already pointed out in our comment on 1:4, that this is a reference to the seven-fold fullness of the Holy Spirit. In Isaiah 11:2, the Holy Spirit is described thus: *the spirit of the LORD shall rest upon him, the spirit of wisdom and understanding, the spirit of counsel and might, the spirit of knowledge and of the fear of the LORD.* That the Holy Spirit should be seen before the throne surely reminds us that we can approach the throne of God only through Him. He is the author of the new birth that is required (John 3:3) if a poor sinner is to get to heaven. He is also the author of the supplications of believers before God's throne during our earthly pilgrimage. *Likewise the Spirit also helpeth our infirmities: for we know not what we should pray for as we ought: but the Spirit itself maketh intercession for us with groanings which cannot be uttered,* Romans 8:26. He helps or lays hold alongside of us in prayer and enables us to come before God with our needs. By Him we draw nigh to God, which results in God drawing nigh to us (James 4:8).

The word *burning* reminds us that He is the *Holy* Spirit. The word is a strong word. It is used by Paul in 1 Cor 13:3 when speaking of the fire which consumes the body of a martyr. It is also used by him when referring (Hebrews 12:18) to the burning fire seen on Mount Sinai. It also is used to describe the lake of fire which is the final destination of the damned (Rev 19:20, 21:8). How contrary is this manifestation of the Holy Spirit to His portrayal by the modern charismatic movement! Those involved in this deception of the devil would have us believe that the Holy Spirit is the author of the circus performances that they call worship, that He has led them into the disorderly and unseemly lifestyle which they prefer to decency and decorum. They further claim that He is the source of the farcical revelations that they spout to their shame. This amounts to a great blasphemy against the Spirit Who is as a burning fire. None who fears the Lord expects such to go unnoticed or unanswered by heaven.

And before the throne there was a sea of glass like unto crystal, verse 6. The crystal-clear purity that was before the throne reminds us of what Paul said to the Hebrews. *Follow peace with all men, and holiness, without which no man shall see the Lord,* Hebrews 12:14. The Lord can be approached only over the sea of glass. Immediately outside the tabernacle before the burnt altar at which the priests sacrificed the offerings, there was a laver containing clean water in which the priests were required to wash before entering upon their service in the house of God. It, like the heavenly sea, reminds us all that nothing unclean shall enter God's presence or do His service.

The four and twenty elders fall down before him that sat on the throne, and worship him that liveth for ever and ever, and cast their crowns before the throne, saying, thou art worthy, O Lord, to receive glory and honour and power: for thou hast created all things, and for thy pleasure they are and were created, verses 10-11. Before the throne was a place of worship. And what worship it was! Let this be the pattern for our worship. Men set themselves up as authorities on how God ought to be worshipped. We have already mentioned the charismatic movement and its unseemly antics that some are pleased to call worship. But others err in the opposite direction, introducing formalities and rituals and rites that have no more warrant than do the charismatic capers.

Let us observe the worship in heaven.

1. There was great humility. The worshippers were full of a sense of the Lord's honour and glory. They fell down before the Lord.

2. They displayed great love and affection for the Lord. The word *worship* is derived from a dog licking its master's hand. It is that kissing of the hand that is a token of reverence and love common in the Orient. Our worship ought to be marked by a great outpouring of love for *the Son of God, who loved me, and gave himself for me*, Galatians 2:20.

3. There was a great sense of their own unworthiness. They cast their crowns before the throne. All their triumphs and victories were the Lord's doing.

4. They owned the Lord's sovereignty. He was the Creator of all things and that for His own pleasure. They had no argument with any of the procedures of providence or the acts of God.

Let us seek to make sure that our worship incorporates these essential elements. It then will be a pattern of that which takes place in heaven.

Finally, consider that which was:-

V.   IN THE MIDST AND ROUND ABOUT THE THRONE.

And in the midst of the throne, and round about the throne, were four beasts full of eyes before and behind. And the first beast was like a lion, and the second beast like a calf, and the third beast had a face as a man, and the fourth beast was like a flying eagle, verses 6-7.

The English word *beasts* is likely to give a wrong impression of the creatures here described, since it is the same word that is used to describe the Antichrist in Rev 13:1 and other places. While the words are the same in the English they are very different in the Greek. The Antichrist is literally *a wild beast* while these in the midst of the throne, and round about the throne, are literally *living creatures*. They are heavenly creatures, those who were seen by Isaiah and of whom he speaks in Isaiah 6:1-2. *In the year that king Uzziah died I saw also the Lord sitting upon a throne, high and lifted up, and his train filled the temple. Above it stood the seraphims: each one had six wings; with twain he covered his face, and with twain he covered his feet, and with twain he did fly.* The living creatures seen by Ezekiel very much bear a likeness to those seen by John. *As for the likeness of their faces, they four had the face of a man, and the face of a lion, on the right side: and they four had the face of an ox on the left side; they four also had the face of an eagle*, Ezekiel 1:10. Ezekiel specifically calls the *living creatures* cherubims in chapter 10:20-22. *This is the living creature that I saw under the God of Israel by the river of Chebar; and I knew that they were the cherubims. Every one had four faces apiece, and every one four wings; and the likeness of the hands of a man was under their wings. And the likeness of their faces was the same faces which I saw by the river of Chebar, their appearances and themselves: they went every one straight forward.*

Their close proximity to the throne indicates the exalted position that they occupy in the administration of God. They are most likely the chief of God's angelic beings who ever stand ready to do His bidding and are engaged in His administering of His affairs.

Are there not matters of which we know little? Yet one day we shall know. According to Paul, the glorified saints shall one day exercise power even over angels. *Do ye not know that the saints shall judge the world? and if the world shall be judged by you, are ye unworthy to judge the smallest matters? Know ye not that we shall judge angels? how much more things that pertain to this life?* 1 Corinthians 6:2-3. He who is destined for such glorious heights should endeavour while here on earth to keep himself unspotted from the world, James 1:27.

The sealed book, the slain Lamb and the singing saints
CHAPTER 5

There is gospel order to be observed in this chapter. We see first a scroll, then a sacrifice and finally a song. Every true believer will recognise that order as the one through which the soul passed on its spiritual journey from nature's darkness to the light of God's salvation. They were taken first to the Word of God, which in turn brought them to Christ the bleeding Lamb and then they sang the song of redemption.

I. THE SEALED BOOK.

And I saw in the right hand of him that sat on the throne a book written within and on the backside, sealed with seven seals, 5:1.

1. The authority of the book. In a day when the Bible is despised and its teaching belittled, it is important to remember that the Lord Jesus began His ministry with the Word of God in His hand. His ministry began in the synagogue of Nazareth and of its commencement we read: *And there was delivered unto him the book of the prophet Esaias. And when he had opened the book, he found the place where it was written, The Spirit of the Lord is upon me, because he hath anointed me to preach the gospel to the poor; he hath sent me to heal the brokenhearted, to preach deliverance to the captives, and recovering of sight to the blind, to set at liberty them that are bruised, to preach the acceptable year of the Lord. And he closed the book, and he gave it again to the minister,* *and sat down. And the eyes of all them that were in the synagogue were fastened on him. And he began to say unto them, This day is this scripture fulfilled in your ears,* Luke 4:17-21. When He sent out His disciples to preach the gospel to the world it was with the Word of God in their hands. Paul summed up his message in his memorable words before king Agrippa: *Having therefore obtained help of God, I continue unto this day, witnessing both to small and great, saying none other things than those which the prophets and Moses did say should come: that Christ should suffer, and that he should be the first that should rise from the dead, and should shew light unto the people, and to the Gentiles,* Acts 26:22-23. The Word of God, containing the revelation of His eternal purpose in Christ, how He would die to redeem a people, and the nature and extent of the redemption He would accomplish for them, is forever settled in heaven. It is *in the right hand of him that sat on the throne,* Revelation 5:1. *Heaven and earth shall pass away: but my words shall not pass away,* Mark 13:31.

   2. The description of the book. *Sealed with seven seals.* An understanding of the significance of this sealing of the book may be had by looking at Jeremiah 32:6-12. In this chapter, Jeremiah is depicting the Lord delivering His people and their land into the hands of the Babylonians as a punishment for their sin, verses 2-5. But Jeremiah also prophesied of the return of God's people to their own land in verse 15. The prophet was told to engage in the purchase of a field from his uncle's son and, by so doing, demonstrate that the land of Israel would return one day to the ownership of God's people and that such a purchase would not be a lost investment. The enemy would not always occupy Canaan. It would return one day to God's people. What is particularly interesting was the legal requirement to have two deeds of sale, one sealed and one unsealed (verse 11). When the property was to be redeemed, that is, bought back by the original owner or his descendants, then the redeemer would have to produce the sealed deed to prove his right of ownership. Christ the Redeemer of God's elect possesses a sealed book that is evidence of His right of ownership of a people and all that pertains to their eternal happiness and glory. He made that purchase at Calvary when He offered His blood as the price of redeeming His elect from captivity and condemnation under sin. Christ's elect are His inheritance. He has yet to claim His possession and enter into it.

He will one day. Presently, each child of God is sealed *until the redemption of the purchased possession*, Ephesians 1:14. The day of the opening of the seals and the claiming of His inheritance by Christ draws on. *And when these things begin to come to pass, then look up, and lift up your heads; for your redemption draweth nigh*, Luke 21:28.

3. The contents of the book. Just as the document Jeremiah drew up and sealed contained a description of the location, character and extent of the field he purchased, so the sealed book contains a full description of the purchase Christ made at the cross. In all the promises and prophecies of the Bible, we have a full description of all that pertains to our Saviour's inheritance in the saints.

4. The sorrow at the unopened book. *And I wept much, because no man was found worthy to open and to read the book, neither to look thereon*, verse 4. If none had the authority to open the book and redeem the lost inheritance then indeed it was a time for weeping. But praise God, there is *One Who is worthy to open the book and loose the seals*. It is the Lord Jesus, *the Lion of the tribe of Juda, the Root of David*. He *hath prevailed to open the book, and to loose the seven seals thereof*, verse 5. Man without hope of redemption is a miserable being. Little wonder he spends himself upon entertainment and pleasure. He must by some means seek to drive from his thoughts the truth about the dire circumstances of his soul. Yet for all that, he will not hearken to the gladsome tidings of salvation in Christ. Oh poor sinner, bowed down under a terrible burden of sin that will press you down to your grave and eternal hell, yet you are blind and deaf to hope and cheer as set before you in the gospel of Christ!

II. THE SLAIN LAMB.

1. The description of the Redeemer. *Behold, the Lion of the tribe of Juda, the Root of David, hath prevailed to open the book, and to loose the seven seals thereof. And I beheld, and, lo, in the midst of the throne and of the four beasts, and in the midst of the elders, stood a Lamb as it had been slain*, verses 5-6.

Christ is both a Lion and a Lamb. He is the Lion Who conquers our enemies and the Lamb Who atones for our sin. He is the One Whose roar against His enemies is dreadful. *The LORD shall go forth as a mighty man, he shall stir up jealousy like a man of war: he shall cry, yea, roar; he shall prevail against his enemies*, Isaiah 42:13. And at the same time He is the silent sufferer for the sins of His people. *All we like sheep have gone astray; we have turned every one to his own way; and the LORD hath laid on him the iniquity of us all. He was oppressed, and he was afflicted, yet he opened not his mouth: he is brought as a lamb to the slaughter, and as a sheep before her shearers is dumb, so he openeth not his mouth*, Isaiah 53:6-7. Notice that it is not as a Lion but as a Lamb that the Saviour stands in the midst of the throne. So shall He ever be throughout eternity to His people. Even when He is invested with all the power and glory of the throne of heaven, He will still be as a Lamb to His people. It is interesting to note that the word *Lamb* denotes a *little lamb*. There seems to be an accentuating of the gentleness of the Saviour.

A Lamb as it had been slain, having seven horns and seven eyes, which are the seven Spirits of God sent forth into all the earth, verse 6. The horns denote *power and strength*. The eyes denote *knowledge and understanding*. The number seven denotes fullness. The Saviour here is depicted as having all power and authority and all knowledge and One endued with the fullness of the Holy Spirit. Nothing can resist the Saviour's power and nothing can escape the Saviour's observation. We need not fear serving the One Who may truly say, *All power is given unto me in heaven and in earth*, Matthew 28:18.

2. The credentials of the Redeemer. He is the royal Redeemer. As prophesied in Genesis 49:10, Christ came of the tribe of Judah. *The sceptre shall not depart from Judah, nor a lawgiver from between his feet, until Shiloh come; and unto him shall the gathering of the people be.* There is a testifying here to the true humanity of our Redeemer also. He was of *the Root of David.* Paul stated the truth of Christ's humanity when he said: *Concerning his Son Jesus Christ our Lord, which was made of the seed of David according to the flesh*, Romans 1:3. There is also a further emphasising of His royalty when it is stated that the Saviour is the offspring of David.

3. The victory of the Redeemer. He was *slain* but *standing.* As He stated in 1:18: *I am he that liveth, and was dead; and, behold, I am alive for evermore, Amen; and have the keys of hell and of death.* This is a pictorial declaration of what Peter said in Acts 5:30-31. *The God of* *our fathers raised up Jesus, whom ye slew and hanged on a tree. Him hath God exalted with his right hand to be a Prince and a Saviour, for to give repentance to Israel, and forgiveness of sins,* Acts 5:30-31.

4. The claiming of the possession. When the Lamb takes the book there erupts in heaven a glorious chorus of praise. The elders and the angelic beings join in harmony, verses 7-8. Note the reference to the vials full of the prayers of the saints, What has just happened is something for which the saints of all ages have prayed. The Redeemer is about to claim His kingdom. Did He not instruct us to pray: *Thy kingdom come*? Matthew 6:10. The joy that is here recorded as breaking forth is in anticipation of the approaching moment of Christ claiming His kingdom.

III.   THE SINGING SAINTS.

What a song this is!

1. It is of the worthiness of Christ. After they fall before the Lamb, they sing of His worth. That is what good hymnology, heaven's hymnology, centres upon. It was sung with the utmost reverence and humility. What a lesson for us all in this day of hymn writers and singers who feel it right to ape both the style and the language, the lyrics and melodies of the world's singers and crooners!

2. It is of the work of Christ. His blood-shedding and its consequences occupy their praise. *For thou wast slain, and hast redeemed us to God by thy blood out of every kindred, and tongue, and people, and nation,* verse 9. How very, very much we owe to the blood shed upon the cross!

3. It is of the worthlessness of sinners. Those who escape hell and gain heaven had to be redeemed by another. They could not redeem themselves. Elementary as this may appear, there is no truth so resisted by the human mind. Ever since Cain, who thought he could appease God by the offering of the fruits of his own labours rather than the blood of a sacrifice, man has argued for his own merits and worth. The spirit of the Pharisee is natural to all men. *The Pharisee stood and prayed thus with himself, God, I thank thee, that I am not as other men are, extortioners, unjust, adulterers, or even as this publican. I fast twice in the week, I give tithes of all that I possess,* Luke 18:11-12. Only grace can bring a sinner to see his own unworthiness and make him to pray, *God be merciful to me a sinner,* Luke 18:13.

4. It is of the wonder of redemption. *And hast made us unto our God kings and priests: and we shall reign on the earth*, verse 10. Here is what we are: kings and priests. Note again that before we can exercise the intercessory role of a priest we must enjoy the victorious life of a king. As kings we reign over sin in the power of the Saviour's life. *For sin shall not have dominion over you*, Romans 6:14. Thus Paul rejoiced in victory through Christ. *I am crucified with Christ: nevertheless I live; yet not I, but Christ liveth in me: and the life which I now live in the flesh I live by the faith of the Son of God, who loved me, and gave himself for me*, Galatians 2:20. On the high ground of victory we may, like Moses, lift up our hands in victorious praying, (Exodus 17:11). The rod of Moses was as a king's sceptre. When he held it out demonstrations of power took place. He who stands as a king and intercedes as a priest will see mighty answers to prayer.

The future role of the child of God is here depicted. *We shall reign on the earth.* There is a time when the saints shall reign with Christ upon the earth. *Blessed and holy is he that hath part in the first resurrection: on such the second death hath no power, but they shall be priests of God and of Christ, and shall reign with him a thousand years*, Revelation 20:6. Paul uses this future judicial role as an argument in 1 Corinthians why Christians should not go to court in order to settle their differences. If they will one day hold high office, why can they not now seek the wisdom and grace to settle small matters of dispute? *Do ye not know that the saints shall judge the world? and if the world shall be judged by you, are ye unworthy to judge the smallest matters? Know ye not that we shall judge angels? how much more things that pertain to this life?* 1 Corinthians 6:2-3. It doth not yet appear what those presently called the *foolish*, the *weak*, the *base*, the *despised* and the *things which are not* shall be in the manifestation of Christ's kingdom.

The chapter ends with the universe joining in the song of praise *unto him that sitteth upon the throne, and unto the Lamb for ever and ever*, verse 13. This song has been increasing in fervour and volume. The participants increase in number as you study verses 8, 12 and 13. This universe shall yet echo to the sound of creation hailing *Jesus Christ as Lord, to the glory of God the Father*, Philippians 2:10-11.

The opening of the seals
CHAPTER 6

The explanation of the significance of the sealed book was seen in our consideration of Jeremiah, chapter 32. The Church of Christ is a purchased Church. Its members are a redeemed people awaiting the day of their entering into the full experience of their redemption. That day will dawn with the return of Christ to this earth in glory. For that day we watch. The phrase *Come and see* is repeated by one of the four living creatures or angelic beings, as the seals are opened, verses 1, 3, 5, 7. It is God's will that we know something of the events that will take place before the coming of the Son of Man. The believer should observe the times and seasons in order to mark the approach of that day. When the signs, that the Saviour has told us will herald His return, begin to come to pass, *then look up, and lift up your heads; for your redemption draweth nigh,* Luke 21:28.

The Holy Ghost's work is to seal us in Christ and our partaking of His grace is the earnest, or the down-payment, of our inheritance until *the redemption of the purchased possession,* Ephesians 1:14.

I.   THE FOUR HORSEMEN, VERSES 1-8.

In these verses, John sees a series of horsemen riding forth as the first four seals are opened. They and their horses and the events which are linked with them are described.

When Elisha would have his servant reassured regarding the protective power of God that was about them both, in the face of the threat posed by the soldiers of the Syrian king, who had been sent to capture the prophet, he prayed, *LORD, I pray thee, open his eyes, that he may see.* God answered that prayer, for the LORD *opened the eyes of the young man; and he saw: and, behold, the mountain was full of horses and chariots of fire round about Elisha,* 2 Kings 6:17. The symbol of God's sovereign power over the nations is, most appropriately, the most devastating weapon of war then known to man - horses and chariots. The unique superiority of God's power is seen in that they were horses and chariots of fire. What is depicted by these four horsemen is the sovereign power of God at work amongst the nations at the close of this age.

1. The white horse.   Christ is here depicted. It is, as it were, a preview of that scene given in greater detail in chapter 19:11-21. The Saviour's coming being depicted first is out of sequence since the events linked with the other three horses take place before the Saviour's return. The going forth of Christ, conquering, and to conquer, is mentioned first in order to comfort and strengthen the saints and to remind them that those things which shall come to pass upon the earth are under the direct control of the Lord and that they will culminate in His glorious return.

The Saviour used this method of revealing the end before the events that lead up to the end, in order to reassure His disciples, when showing them some distressing truths in Mark 8: 27-31. Before He began to teach them about His rejection by Israel, the suffering that He must endure and the death He must die, the Lord Jesus sought to draw powerfully the disciples' attention to Who He was, by asking the question: *Whom do men say that I am?*   Peter's answer on behalf of the disciples was most striking. *Thou art the Christ.* Only when this truth had been reconfirmed among them, did the Saviour go on to deal with the distressing truth of His rejection. Nor did He tell them all at this juncture. Progressively, He revealed the awful truth about His crucifixion.

That it may be seen that our observation has substance, I direct the reader to other occasions when the Lord revealed distressing truths to His servants, but before doing so sought to establish in their minds the glorious victory that ultimately would be theirs. In Genesis 15, the Lord came to Abraham in a vision and showed him the end for which he had been chosen. *And he brought him forth abroad, and said, Look now toward heaven, and tell the stars, if thou be able to number them: and he said unto him, So shall thy seed be. And he believed in the LORD; and he counted it to him for righteousness. And he said unto him, I am the LORD that brought thee out of Ur of the Chaldees, to give thee this land to inherit it,* Genesis 15:5-7. After showing him the certainty of His purpose in Abraham's life, the Lord then showed him the horror of the years of bondage and affliction that would come upon his descendants before the fulfilment of that promise. *And when the sun was going down, a deep sleep fell upon Abram; and, lo, an horror of great darkness fell upon him. And he said unto Abram, Know of a surety that thy seed shall be a stranger in a land that is not theirs, and shall serve them; and they shall afflict them four hundred years,* Genesis 15:12-13.

The sequence of events in the conversion of Saul of Tarsus is but another example of this method of teaching employed by the Lord. Saul is shown the Saviour in His glory before he is shown the great things he must suffer for the Saviour's name's sake (Acts 9:16).

Thus the Lord, here in Revelation chapter 6, shows His triumphant return before He shows the dreadful events that will precede that return. He Who knows the end from the beginning would have us confidently know that things will end in His triumphant glory, before He shows us the terrible events that will come before that happy and victorious conclusion. Consequently, the dreadful events will cause those taught of the Lord to look up in expectation of their redemption drawing nigh.

He that sat on him had a bow. The bow is a weapon that is employed at a distance. In Revelation 19, the Lord Jesus is seen coming again carrying a sword, the weapon of close combat. The going forth of the horsemen in Revelation 6 symbolises the Saviour's first strike against His enemies, hence He uses a bow. His attack will conclude with Him drawing His sword and coming to close quarters with His enemies at His return.

2. The red horse. Here is the symbol of lawlessness. *And there went out another horse that was red: and power was given to him that sat thereon to take peace from the earth, and that they should kill one another: and there was given unto him a great sword,* verse 4. The word peace is translated *quietness* in Acts 24:2. *And when he was called forth, Tertullus began to accuse him, saying, Seeing that by thee we* *enjoy great quietness, and that very worthy deeds are done unto this nation by thy providence.* Here it refers to national tranquillity. The end of this age is to be marked by growing restlessness and lawlessness. That is the clear statement of Holy Scripture. *This know also, that in the last days perilous times shall come. For men shall be lovers of their own selves, covetous, boasters, proud, blasphemers, disobedient to parents, unthankful, unholy, without natural affection, trucebreakers, false accusers, incontinent, fierce, despisers of those that are good, traitors, heady, highminded, lovers of pleasures more than lovers of God; having a form of godliness, but denying the power thereof: from such turn away,* 2 Timothy 3:1-5. The features which Paul says will characterise the last days are the antithesis of decency and order. The earth will grow progressively worse. *But evil men and seducers shall wax worse and worse, deceiving, and being deceived,* 2 Timothy 3:13.

It is God Who keeps this world under restraint, otherwise it would be a veritable hell. The old world in Noah's day and the cities of Sodom and Gomorrah are examples of what man will degenerate into, unless divinely restrained. What peace and order is enjoyed in this world is given of God. *And I will give peace in the land, and ye shall lie down, and none shall make you afraid: and I will rid evil beasts out of the land, neither shall the sword go through your land,* Leviticus 26:6. Where there is a despising of His word and a rebelling against His order then lawlessness and death will follow. He Who can give peace can take it away. *Hear ye the word of the LORD, O kings of Judah, and inhabitants of Jerusalem; Thus saith the LORD of hosts, the God of Israel; Behold, I will bring evil upon this place, the which whosoever heareth, his ears shall tingle. . . . . I will cause them to fall by the sword before their enemies, and by the hands of them that seek their lives: and their carcasses will I give to be meat for the fowls of the heaven, and for the beasts of the earth,* Jeremiah 19:3-7.

And that they should kill one another. Man was not long a sinner until he was a killer. *And Cain talked with Abel his brother: and it came to pass, when they were in the field, that Cain rose up against Abel his brother, and slew him,* Genesis 4:8. Murder is one of the trademarks of a departure from God and an abandoning of His law.

This trademark is everywhere evident today. Who is safe upon the streets of the land? The most brutal crimes are carried out randomly upon men, women and children. Political parties make it an issue of top priority, for they know that the nation will vote for the party that deals effectively with public disorder. Yet, despite repeated attempts to come to grips with the problem, crime continues to rise and takes on ever more ominous and frightening dimensions.

3. The black horse. Here is shortage and want. The pair of balances held by its rider must surely symbolise the merchant. Accompanying this horse is the cry, *A measure of wheat for a penny, and three measures of barley for a penny; and see thou hurt not the oil and the wine*. Such a price was a highly inflated price to pay for such measures of foodstuff at the close of the first century. It would have been an astounding price to the readers of John's book. Want of food will plague this world before the return of Christ.

4. The pale horse. This yellowish pale horse is the harbinger of great ill. Death is the title of its rider and Hell attends him. He has power and authority to kill. One quarter of the earth will feel his power for he will kill by war (*sword*), famine (*hunger*), with death (*disease*) and by the wild beasts.

The Greek word for earth, *ge*, may mean the whole world or a limited area of the earth such as the region around the Mediterranean Sea which features so much in this book. An example of the two usages of the word are found in Matthew. In Matthew 2:21 we read, *And he arose, and took the young child and his mother, and came into the land of Israel* (ge) and in Matthew 5:5, *Blessed are the meek: for they shall inherit the earth* (ge). I am of the opinion that it refers here to the prophetic earth, the region around the Mediterranean Sea, being swept by death so as to destroy one quarter of its population.

We hear of terrible famines and disasters that result in the death of countless thousands. Often the disasters are made worse by the slow response of richer nations to help. Helping is not without its difficulties, for simply to pour aid into a stricken country may so destabilise the economy of the country as to exacerbate the problem and make it virtually impossible for a recovery to take place. Despite the difficulties, it is more often greed and self-concern that hinder assistance being given. As man's wickedness increases then it stands to reason that humanitarian response to the distress of others will correspondingly decline. Man by nature reasons, *Am I my brother's keeper*? It is the grace of God alone that teaches men that all the law is fulfilled in one word, even in this; *Thou shalt love thy neighbour as thyself,* Galatians 5:14.

The sequence of the red, the black and the pale horses is to be noted carefully. Lawlessness gives rise to disorder which in turn gives rise to famine and want which in turn gives rise to widescale death and destruction. In this world, God has decreed that happiness follow holiness. *Godliness is profitable unto all things, having promise of the life that now is, and of that which is to come,* 1 Timothy 4:8. The principle set forth in the parable of the prodigal son is everywhere at work. When we leave the order and discipline of the Father's house then we will descend into chaos and want. That is the course that this world is set upon. We ought not to be surprised at these prophecies of disaster and doom. Rather, we ought to *take heed . . . unto the doctrine; continue in them: for in doing this thou shalt both save thyself, and them that hear thee,* 1 Timothy 4:16.

II. THE MARTYRS UNDER THE ALTAR, VERSES 9-11.

The scene changes to that of heaven. As the fifth seal is opened, John sees the souls of the martyred saints of God. As events on earth move toward the culmination of this age, so in heaven there is a corresponding awareness of the nearing of the end. Consider:-

1. The martyrs' crime. *And when he had opened the fifth seal, I saw under the altar the souls of them that were slain for the word of God, and for the testimony which they held,* verse 9. It is a capital offence to believe in Christ Jesus as far as this world is concerned. That all the believers have not been slain and made to share in the fate of the Saviour and His martyrs is but evidence of the watchcare God exercises over His flock. How could sheep survive in a world of wolves, if supernatural protection were not provided for them?

These were slain for their believing of the Word of God and for declaring that they believed it. The word *testimony* carries the meaning to *wear.* It was for the public associating with the Lord Jesus by wearing His testimony that these believers were slain.

2. The martyrs' cry. It will appear strange to some that the souls of just men made perfect should cry for vengeance but that is the cry recorded. *And they cried with a loud voice, saying, How long, O Lord,* *holy and true, dost thou not judge and avenge our blood on them that dwell on the earth?* Verse 10. It is part of the blind folly of men that they should deceive themselves into believing that vengeance has no place in the order of God. How wrong sinful man is!

The word *loud* is the Greek word *megas* which we see associated with that which is greater than normal such as megastore. In mathematics the prefix mega indicates multiplying by a factor of 1 million. -This was an powerful cry that could not be ignored.

It was a cry for vengeance. The invoking of the titles of the Lord, holy and true, shows that the petitioners expected the holiness and truth of God to grant them vengeance. God is indeed obligated to avenge His people who have suffered at the hands of evil men. *Dearly beloved, avenge not yourselves, but rather give place unto wrath: for it is written, Vengeance is mine; I will repay, saith the Lord. Therefore if thine enemy hunger, feed him; if he thirst, give him drink: for in so doing thou shalt heap coals of fire on his head. Be not overcome of evil, but overcome evil with good*, Romans 12:19-21. Since it is not permitted for us to avenge ourselves of the wrongs done against us, as that is God's prerogative, these martyred souls cry unto God for Him to keep His word.

Judge and avenge our blood. Justice and vengeance will be linked in the punishment that the perpetrators of this wickedness against the people of God will receive.

3. The martyrs' comfort. *And white robes were given unto every one of them; and it was said unto them, that they should rest yet for a little season, until their fellowservants also and their brethren, that should be killed as they were, should be fulfilled,* verse 11. They were given white robes and told to rest (the word means to take refreshment). The white robe was the garment of the overcomer, 3:5. They had an ignominious exit from this world as far as men were concerned, but a most glorious entrance into heaven.

It should be noticed that their cry for vengeance was not rebuked. Rather, it was implicitly responded to in a positive fashion. In a little season, their cry would be answered.

The promise of vengeance is part of the comfort of the saints. The unbelieving, so-called 'Christian', who abounds in the ecumenical denominations, will reject such a notion as that just stated. Yet it is nevertheless true. *Say to them that are of a fearful heart, Be strong, fear not: behold, your God will come with vengeance, even God with a recompence; he will come and save you,* Isaiah 35:4. *And to you who are troubled rest with us, when the Lord Jesus shall be revealed from heaven with his mighty angels, in flaming fire taking vengeance on them that know not God, and that obey not the gospel of our Lord Jesus Christ: who shall be punished with everlasting destruction from the presence of the Lord, and from the glory of his power; when he shall come to be glorified in his saints, and to be admired in all them that believe (because our testimony among you was believed) in that day,* 2 Thessalonians 1:7-10. The thought of the just retribution, that shall be dealt out by the Lord when He comes again, gives comfort to the saints on earth as well as those in heaven.

4. The martyrs' companions. *And it was said unto them, that they should rest yet for a little season, until their fellowservants also and their brethren, that should be killed as they were, should be fulfilled,* verse 11.

There was yet but a little season of the age to run, after which their cry would be answered. In that little season, there were yet martyrs who must die for the Lord. Martyrdom is not a mark of the devil's triumph over the church of Christ. Rather, each death is but part of the great *purpose of him who worketh all things after the counsel of his own will,* Ephesians 1:11. Just as the devil thought that he had triumphed over God by the slaying of Christ, so he likewise considers the slaying of the saints as a victory. He has been wrong on both counts. As the death of Christ was central to the eternal purpose of God to redeem His people and deliver them from eternal damnation, so the death of His saints, oftentimes in the most cruel of circumstances, is also part of His grand design. Time has proved again and again that 'the blood of the martyrs of Christ has been the seed of the church.'

III. THE WRATH OF THE LAMB, VERSES 12-17.

The opening of the sixth seal presents us with a scene that heralds the end of the age. It is a scene not unfamiliar to the people of God for it has been often spoken of by the prophets. For instance, Isaiah spoke of it some 700 years before Christ. *Behold, the day of the LORD cometh, cruel both with wrath and fierce anger, to lay the land desolate: and he shall destroy the sinners thereof out of it. For the stars of heaven and the constellations thereof shall not give their light: the sun shall be darkened in his going forth, and the moon shall not cause her light to shine. And I will punish the world for their evil, and the wicked for their iniquity; and I will cause the arrogancy of the proud to cease, and will lay low the haughtiness of the terrible. I will make a man more precious than fine gold; even a man than the golden wedge of Ophir. Therefore I will shake the heavens, and the earth shall remove out of her place, in the wrath of the LORD of hosts, and in the day of his fierce anger,* Isaiah 13:9-13. We have records of the Saviour's repeating of the prophet's description in Matthew 24: 29-30 and in Luke 21:25-27.

1. The forerunners of the end, verses 12-14. As the servants of a great personage go before to announce the arrival of their master, so the creation heralds the coming of Christ.

A great earthquake. The earth shook under the first judgment when the bowels of the earth were broken open in the days of Noah. It shook again when the Lord descended upon Sinai to give the law to Israel. It shook when the Son of God yielded up His life for His elect. It will shake again in a universal fashion when the Saviour returns to judge the earth.

The sun became black as sackcloth of hair, and the moon became as blood. The hiding of the light of the sun and the darkening of the face of the moon rightly set forth the end of the day of mercy and gospel light for this age. The darkness that embraced the land, when the Saviour died, symbolised the darkness that fell upon Israel as they rejected their Messiah. It spoke of the darkness of soul that they entered into as a result of their sinful refusal of Christ. Like darkness shall fall upon the world just before the Saviour returns and it will herald the eternal darkness of damnation that shall fall upon the Christ-rejecter, 2 Thessalonians 1:7-10. The mention of the two great heavenly lights, one connected with the day and the other with the night (Genesis 1:16), suggests that this is a phenomenon universally seen.

And the stars of heaven fell unto the earth, even as a fig tree casteth her untimely figs, when she is shaken of a mighty wind, verse 13. Will not these things attract men's eyes upward? Unregenerate man, like the dumb brute, is a creature of the downward look. These events will have him look up and consider a realm to which his thoughts rarely, if ever, turned. A passing distant comet has the world gazing out into space in order to catch a glimpse of the tiny speck of light. What puzzlement, what fear, what dread will seize the hearts of men when the stars begin to fall!

The word *fell* is a word that simply means to descend from one level to another. Thus, the wise men *fell down* before the infant Saviour, Matthew 2:11. So the stars will descend from the heights in heaven. The word *unto* is a Greek word translated by the English word *toward* in quite a few places in the New Testament. For example, the word *toward* appears in Acts 1:10, 8:28 and 28:14. Perhaps these verses will give us a clearer understanding of the scene depicted here. It is not a matter of the stars falling onto the earth since, being many hundreds of times larger than the earth, such a collision would destroy it. The stars will move or descend toward the earth and those permanent signposts in the skies, by which men have traversed the continents and the oceans on their journeys of discovery from time immemorial, will declare by their moving that the dissolution of the present order of things in creation is approaching.

And the heaven departed as a scroll when it is rolled together. We cannot begin to imagine just what this will be like. The scroll is the ancient roll of parchment upon which the Holy Scriptures were written. When a passage was being read, the document was unrolled from one spool on to another until the desired portion was reached. The two spools were moved apart so that the passage could be read. When it was finished with, the two spools were rolled toward each other and thus the scroll was closed up. This is the likeness used when God shall roll together the vaulted expanse of the sky where the clouds are presently to be seen.

And every mountain and island were moved out of their places. This gives us some measure of the extent of the first mentioned phenomenon, the earthquake. It will alter the face of creation.

We cannot conceive the terror that will grip men's hearts when such events occur. All that they have been assured by and have been certain of will suddenly shake and fall. The Christ-rejecter has long been accustomed to turning to the unchanging creation and saying, *Where is the promise of his coming? for since the fathers fell asleep, all things continue as they were from the beginning of the creation*, 2 Peter 3:4. Only those who share the psalmist's confidence will remain calm and unfrightened. *God is our refuge and strength, a very present help in trouble. Therefore will not we fear, though the earth be removed, and though the mountains be carried into the midst of the sea; though the waters thereof roar and be troubled, though the mountains shake with the swelling thereof. Selah. There is a river, the streams whereof shall make glad the city of God, the holy place of the tabernacles of the most High. God is in the midst of her; she shall not be moved: God shall help her, and that right early. The heathen raged, the kingdoms were moved: he uttered his voice, the earth melted. The LORD of hosts is with us; the God of Jacob is our refuge. Selah. Come, behold the works of the LORD, what desolations he hath made in the earth. He maketh wars to cease unto the end of the earth; he breaketh the bow, and cutteth the spear in sunder; he burneth the chariot in the fire. Be still, and know that I am God: I will be exalted among the heathen, I will be exalted in the earth. The LORD of hosts is with us; the God of Jacob is our refuge. Selah.* Psalm 46:1-11. Surely God's people will think upon and sing this psalm on that great day.

2. The fear of God. *And the kings of the earth, and the great men, and the rich men, and the chief captains, and the mighty men, and every bondman, and every free man,* verse 15. The seven-fold listing of the categories of mankind shows that the Lord is speaking of all the ungodly. Here are those among whose ranks the Lord Jesus never received any honour. It is clear that they are acquainted with the truth of God for they are familiar with the day of God's wrath and its coming. They are those who blasphemed His name and mocked His Word and despised His people. This description is representative of the various classes that make up the entire population of the world. All rejecters of Christ alive when He shall come again will be filled with an indescribable dread and fear. What unholy boldness men showed at the cross when they mocked the Son of God in His death agonies! That wicked defiance of God has continued long throughout the ages of mercy, when God has been pleased to restrain His wrath and deal with sinners in mercy and grace. Now the day of such restraint is over and Christ the King is returning to avenge Himself on His enemies. This is the fulfilling of that depicted in parables such as the one recorded in Matthew 22:1-14.

3. The folly of sinners. *And said to the mountains and rocks, Fall on us, and hide us from the face of him that sitteth on the throne, and from the wrath of the Lamb: for the great day of his wrath is come; and* *who shall be able to stand?* Verses 16-17. Many entertain the foolish notion that they would believe on Christ, had they seen Him in the flesh as did the disciples. Here are millions who see Him coming in His glory but they do not fall in repentance and worship Him. No, they continue to defy Him and seek to escape from Him, thus showing their ignorance of His power and omnipotence. They believe they can yet hide from Him and thus escape His wrath. The evil fallen nature that they inherited from Adam is clearly seen at work. Adam sought to hide from the same Lord after he had eaten the forbidden fruit. *And they heard the voice of the LORD God walking in the garden in the cool of the day: and Adam and his wife hid themselves from the presence of the LORD God amongst the trees of the garden*, Genesis 3:8. The passage of millenniums from the dawn of time has not seen depraved men becoming wiser or gaining any knowledge of God. They recognise that the great day of wrath is come and that they need shelter, but show no knowledge that there is no shelter in all this world from His judgment. They realise that none shall stand before Him but do not know the means of deliverance. Such things cannot be known by natural man. The truth of salvation must be revealed unto us by God's Spirit. Man must be born again, otherwise he will remain in ignorance of the things of God. God must impart heavenly light to his soul before he can understand. If we have a knowledge of God today, it is because God, *who commanded the light to shine out of darkness, hath shined in our hearts, to give the light of the knowledge of the glory of God in the face of Jesus Christ*, 2 Corinthians 4:6.

Who shall be able to stand? Verse 17. Who indeed? There are some who will be able to stand. *Therefore the ungodly shall not stand in the judgment*, Psalm 1:5. The ungodly shall not but the redeemed shall. Chapter 7:9 tells us that *a great multitude, which no man could number, of all nations, and kindreds, and people, and tongues, stood before the throne, and before the Lamb, clothed with white robes, and palms in their hands.* Further on in chapter 7, we are told that those who thus stand before the Lord are *they who have washed their robes, and made them white in the blood of the Lamb. Therefore are they before the throne of God, and serve him day and night in his temple: and he that sitteth on the throne shall dwell among them*, verses 14-15.

There is no hope of us standing before the Lord in the day of judgment other than having had our sins washed away in the Saviour's blood and clothed in His righteousness. Those who have been thus washed and are standing before God, trusting in the merits of Christ's life and atoning death, will not be condemned but received into glory. *Therefore being justified by faith, we have peace with God through our Lord Jesus Christ*, Romans 5:1. *There is therefore now no condemnation to them which are in Christ Jesus, who walk not after the flesh, but after the Spirit*, Romans 8:1.

The numbered and the numberless multitudes
CHAPTER 7

The events of the visions recorded in this chapter take place after the opening of the sixth seal, so they belong to the time of the very end. I believe they belong to that period spoken of by the Lord Jesus as the time when *there shall be great tribulation, such as was not since the beginning of the world to this time, no, nor ever shall be*, Matthew 24:21. It is the time of Antichrist's reign. Those who enter heaven at this time are referred to as *they which came out of great tribulation, and have washed their robes, and made them white in the blood of the Lamb*, verse 14.

This chapter indicates that, at the time of the end, there will be a limited work done amongst the people of Israel, verses 1-8. The chapter also deals with the extensive work that will be wrought amongst the Gentiles, verses 9-17.

I.   THE ANGELS HOLDING THE WINDS.

And after these things I saw four angels standing on the four corners of the earth, holding the four winds of the earth, that the wind should not blow on the earth, nor on the sea, nor on any tree, verse 1.

We are again presented with the truth that angels have an important role in God's administration of the earth and particularly with regard to the affairs of the elect. It was the Saviour Who warned, *Take heed that ye despise not one of these little ones; for I say unto you, That in heaven their angels do always behold the face of my Father which is in heaven*, Matthew 18:10. Do not these words make it clear that, with regard to the wellbeing of little ones that believe in the Lord Jesus, there are angels with special duties to watch over them? Angels have often communicated God's word to His people. I am sure that as well as those occasions of visible angelic activity, such as surrounded the birth of Christ, there is ongoing invisible angelic activity surrounding all of God's elect.

In the Bible, the wind is often the symbol of destructive power. I recognise that it is used at times of the work of the Holy Spirit such as in John 3:8. But it is also used to symbolise the destructive forces of evil at work in this world. Just as there are occasions when the wind blows so as to aid mankind - propel ships, power windmills, dry crops and refresh the weary - so also there are occasions when it works much evil - destructive storms on land and sea.

In verse 1, the winds symbolise destructive forces capable of hurting the earth, verses 2-3. Often God has depicted His judgments upon men because of their sins as destructive winds. *And upon Elam will I bring the four winds from the four quarters of heaven, and will scatter them toward all those winds; and there shall be no nation whither the outcasts of Elam shall not come. For I will cause Elam to be dismayed before their enemies, and before them that seek their life: and I will bring evil upon them, even my fierce anger, saith the LORD; and I will send the sword after them, till I have consumed them: and I will set my throne in Elam, and will destroy from thence the king and the princes, saith the LORD*, Jeremiah 49:36-38. *Thus saith the LORD; Behold, I will raise up against Babylon, and against them that dwell in the midst of them that rise up against me, a destroying wind; and will send unto Babylon fanners, that shall fan her, and shall empty her land: for in the day of trouble they shall be against her round about*, Jeremiah 51:1-2.

In the book of Daniel we are told much about the developments that will take place at the end of this age, especially with regard to the rise of the Antichrist. We read in chapter 7:2-3, *Daniel spake and said, I saw in my vision by night, and, behold, the four winds of the heaven strove upon the great sea. And four great beasts came up from the sea, diverse one from another.* Here are the winds at work bringing about the formation of the four great kingdoms with which God chiefly links the affairs of His people: the Babylonian, the Medo-Persian, the Grecian and the Roman empires. All of these empires were centred upon the Great Sea or the Mediterranean Sea. It is out of this sea that the Antichrist shall arise, according to Revelation 13:1. His likeness will be depicted by a combination of the chief features that Daniel was inspired to use when depicting the four great world empires. We shall deal with this matter in more detail when we come to chapter 13. Suffice to say that the winds are symbolising those forces that bring about the rise of antichristianity.

The winds are again referred to in Zechariah 5:9-11. *Then lifted I up mine eyes, and looked, and, behold, there came out two women, and the wind was in their wings; for they had wings like the wings of a stork: and they lifted up the ephah between the earth and the heaven. Then said I to the angel that talked with me, Whither do these bear the ephah? And he said unto me, To build it an house in the land of Shinar: and it shall be established, and set there upon her own base.* The ephah is a commercial dry measure or the receptacle or jar that held that amount. It is therefore a very apt symbol of commercial enterprise. The ephah that Zechariah saw contained a woman who was termed wickedness. It is the term that has ever been linked with the forces of antichristianity and apostasy. The title wicked or wicked one is used of the devil and of the Antichrist. (See Matthew 13:19, 38; Ephesians 6:16; 1 John 2:13, 14, 3:12, 5:18; 1 Thessalonians 2:8.) That ephah was borne by two flying creatures, with the power of the wind in their wings, to the land of Shinar, the ancient name for Babylon. It was in Shinar that wicked men first organised themselves into a confederacy against the Lord and built the tower of Babel (Genesis 11:1-9). It is to this ancient seat of rebellion that the winds are seen to be carrying wickedness for the final and full manifestation of apostasy and rebellion in the kingdom of Antichrist. The word *established* means to *confirm, to fix.* That which the Lord has hindered from becoming established He is going to cease to restrain. It will be allowed to take a firm root. He had restrained this spirit of lawlessness on the occasion of the building of the tower of Babel, Genesis 11:1-9, and on many other occasions. But the time is coming when it will please the Lord to lift His restraints upon this power for evil and allow it to develop. There is a time of unrestrained wickedness coming upon this earth. Turbulence and upheaval are what await this world as man ever strives to be rid of the restraint of God's law and rule. It is what the Psalmist saw coming to pass. *Why do the heathen rage, and the people imagine a vain thing? The kings of the earth set themselves, and the rulers take counsel together, against the LORD, and against his anointed, saying, Let us break their bands asunder, and cast away their cords from us*, Psalm 2:1-3. When once the angels of God release the winds that they presently restrain, then unparalleled storms of sin and rebellion will be experienced upon this earth. Every structure of moral rectitude that gospel influence has erected in the past will be shaken and uprooted. It was to this that Paul referred when he said, *This know also, that in the last days perilous times shall come*, 2 Timothy 3:1. Evil will become good and black will become white.

God presently exercises a restraint upon evil. That restraint incorporates the witness of His remnant people. It is today as it was in the day of Isaiah. *Except the LORD of hosts had left unto us a very small remnant, we should have been as Sodom, and we should have been like unto Gomorrah*, Isaiah 1:9. The influences of God's remnant are such that there is a hindering of the development of apostasy to the dimensions that it desires. But that restraint will be lifted as God gives evil men their way. *And now ye know what withholdeth that he might be revealed in his time. For the mystery of iniquity doth already work: only he who now letteth will let, until he be taken out of the way. And then shall that Wicked be revealed, whom the Lord shall consume with the spirit of his mouth, and shall destroy with the brightness of his coming*, 2 Thessalonians 2:6-8. The word *withholdeth* (Greek- *katecho*) means *to restrain*. The word *letteth* is the same Greek word translated by a different English word. Thus the restraint shall end when God decrees and there shall be a manifesting of the Antichrist, wickedness personified.

Before God's restraint finally ends there will be an ingathering of the elect of Israel. God restrains the gathering forces of Antichristianity that would eradicate every reference and witness to God and His truth from the earth, so that twelve times twelve thousand of all the tribes of Israel are redeemed before there is an unleashing of wickedness, verses 4-8. As Shadrach, Meshach and Abednego were preserved amidst the fire kindled by Nebuchadnezzar's wrath, so the Lord will preserve a small remnant of Israel from the wrath of Antichrist and bring them to saving faith and repentance. It is to this time that Zechariah refers in his prophecy. *And it shall come to pass, that in all the land, saith the LORD, two parts therein shall be cut off and die; but the third shall be left therein. And I will bring the third part through the fire, and will refine them as silver is refined, and will try them as gold is tried: they shall call on my name, and I will hear them: I will say, It is my people: and they shall say, The LORD is my God*, Zechariah 13:7-9.

It should be noted that conversion can take place only when evil is restrained. Do we pray enough against the evil forces at work in our land? During the advance of apostasy in our land, it has been the singular complaint of God's people that it has become increasingly difficult to see sinners saved. As the rising of the sun dispels the darkness of the night and as the setting of the sun brings darkness, so it is in the realm of evangelism. Sunshine and darkness cannot dwell together.

This truth is illustrated in the history of Israel. *So Moab was subdued that day under the hand of Israel. And the land had rest fourscore years*, Judges 3:30. The subduing of the enemy resulted in prosperity for Israel.

It is illustrated in nature. *And some fell among thorns; and the thorns sprung up, and choked them*, Matthew 13:7. The farmer must constantly combat the growth of weeds if he is to enjoy a bountiful harvest.

It is illustrated in the experience of the believer. *For the flesh lusteth against the Spirit, and the Spirit against the flesh: and these are contrary the one to the other: so that ye cannot do the things that ye would. But I see another law in my members, warring against the law of my mind, and bringing me into captivity to the law of sin which is in my members. For to be carnally minded is death; but to be spiritually minded is life and peace. For if ye live after the flesh, ye shall die: but if ye through the Spirit do mortify the deeds of the body, ye shall live. I am crucified with Christ: nevertheless I live; yet not I, but Christ liveth in me: and the life which I now live in the flesh I live by the faith of the Son of God, who loved me, and gave himself for me. And they that are Christ's have crucified the flesh with the affections and lusts.* (Galatians 5:17; Romans 7:23; Romans 8:6; Romans 8:13; Galatians 2:20; Galatians 5:24.)

It is a truth plainly taught by the Lord Jesus. *No man can enter into a strong man's house, and spoil his goods, except he will first bind the strong man; and then he will spoil his house*, Mark 3:27.

The word *holding*, in Revelation 7:1, means to *arrest*. It is used of the arrest of John the Baptist and of the Lord Jesus, Matthew 14:3, 21:46, 26:48. We need to pray for an arresting of the power of the devil in order that we may see an advance in the work of saving sinners.

II. THE NUMBERED MULTITUDE SEALED.

And I saw another angel ascending from the east, having the seal of the living God:, and he cried with a loud voice to the four angels, to whom it was given to hurt the earth and the sea, saying, Hurt not the earth, neither the sea, nor the trees, till we have sealed the servants of our God in their foreheads, Revelation 7:2-3.

The salvation of this remnant is according to the workings of God's grace in all ages. It is likened to the sealing of a people. In Ezekiel chapter 9, we have a people marked or sealed before judgment fell. Each one that received the mark was to be spared in the judgment, Ezekiel 9:1-6. That event was a foreshadowing of that which is to take place again in Jerusalem at the end of this age.

1. The angel with the seal ascends from the east. That is the quarter from which the new light of each day arises. How often the rising of the sun is used to illustrate the illuminating work of grace that must take place in a sinner's heart if he is to be saved! Indeed, the Lord Jesus is called the *Sun of Righteousness* Whose rising brings saving health to those upon whom His beams fall (Malachi -4:2). God shall be pleased to visit a remnant of His ancient people Israel at the end of this age with saving grace.

2. The work is likened to a sealing. The process of sealing in the Holy Scriptures is linked with securing. *So they went, and made the sepulchre sure, sealing the stone, and setting a watch*, Matthew 27:66. *And cast him into the bottomless pit, and shut him up, and set a seal upon him, that he should deceive the nations no more, till the thousand years should be fulfilled: and after that he must be loosed a little season*, Revelation 20:3. How secure the child of Christ is! *And I give unto them eternal life; and they shall never perish, neither shall any man pluck them out of my hand*, John 10:28.

The process is also linked with identification. *So she wrote letters in Ahab's name, and sealed them with his seal, and sent the letters unto the elders and to the nobles that were in his city, dwelling with Naboth,* 1 Kings 21:8. *If I be not an apostle unto others, yet doubtless I am to you: for the seal of mine apostleship are ye in the Lord,* 1 Corinthians 9:2. God puts a mark upon all of His children that identifies them as His. It is a mark which, like a king's seal, dare not and cannot be copied. *But ye are not in the flesh, but in the Spirit, if so be that the Spirit of God dwell in you. Now if any man have not the Spirit of Christ, he is none of his,* Romans 8:9. It befits us all to ascertain whether or not this mark is upon us.

3. It was a prominent mark. They were sealed in their foreheads. Whenever we meet someone, eye contact is the first element of the contact we make with that person. Before we shake hands or exchange verbal greetings we make eye contact. The first thing that is seen and noticed about this people sealed is the mark upon their forehead, just between their eyes. A noticing of it cannot be avoided. The first time that the forehead is mentioned in Holy Scripture is in Exodus 28:36-38. It has to do with the mitre worn by the high priest of Israel. *And thou shalt make a plate of pure gold, and grave upon it, like the engravings of a signet, HOLINESS TO THE LORD. And thou shalt put it on a blue lace, that it may be upon the mitre; upon the forefront of the mitre it shall be. And it shall be upon Aaron's forehead, that Aaron may bear the iniquity of the holy things, which the children of Israel shall hallow in all their holy gifts; and it shall be always upon his forehead, that they may be accepted before the LORD,* Exodus 28:36-38. Holiness must be engraved prominently upon the life of the true child of God. *Therefore if any man be in Christ, he is a new creature: old things are passed away; behold, all things are become new,* 2 Corinthians 5:17. The creation of a holy people lay behind the eternal plan of redemption. *Who gave himself for us, that he might redeem us from all iniquity, and purify unto himself a peculiar people, zealous of good works,* Titus 2:14. The rule of holiness does not change from age to age. That which governed the conduct of first century believers governs us today. It is a fallacy to speak of holy conduct and behaviour as being old-fashioned. *For whom he did foreknow, he also did predestinate to be conformed to the image of his Son, that he might be the firstborn among many brethren,* Romans 8:29. Likeness to Christ ever has been, and ever will be, the norm of holiness. *But as he which hath called you is holy, so be ye holy in all manner of* *conversation; because it is written, Be ye holy; for I am holy*, 1 Peter 1:15-16.

4. It was a permanent mark. Seals are made to last and not fade away. God's work of regeneration and sanctification are lasting works. They shall not be undone by any hand. *For the writing which is written in the king's name, and sealed with the king's ring, may no man reverse*, Esther 8:8. That which was true of the handiwork of king Ahasuerus is even more true of the work of Jehovah.

5. It was a distinguishing mark. What a difference the mark of God upon the life of a person makes! It most certainly sets them apart. *Now when they saw the boldness of Peter and John, and perceived that they were unlearned and ignorant men, they marvelled; and they took knowledge of them, that they had been with Jesus*, Acts 4:13. This is an age of conformity! An age when the worldling wishes to be individualistic, by being just like everyone else! Fads and phases come and go like waves upon the surface of the ocean, as the worldly masses slavishly follow the dictates and follies of the fashion mandarins of London, Paris – and New York. The world's so-called celebrities act as clothes horses for these ludicrous creations. Today's height of fashion is reminiscent of the old duds my mother wore to feed the hens! It seems that today's modern young women count it most elegant to borrow their grandfathers' old boots and parade themselves in them!

The follies of this apostate and rebellious age are but a repetition of those of former ages. Who can read Isaiah 3:16-24, without recognising the spirit that is abroad today? *Moreover the LORD saith, Because the daughters of Zion are haughty, and walk with stretched forth necks and wanton eyes, walking and mincing as they go, and making a tinkling with their feet: therefore the Lord will smite with a scab the crown of the head of the daughters of Zion, and the LORD will discover their secret parts. In that day the Lord will take away the bravery of their tinkling ornaments about their feet, and their cauls, and their round tires like the moon, the chains, and the bracelets, and the mufflers, the bonnets, and the ornaments of the legs, and the headbands, and the tablets, and the earrings, the rings, and nose jewels, the changeable suits of apparel, and the mantles, and the wimples, and the crisping pins, the glasses, and the fine linen, and the hoods, and the vails. And it shall come to pass, that instead of sweet smell there shall be stink; and instead of a girdle a rent; and instead of well set hair baldness; and instead of a stomacher a girding of sackcloth; and burning instead of beauty.*

With such sinful absurdity the child of God should have no part. The injunction of Paul to the church at Rome is still in force for us all today. *And be not conformed to this world: but be ye transformed by the renewing of your mind, that ye may prove what is that good, and acceptable, and perfect, will of God,* Romans 12:2.

6. Those so marked were called servants of God. We are marked to serve. The Greek word *doulos,* translated *servant,* literally means *slave.* We ought to have no mind or will but that of our Master, the Lord Jesus Christ.

We must note that two names are not used in the list of the tribes. They are those of Ephraim and Dan. The meaning of these names give us, I believe, a reason why they are omitted here. Ephraim means fruitful and Dan means judge. The period of limited blessing set forth in this portion is not the time of Israel's fruitfulness and the time of her judging the world has not yet come. That time shall come after the Saviour returns. To this time Christ referred while dining with His disciples in the upper chamber. *Ye are they which have continued with me in my temptations. And I appoint unto you a kingdom, as my Father hath appointed unto me; that ye may eat and drink at my table in my kingdom, and sit on thrones judging the twelve tribes of Israel,* Luke 22:28-30. But that matter is a subject for a later study.

III. THE NUMBERLESS MULTITUDE.

After this I beheld, and, lo, a great multitude, which no man could number, of all nations, and kindreds, and people, and tongues, stood before the throne, and before the Lamb, clothed with white robes, and palms in their hands, verse 9.

Those redeemed, referred to in verses 2-8, were of the children of Israel. The multitude mentioned in the remainder of the chapter is from all nations, and kindreds, and people, and tongues. They are those who will suffer for Christ during the great tribulation for *these are they which came out of great tribulation, and have washed their robes, and made them white in the blood of the Lamb,* 7:14.

We live in *the times of the Gentiles.* It is with them that God deals in mercy, having rejected the people of Israel for a season. *I say then,*

Have they stumbled that they should fall? God forbid: but rather through their fall salvation is come unto the Gentiles, for to provoke them to jealousy, Romans 11:11. Paul's action, following the opposition to the gospel that he experienced in the synagogue in Corinth, is symbolic of God's reaction to Israel's rejection of the Lord Jesus Christ. *And when they opposed themselves, and blasphemed, he shook his raiment, and said unto them, Your blood be upon your own heads; I am clean: from henceforth I will go unto the Gentiles,* Acts 18:6.

What a great multitude of sinners have availed themselves of God's grace! The word *lo,* in verse 9, is one that is used to draw attention to something remarkable. There is nothing in all this world more remarkable than that a sinner should stand justified, uncondemned before God in glory. They, who deserve eternal damnation, enjoy, instead, intimate and blessed fellowship with God. We echo the words of Hannah's rejoicing. *The LORD maketh poor, and maketh rich: he bringeth low, and lifteth up. He raiseth up the poor out of the dust, and lifteth up the beggar from the dunghill, to set them among princes, and to make them inherit the throne of glory: for the pillars of the earth are the LORD'S, and he hath set the world upon them,* 2 Samuel 2:7-8. The poor and the beggarly are lifted out of the dust and the dung of their own depravity and made to inherit the throne of Glory. Sin could have made us no lower. Grace and mercy could have lifted us no higher. Saved sinners will share Christ's throne. *To him that overcometh will I grant to sit with me in my throne, even as I also overcame, and am set down with my Father in his throne,* Revelation 3:21. We are joint-heirs with the Lord Jesus. What a glorious prospect is ours! *And if children, then heirs; heirs of God, and joint-heirs with Christ; if so be that we suffer with him, that we may be also glorified together. For I reckon that the sufferings of this present time are not worthy to be compared with the glory which shall be revealed in us,* Romans 8:17-18.

Look at what the saved sinner will enjoy in glory.

1. Their closeness. They are *before the throne of God.* That is emphasised in verse 9 and verse 15. Sin separated us from God, but see what grace has accomplished for the redeemed.

2. Their clothing. The white robe signified not only purity but great dignity. The wearing of such a garment by a Roman official signified the holding of high office.

3. Their cry. They who on earth were heard often to groan, in heaven cry aloud with joy. The sighing of Ezekiel 9:4 has given way to the singing of heaven. It is the sound of victory. Christ has triumphed over all His enemies and brought His people to heaven, to rest and to everlasting joy.

4. Their cleansing. Lot was *vexed with the filthy conversation of the wicked*, 2 Peter 2:7. Such has been the experience of all of God's saints. The *sound* of sin is vexing never mind the *sight* and the *stain* of it. How happy will the redeemed be in the sinless atmosphere of heaven!

5. Their comforts. They serve God, verse 15. This is what they had longed to do, but were ever hindered from doing perfectly by the infirmities of the flesh. *O wretched man that I am! who shall deliver me from the body of this death? I thank God through Jesus Christ our Lord. So then with the mind I myself serve the law of God; but with the flesh the law of sin*, Romans 7:24-25.

6. Their company. They have the company of God. The words of the angels to the despondent disciples on Mount Olivet, *Ye men of Galilee, why stand ye gazing up into heaven?* surely touch upon the feelings often experienced by the Christian. Such loneliness will be over in heaven for *He that sitteth on the throne shall dwell among them.* Notice the tender attention they will receive. *For the Lamb which is in the midst of the throne shall feed them, and shall lead them unto living fountains of waters: and God shall wipe away all tears from their eyes*, verse 17. During this earthly pilgrimage, God oftentimes makes us to cry. *Thou feedest them with the bread of tears; and givest them tears to drink in great measure*, Psalm 80:5. The chastening that brought forth such tears was always for our benefit and wrought because of love. But in heaven there are no more tears. God Himself shall wipe them all away. All trouble is at an end for the child of God. They have reached the Father's house and the journey is over.

The period of the seventh seal

CHAPTERS 8 AND 9

The further you go in a study of the book of the Revelation, the more detailed becomes the subject matter of the visions. The nearer we get in our study to the event of the ages, the return of Christ, the greater the detail of the information given. It is akin to the record of history. The further back you go, the less detailed are the records available. It may be likened to the information we would give to someone travelling to our home who is a complete stranger in the area. The first section of the journey would require few directions. It would be sufficient for directions to be given that would place the traveller on the road that would lead to our home. It would be necessary to become more specific only as he neared his destination. Then he would need increasingly detailed information of turn offs and prominent landmarks until he was guided to our door. So it is with prophecy. As we are taken nearer to the return of Christ, the significant and graphic pointers that herald that event are given in increasing detail and numbers.

The period of the opening of the seventh and last seal is divided into seven smaller periods, the beginning of each one being signalled by the sounding of a trumpet.

In this study we shall look at six of those trumpets.

I.   THE SILENCE IN HEAVEN.

And when he had opened the seventh seal, there was silence in heaven about the space of half an hour, Revelation 8:1.

This silence has been likened to the hush that descends upon a battlefield before the commencement of hostilities. God is about to stretch out His hand upon the earth in judgment. The trumpet, the ancient instrument of communication on the battlefield, is about to sound its commands. All heaven listens attentively for the signal that will herald the final phase of the conflict of the ages.

1. The sinfulness of men has provoked these judgments. *And the rest of the men which were not killed by these plagues yet repented not of the works of their hands, that they should not worship devils, and idols of gold, and silver, and brass, and stone, and of wood: which neither can see, nor hear, nor walk: neither repented they of their murders, nor of their sorceries, nor of their fornication, nor of their thefts*, Revelation 9:20-21. Here is a six-fold description of mankind generally. Six being the number of man, we have a picture of what man will become as he progressively breaks free of all moral restraint.

Devil worship. The final apostasy will centre upon the total rejection of God. Man is an atheist at heart. *The fool hath said in his heart, There is no God*, Psalm 14:1. The end of this age will see open and blatant denial of God and the worship of the devil. *For that day shall not come, except there come a falling away first, and that man of sin be revealed, the son of perdition; who opposeth and exalteth himself above all that is called God, or that is worshipped; so that he as God sitteth in the temple of God, shewing himself that he is God*, 2 Thessalonians 2:3-4. *And they worshipped the dragon which gave power unto the beast: and they worshipped the beast, saying, Who is like unto the beast? who is able to make war with him?* Revelation 13:4.

Idol worship. Man has surely reached his lowest level of intellectual turpitude when he bows in worship before an idol of metal or wood or stone. It is on the increase in this age. In lands, where the gospel swept it away at the reformation, it is returning with a vengeance. It has become almost fashionable to become an idol-worshipping Romanist. Hundreds, if not thousands of members of the Church of England have been led by their disaffected clerics into the fold of Rome. Among these blind and deluded devotees have been ministers of the British Government, members of the Royal family and celebrities from the world of so-called entertainment. The shameful display of Mary-worship at Walsingham in Norfolk, England, when the Romish doll is paraded with great pomp and ceremony through the tiny village, amidst much chanting of 'Ave Maria' and swilling of beer by monks and priests, is an example of the evil traditions of the dark ages. It is true of them as it had been of the believers at Corinth before their conversion to Christ. *Ye know that ye were Gentiles, carried away unto these dumb idols, even as ye were led*, 1 Corinthians 12:2. The worship of idols is but a cover for the worship of devils, though I am sure that few of the worshippers realise this. *What say I then? that the idol is any thing, or that which is offered in sacrifice to idols is any thing? But I say, that the things which the Gentiles sacrifice, they sacrifice to devils, and not to God: and I would not that ye should have fellowship with devils*, 2 Corinthians 10:19-20.

Murder. Where there is subservience to the devil there will be murder for *he was a murderer from the beginning*, John 8:44. Not only will murder become more frequent, but it will become accepted. By that I mean, it will not be considered with the abhorrence that is in keeping with such an awful crime. The punishment laid down for it in God's law, capital punishment, has been almost universally abolished. Mitigating circumstances will be increasingly promulgated, as in some recent cases where women, who had murdered their common-law husbands in retaliation for beatings and were given a jail sentence for murder, were released from prison, when it was decided by the courts that they were not really guilty of murder and that a much shorter sentence would be more appropriate. A new attitude to murder is also seen in the public 'rehabilitation' of men such as Gerry Adams and Martin McGuinness who are associated with the IRA terror campaign in Northern Ireland, in which many hundreds of Protestants have been brutally murdered, simply because they were Protestants. It is quite in order, but a few short months after the last IRA murder, for Government ministers to be seen shaking hands with these guilty men and smiling and posing for the press, as they enter talks with these erstwhile terrorists who have never unequivocally renounced terrorism or repented of their crimes.

Sorcery. This practice will become very common in the last days of this age. The word for sorcery is *pharmakeia* from which we get *pharmacist*. It is linked with the administration of drugs. It literally refers to enchantment with drugs. Drug-taking is a practice that is becoming ever more common. A recent survey commissioned by the Institute for the Study of Drug Dependence indicated that pupils at school who do not take drugs will soon be the exception. Some 80% of 700 school attenders, interviewed in Manchester and Liverpool in England, acknowledged that they had been offered drugs before they were 16 and more than half of them had tried them. It has been claimed by the authors of the survey that over the next few years, particularly in urban areas, 'non-drug-trying adolescents will be a minority group. In one sense they will be the deviants' (National press, 25/7/95). Link this drug-taking with the rise of interest in the occult and you can see that which is spoken of in this chapter coming to pass. 'Mystic Meg' is a rather comical female who, for a time, was featured each week in the choosing of the numbers for the national lottery in the United Kingdom. That 'figure of fun' will become more and more a 'figure of fear', as increasing darkness takes hold upon the mind of the nation.

Fornication. Illicit sexual behaviour of all forms is becoming increasingly accepted in society. The heir to the British throne, Prince Charles, has openly acknowledged that he has committed adultery. That, it seems, has not jeopardised his right of succession to the throne. So too has his former wife, Princess Diana. Such an acknowledgement has not damaged her public standing in the eyes of the majority in the nation. United States President, Bill Clinton and the late François Mitterand, a former president of France, are two other international figures who openly acknowledged their infidelity. A recent report by a committee within the Church of England called for the abandoning of the term 'living in sin', because it was offensive when referring to those who co-habited outside of marriage. Similar noises have been heard from other religious camps. Sodomy has been legalised. Sodomite couples have even been considered as suitable for the adoption of children. In certain circumstances it is punishable by law for one to express abhorrence of this detestable and wicked practice. The brasen adherents of this shameful defiance of God's law are becoming ever more open and bold. There are even sodomites in the ministry of some ecumenical denominations. Many of them occupy prominent positions of power.

All of this points to the increasing moral corruption which will trigger God's judgments, even as it did in Noah's day and in Lot's day.

Theft. Theft may seem a minor thing, a thing that has been a common practice throughout the ages. Common it may be, but I am sure that it will reach new depths as this age advances toward its close. Dishonesty, the seedbed of theft, is more prevalent now than ever before. It has become quite acceptable for those who are otherwise quite respectable members of society to steal from employers, from shops, from just about anybody when an opportunity arises. A robbery recently took place in Dublin, Republic of Ireland, but the robber was soon hotly pursued by the police. As he ran, bank notes began to fall from the leg of his trousers down which he had stuffed his loot. Passers-by grabbed what they could and were most reluctant to hand it over to the police. Hundreds of pounds were never recovered, having been taken by citizens who felt that it was quite in order to hold on to such a windfall.

A phrase has become very prevalent in the utterances of those expressing the view that life has been unkind to them. They say they have a 'right' to a house, to a substantial and steady income, to an underpinning of their lifestyle by government funds, to just about whatever takes their fancy. Such a view is the product of the so-called 'welfare state' and has been promoted by successive political parties urging upon the electorate an expectation of such 'rights' in order to win support and ultimate political power. The populace, having been urged to demand these 'rights', naturally expect them. Where it is commonly believed that we have a right to that which others seem to be enjoying, then it is a short step to concluding that, all other avenues to our obtaining it being apparently closed, we have a right to take it. Of course, such thinking lies behind the moral theology of Rome. Her great 'moralist,' Alphonso Ligouiri, teaches that, if our neighbour has an abundance of that which we have need of, it is no sin to steal from him. Such teaching has produced the thinking in countries such as Italy, Portugal, the Irish Republic and Spain that has resulted in the fraudulent appropriation of countless millions of pounds by citizens claiming grants from the funds of the European Community to which they have no rights. Dishonesty will reach epidemic proportions before the end of the age.

2. The prayers of believers have produced these judgments. *And another angel came and stood at the altar, having a golden censer; and there was given unto him much incense, that he should offer it with the prayers of all saints upon the golden altar which was before the throne. And the smoke of the incense, which came with the prayers of the saints, ascended up before God out of the angel's hand. And the* *angel took the censer, and filled it with fire of the altar, and cast it into the earth: and there were voices, and thunderings, and lightnings, and an earthquake*, Revelation 8:3-5.

The prayers of all saints regarding the wickedness of this world are going to be answered. The believer has ever been vexed by the sin taking place around him. That vexation has given rise to prayers and they will be answered. Some of the utterances of David are representative of the feelings of the child of God amidst the wickedness of this world. *Horror hath taken hold upon me because of the wicked that forsake thy law. Rivers of waters run down mine eyes, because they keep not thy law. I beheld the transgressors, and was grieved; because they kept not thy word*, Psalm 119:53, 136, 158. The prayers of God's people will bring God's judgment upon the earth. *Mine eye also shall see my desire on mine enemies, and mine ears shall hear my desire of the wicked that rise up against me*, Psalm 92:11. *And shall not God avenge his own elect, which cry day and night unto him, though he bear long with them?* Luke 18:7. We have already seen that even in heaven the saints continue to pray such prayers, Revelation 6:10-11. The *little season*, mentioned in 6:11, is coming to an end and the time of wrath and vengeance draws near.

3. It should be noticed that the instruments associated with gospel mercy are now used in judgment. The trumpet is first mentioned in the Bible as the instrument that featured in the announcement of the law of God to Israel. The censer was the symbol of intercession at which the high priest ministered on behalf of Israel. These now become the instruments of judgment. Paul called the preacher of the gospel a *savour of death unto death* or a *savour of life unto life*, 2 Corinthians 2:16. That, which saves those who believe it, will damn those who reject it. It was to this truth Christ referred when He said, *Do not think that I will accuse you to the Father: there is one that accuseth you, even Moses, in whom ye trust*, John 5:45. The words of life shall become the words of condemnation to those who refused to obey them.

II. THE DEVASTATION ON THE EARTH.

1. Creation is at first the chief subject of judgment. *And the seven angels which had the seven trumpets prepared themselves to sound.*

The first angel sounded, and there followed hail and fire mingled with blood, and they were cast upon the earth: and the third part of trees was burnt up, and all green grass was burnt up, 8:6-7. In the judgments we may observe the gradual procedure of God. The inanimate creation is the first to feel His wrath and natural forces are employed by the Lord. A similar commencement to the judgments in Egypt may be observed. There the first judgments fell chiefly upon the creatures of the fields and then increasingly affected men. There all the judgments involved only natural phenomena.

And the second angel sounded, and as it were a great mountain burning with fire was cast into the sea: and the third part of the sea became blood; and the third part of the creatures which were in the sea, and had life, died; and the third part of the ships were destroyed, verses 8-9. The second trumpet brings a judgment that results in a third of the creatures in the sea and a third of the ships and their crews and passengers being destroyed.

And the third angel sounded, and there fell a great star from heaven, burning as it were a lamp, and it fell upon the third part of the rivers, and upon the fountains of waters; and the name of the star is called Wormwood: and the third part of the waters became wormwood; and many men died of the waters, because they were made bitter, verses 10-11. The third judgment brings a poisoning of a third of the waters and many men die as a result.

And the fourth angel sounded, and the third part of the sun was smitten, and the third part of the moon, and the third part of the stars; so as the third part of them was darkened, and the day shone not for a third part of it, and the night likewise, verse 12. The fourth judgment, with its darkening of the sun, will likewise bring great discomfort to men.

2. A woeful pronouncement. *And I beheld, and heard an angel flying through the midst of heaven, saying with a loud voice, Woe, woe, woe, to the inhabiters of the earth by reason of the other voices of the trumpet of the three angels, which are yet to sound,* verse 13. If men only realised what their sin will bring upon their heads, they would understand why even the angels utter a groan at the prospects faced by sinners. This verse makes clear that the three woes are synonymous with the last three trumpets.

III. AN INVASION FROM HELL.

This triple woe pronounced by the angel indicates a significant new phase of the judgments as their severity increases. The Lord no longer confines Himself to using natural forces as instruments of judgment. Now He releases the powers of hell upon men. It should be noticed also that men are now the only target of judgment. *And it was commanded them that they should not hurt the grass of the earth, neither any green thing, neither any tree; but only those men which have not the seal of God in their foreheads. . . . and their power was to hurt men five months. . . for to slay the third part of men. . . . By these three was the third part of men killed, by the fire, and by the smoke, and by the brimstone, which issued out of their mouths*, Revelation 9:4, 10, 15, 18.

1. The likeness of these invaders, verses 7-10.

They are described as warhorse-like locusts, verse 7. What an image of furious activity! Both creatures are noted for fury and voracity. The war horse is described in Job 39:19-25 as a creature without fear. Against the locust man, even modern man, has no defence.

They wear crowns of gold, verse 7. Unto them was given power, verses 3, 5, 10. The word *power* means that they had the *authority* as well as the *ability* to hurt men. They could not be resisted by men for they had divinely-given jurisdiction over their victims.

They have faces like men, verse 7. The idea suggested is that of intelligence. They would deceive men all the more easily, being given the knowledge of men.

They have hair like women, verse 8. Men with long female-like hairstyles have become part of the gender confusion in which modern society indulges—. It speaks of effeminacy and sensuality. If the shaven head in Old Testament times was the symbol of mourning, then the opposite surely denotes revelry. *Cut off thine hair, O Jerusalem, and cast it away, and take up a lamentation on high places; for the LORD hath rejected and forsaken the generation of his wrath*, Jeremiah 7:29. The Grecian and Roman empires, in keeping with former empires, came to an end in a wave of wanton seeking after the gratifications of the flesh. That same spirit will manifest itself to an unparalleled degree in the last days of this age.

They have teeth like a lion, verse 8. Satan is lion-like in his cruel harassment of men. *Be sober, be vigilant; because your adversary the* *devil, as a roaring lion, walketh about, seeking whom he may devour*, 1 Peter 5:8. Fierce and cruel will be the regime that the devil will be permitted to inflict upon men.

They have breastplates of iron, verse 9. They will be impervious to resistance and to all appeals for clemency. Their breast, the seat of emotion and tenderness, will be bound about with iron-like harshness.

They have wings. Flying is the fastest means of transport known to man. With what rapidity this dark plague of evil will spread across the world! It will penetrate to all areas. The Romans needed roads to conquer. Wings make roads obsolete. There are few truly remote areas left in the world. There will be no hiding away from what is coming upon the world.

They have stings. They injured rather than killed. They tortured rather than slew. They shall so afflict that men shall desire death. *And in those days shall men seek death, and shall not find it; and shall desire to die, and death shall flee from them*, verse 6.

2. The leader of these invaders. *And they had a king over them, which is the angel of the bottomless pit, whose name in the Hebrew tongue is Abaddon, but in the Greek tongue hath his name Apollyon*, verse 11. This was not 'mindless' violence and disorder. It was executed under the directions of the devil. It must be said, that while much of the violence in which men engage seems to be without reason or purpose, in truth there is no such thing as 'mindless' violence. There is a mind behind it all - Satan's. The invasion begins with a falling star. *And the fifth angel sounded, and I saw a star fall from heaven unto the earth: and to him was given the key of the bottomless pit*, verse 1. I believe the star refers to the devil. He is depicted in Holy Scripture as gathering to himself a portion of the angels of heaven who followed him in his rebellion against God. The words of Isaiah 14:12-15 are a reference to Satan's fall into rebellion. There again there is a reference to the stars of God and Satan's desire to rule over God's host. *How art thou fallen from heaven, O Lucifer, son of the morning! how art thou cut down to the ground, which didst weaken the nations! For thou hast said in thine heart, I will ascend into heaven, I will exalt my throne above the stars of God: I will sit also upon the mount of the congregation, in the sides of the north: I will ascend above the heights of the clouds; I will be like the most High. Yet thou shalt be brought down to hell, to the sides of the pit*, Isaiah 14:12-15.

God shall permit the devil to release upon the world the hellish powers that mercy has long restrained. Under king Satan, this dark host will come forth to plague men.

3. The limits of this invasion. There is a three-fold limitation upon it.

It is limited in the power it exercises. *And to them it was given that they should not kill them,* verse 5. What power God exercises over the devil! A similar restriction to that placed upon Satan, when he was permitted to afflict Job, will be placed upon him on this occasion. *And the LORD said unto Satan, Behold, he is in thine hand; but save his life,* Job 2:6. While Job's afflictions were to test the man of God and to show forth God's gracious power to keep His children, such will not be the purpose of God on this occasion. The subjects of Satan's attack will not be killed, but they will be tormented. The word *torment* (verse 5) is the word so often used by unclean spirits when referring to their future punishment. *And, behold, they cried out, saying, What have we to do with thee, Jesus, thou Son of God? art thou come hither to torment us before the time?* Matthew 8:29. This clearly indicates just what wicked men will endure at the devil's hands at the end of this age.

It is limited in the time that it will last. *And their power was to hurt men five months,* verse 10.

It is limited in those targeted. *And it was commanded them that they should not hurt the grass of the earth, neither any green thing, neither any tree; but only those men which have not the seal of God in their foreheads,* verse 4. Let every child of God rejoice that even in the midst of hell's invasion there will be the barrier of redeeming blood that will keep the messenger of suffering from the door. Those with the seal of Christ upon them need fear no evil. *When thou passest through the waters, I will be with thee; and through the rivers, they shall not overflow thee: when thou walkest through the fire, thou shalt not be burned; neither shall the flame kindle upon thee. For I am the LORD thy God, the Holy One of Israel, thy Saviour,* Isaiah 43:2-3.

IV. THE SATANIC INFLUENCE OF ANTICHRIST'S KINGDOM.

Loose the four angels which are bound in the great river Euphrates, 9:14. Here is an unloosing of the evil power that resides in

Babylonianism. It is that releasing from restraint about which we have already made some comments. As Lazarus was loosed from the restraints of his grave clothes (John 11:44), even so shall there be a liberating of powers of evil angels, which are presently bound in the region of the Euphrates river.

Babylonianism will be a system not only of commerce and false religion. It will have a military arm. The loosing of the evil angels is swiftly followed by reference to a great army of *two hundred thousand thousand*, verse 16. This army was to be the instrument by which one third of the men were killed. It is most likely that it is one third of the male population of the prophetic earth, the area around the Great or the Mediterranean Sea.

Great slaughter shall mark the advance of antichristianity. Apostasy and misery go hand in hand. Northern Ireland over the last 30 years ought to have learned this lesson. So ought the rest of the United Kingdom. Even the long-safe sanctuary of the infants' school has been breached by the devilish cruelty that has followed in the footsteps of national apostasy, as was witnessed at Dunblane in Scotland not long ago.

The mighty Angel and the commissioning of the prophet
CHAPTERS 10

The focus of the prophecy is becoming narrower. The subject matter is becoming more precise and definite. A wider view of the developments in the world, particularly in that area known as the prophetic earth, the territory around the Mediterranean Sea, has been dealt with in the chapters 6-9. In chapters 11-13, the subject matter will become more narrow still and will be very concentrated with regard to persons, places and the period of time.

This chapter 10 acts like an introduction to what follows in the succeeding chapters. While the subject matter of chapters 11-13 will be the earth under the rule of the devil through his puppets, the Antichrist and the False Prophet, here in chapter 10 we are given a larger preview of the One *stronger than the strong man* coming in power and great glory to overthrow the devil's rule and claim the earth as His own. We have already commented, at the beginning of our study of chapter 6, upon the matter of the Lord giving a preview of His coming, before He reveals what will actually take place before His coming, in order to strengthen His disciples. Here again, the Saviour reveals to John, and through John to His Church universal, the wickedness that will fill the earth just prior to His return. But before He does so, He reminds them of the brevity of that period when evil will be permitted to conquer and of the certainty of His return in all-conquering power.

Let us ever remember that the purpose of this revelation is to bless the reader, not to depress him. *Blessed is he that readeth, and they that hear the words of this prophecy, and keep those things which are written therein: for the time is at hand,* 1:3. The Saviour would still have us *come and see,* 6:1. The truth of the Saviour's triumphant return is to be the inspiration of believers in evil times. *For the grace of God that bringeth salvation hath appeared to all men, teaching us that, denying ungodliness and worldly lusts, we should live soberly, righteously, and godly, in this present world; looking for that blessed hope, and the glorious appearing of the great God and our Saviour Jesus Christ; who gave himself for us, that he might redeem us from all iniquity, and purify unto himself a peculiar people, zealous of good works,* Titus 2:11-14. As the night of apostasy grows ever darker, let us look with all the more fervency for the dawn of the Day of the Lord.

I.   THE MIGHTY ANGEL, VERSES 1-7.

The mighty angel referred to in verse 1 represents the Lord Jesus, the Angel of the Covenant. Of that we can have little doubt since the description is one that befits deity alone.

1. His descent. He did not fall as did the star, the devil, in 9:1. Rather it is a controlled and dignified descent. The word *fall* in 9:1 is a translation of *pipto* which carries the meaning of being *thrust down.* It refers to a descent that is not under one's control. Matthew 7:25, 15:14 and 17:15 will give just some examples of its use. On the other hand, the Greek word *katabaino* that is translated *come down* in 10:1 carries a very different meaning. It means a descending that is deliberate and controlled. A few references showing the use of the word will demonstrate what is said: Matthew 3:16; 8:1; John 3:13; 5:4; 6:33. Perhaps the best definition of the two Greek words is found in Acts 20:9-10. *And there sat in a window a certain young man named Eutychus, being fallen into a deep sleep: and as Paul was long preaching, he sunk down with sleep, and fell down (pipto) from the third loft, and was taken up dead. And Paul went down (katabaino), and fell on him, and embracing him said, Trouble not yourselves; for his life is in him.* This shows the contrast between the two words very clearly. The first is a falling down uncontrollably from a great height by a young man who has fallen asleep and the second, a deliberate and measured descent by Paul as he came to his aid.

The Lord will come again in His own appointed time, for He is Lord of time and eternity and none can resist what He wills to do.

2. His description. *And I saw another mighty angel . . . . clothed with a cloud: and a rainbow was upon his head, and his face was as it were the sun, and his feet as pillars of fire: and he had in his hand a little book open: and he set his right foot upon the sea, and his left foot on the earth, and cried with a loud voice, as when a lion roareth,* verses 1-3.

He was clothed with a cloud. It is the garment of divine majesty. *And the LORD went before them by day in a pillar of a cloud, to lead them the way; and by night in a pillar of fire, to give them light; to go by day and night,* Exodus 13:21. *And then shall appear the sign of the Son of man in heaven: and then shall all the tribes of the earth mourn, and they shall see the Son of man coming in the clouds of heaven with power and great glory,* Matthew 24:30.

A rainbow was upon His head. This is the symbol of the covenant of mercy and grace. It is upon His head, for He has ever that covenant upon His mind, as He pursues the interests of the people of that covenant. This same rainbow was seen about the throne in heaven in chapter 4:3. The earth is about to be brought under the rule and power of that throne as the Saviour establishes His kingdom.

His face was as the sun. What Christ is to His people, *as the sun shineth in his strength* (1:16), even so will He be one day to the whole earth. The return of the Saviour will herald the dawn of a new day for Jerusalem, Israel and the whole world. *Arise, shine; for thy light is come, and the glory of the LORD is risen upon thee. For, behold, the darkness shall cover the earth, and gross darkness the people: but the LORD shall arise upon thee, and his glory shall be seen upon thee. And the Gentiles shall come to thy light, and kings to the brightness of thy rising,* Isaiah 60:1-3. On that day the Lord shall arise as the *Sun of righteousness . . with healing in his wings,* Malachi 4:2.

His feet were as pillars of fire. He shall tread this earth in holiness and establish righteousness with everlasting firmness. His feet shall be planted as pillars, never to be moved again.

In His hand was a little book open. It is the book of chapter 5, verse 1, but now the seals are opened and the Saviour is coming to claim

His inheritance according to the ancient rite instituted in Israel, Jeremiah 32:6-12.

He cried with the loud voice of a lion. The world is presently deaf to God and His voice, but not so on the day depicted. The lion's roar cannot be ignored. This earth shall be awakened from its indifference and wicked slumbers by that voice, which is to us, most sweet. *Therefore prophesy thou against them all these words, and say unto them, The LORD shall roar from on high, and utter his voice from his holy habitation; he shall mightily roar upon his habitation; he shall give a shout, as they that tread the grapes, against all the inhabitants of the earth,* Jeremiah 25:30. *For thus hath the LORD spoken unto me, Like as the lion and the young lion roaring on his prey, when a multitude of shepherds is called forth against him, he will not be afraid of their voice, nor abase himself for the noise of them: so shall the LORD of hosts come down to fight for mount Zion, and for the hill thereof,* Isaiah 31:4. *The LORD also shall roar out of Zion, and utter his voice from Jerusalem; and the heavens and the earth shall shake: but the LORD will be the hope of his people, and the strength of the children of Israel,* Joel 3:16.

And cried with a loud voice, as when a lion roareth: and when he had cried, seven thunders uttered their voices. And when the seven thunders had uttered their voices, I was about to write: and I heard a voice from heaven saying unto me, Seal up those things which the seven thunders uttered, and write them not, verses 3-4. The roar of the Lion of Judah is followed by the voice of seven thunders. When the apostle attempts to record what was said, he is forbidden. There are things which we as saints cannot know until the dawn of that day. *For now we see through a glass, darkly; but then face to face: now I know in part; but then shall I know even as also I am known,* 1 Corinthians 13:12.

3. His destination. *He set his right foot upon the sea, and his left foot on the earth,* verse 2.

In keeping with what the Lord said to Israel, in Deuteronomy 11:24, *Every place whereon the soles of your feet shall tread shall be yours: from the wilderness and Lebanon, from the river, the river Euphrates, even unto the uttermost sea shall your coast be,* even so shall He lay claim to the whole earth.

But it is not just the stance of a claimant. It is the stance of a conqueror. A conquered earth, long engaged in rebellion against Him, is beneath His feet. *I have trodden the winepress alone; and of the people there was none with me: for I will tread them in mine anger, and trample them in my fury; and their blood shall be sprinkled upon my garments, and I will stain all my raiment,* Isaiah 63:3.

4. His declaration. *And the angel which I saw stand upon the sea and upon the earth lifted up his hand to heaven, And sware by him that liveth for ever and ever, who created heaven, and the things that therein are, and the earth, and the things that therein are, and the sea, and the things which are therein, that there should be time no longer,* verses 5-6.

Here is a strong confirmation of an oath, the contents of which are clear - *that there should be time no longer.* All delay is over. In mercy the Lord does delay His coming. *There shall come in the last days scoffers, walking after their own lusts, and saying, Where is the promise of his coming? for since the fathers fell asleep, all things continue as they were from the beginning of the creation. But, beloved, be not ignorant of this one thing, that one day is with the Lord as a thousand years, and a thousand years as one day. The Lord is not slack concerning his promise, as some men count slackness; but is longsuffering to us-ward, not willing that any should perish, but that all should come to repentance,* 2 Peter 3:3-4, 8-9. The delay is in order to gather in the elect. It is a display of mercy and longsuffering to *us-ward* in faithfulness to His covenant promise.

But the delay will end one day. It will end on the day of the sounding of the trumpet of the seventh angel. That is the last trump referred to in 1 Corinthians 15:52 and 1 Thessalonians 4:16. Then *the mystery of God should be finished, as he hath declared to his servants the prophets,* verse 7. That which is a mystery to the world, but which is revealed to the saints, even the eternal purpose of God's grace in Christ, shall be fully understood by the saints and grasped to some degree by the world for the first time.

Here is the precise yardstick by which we may know ourselves to be truly Christ's. Do we have an understanding of that which is a mystery to the world? Hear the apostle Paul on the matter and examine yourself. *But we speak the wisdom of God in a mystery, even the hidden wisdom, which God ordained before the world unto our glory: which none of the princes of this world knew: for had they known it, they would not have crucified the Lord of glory. But as it is written, Eye hath not seen, nor*

*ear heard, neither have entered into the heart of man, the things which
God hath prepared for them that love him. But God hath revealed them
unto us by his Spirit: for the Spirit searcheth all things, yea, the deep
things of God,* 1 Corinthians 2:7-10. Have your eyes been opened to the
beauty and glory of the man Christ Jesus? Have you knelt before Him
in lowly penitence and confessed your sinfulness and unworthiness?
Have you cast yourself upon His mercy, trusting only for salvation in
the merits of His blood sacrifice upon the cross? Are you awaiting
patiently the day of His return? These are the essential matters of the
soul that must be settled before one can consider oneself a true believer.

II. THE COMMISSIONING OF THE PROPHET, VERSES 8-11.

From the events of the future of verse 7, we are taken back to the
present in verse 8. The mystery of God as declared by the prophets shall
be finished (brought to a close) by the sounding of the last trumpet. But
until that moment, the duty of the servant of God is to continue witnessing. John is spoken to by the Saviour for His is the voice referred to in
verse 8. Verse 8 directs us back to 4:1, and that verse in turn directs us
back to 1:10, and there we learn that the voice was that of the Saviour.
John is reminded that the day of triumph has not yet dawned and that the
hard path of witness-bearing in a hostile world must yet continue awhile.
John also learned that he was not going to end his days upon Patmos for
he is told, *Thou must prophesy again before many peoples, and nations,
and tongues, and kings,* verse 11.

Notice that the Saviour requires John:-

1. To take the book. *And the voice which I heard from heaven
spake unto me again, and said, Go and take the little book which is open
in the hand of the angel which standeth upon the sea and upon the earth,*
verse 8.

No one may serve the Lord who does not take the book of God in
his hand. A true servant of God has laid hold upon the book and accepted it in its entirety. It is the whole book or nothing. Men, today,
who claim to be God's servants, would remove that which they consider
offensive. They do not perceive it as coming from the hand of Christ or
they would not presume to alter and amend it. *This book of the law shall
not depart out of thy mouth; but thou shalt meditate therein day and*

night, that thou mayest observe to do according to all that is written therein: for then thou shalt make thy way prosperous, and then thou shalt have good success, Joshua 1:8.

2. To taste the book. None may preach the gospel who has not personally tasted of its delights. What sort of cook is the one who has never tasted his own cooking? How may a man present a Christ of Whom he knows nothing experimentally?

Notice how sweet the book was in the mouth of the prophet. *And I took the little book out of the angel's hand, and ate it up; and it was in my mouth sweet as honey*, verse 10. So declared David also. *The judgments of the LORD are true and righteous altogether. More to be desired are they than gold, yea, than much fine gold: sweeter also than honey and the honeycomb*, Psalm 19:9-10. *How sweet are thy words unto my taste! yea, sweeter than honey to my mouth!* Psalm 119:103. There is a sweetness in the book which is tasted by those who meditate upon its chief subject - Christ. *My meditation of him shall be sweet: I will be glad in the LORD*, Psalm 104:34. Dear reader, I call upon you now to *taste and see that the LORD is good: blessed is the man that trusteth in him*, Psalm 34:8. To taste is to trust. None has tasted of Christ and His sweet mercy and grace until by faith He is received into the heart, even as food is received into the mouth and swallowed, so as to be assimilated by the eater.

It was sweet in the mouth but bitter in the belly. *As soon as I had eaten it, my belly was bitter*, verse 10. What bitterness of soul is associated with the preaching of God's Word! This was discovered by Ezekiel also. *And when I looked, behold, an hand was sent unto me; and, lo, a roll of a book was therein; and he spread it before me; and it was written within and without: and there was written therein lamentations, and mourning, and woe*, Ezekiel 2:9-10. So bitter was the message that Jeremiah was required to proclaim, that for a time he was unable to declare it. *O LORD, thou hast deceived me, and I was deceived: thou art stronger than I, and hast prevailed: I am in derision daily, every one mocketh me. For since I spake, I cried out, I cried violence and spoil; because the word of the LORD was made a reproach unto me, and a derision, daily. Then I said, I will not make mention of him, nor speak any more in his name. But his word was in mine heart as a burning fire shut up in my bones, and I was weary with forbearing, and I could not stay*, Jeremiah 20:7-9. The bravest of men, John Calvin, John Knox and many others, were overcome for a time by the bitterness of bearing witness to Christ in a day of darkness.

3. To testify of the book. *Thou must prophesy again before many peoples, and nations, and tongues, and kings*, verse 11. When John took up the ministry again, after seeing what he did upon Patmos, it must be said that he preached in the light of the return of Christ as he never had done before. The light of those visions which he had witnessed must have remained with him all his days. He could never have forgotten the view into the future that was granted to him. In this book of the Revelation, John has shared with us this vision of Christ's return. It behoves God's people generally, and preachers in particular, to live and witness in the light of those *things which must shortly come to pass*, 1:1. Was not this the substance of the solemn charge which Paul laid upon Timothy and which has been laid upon virtually every minister ever since at his ordination service? *I charge thee therefore before God, and the Lord Jesus Christ, who shall judge the quick and the dead at his appearing and his kingdom; preach the word; be instant in season, out of season; reprove, rebuke, exhort with all longsuffering and doctrine*, 2 Timothy 4:1-2. May Christians draw strength from the glory of that day to press on fervently, and may they be spurred on by the terror of that day to witness faithfully to poor lost sinners. So lived the apostle Paul. *For we must all appear before the judgment seat of Christ; that every one may receive the things done in his body, according to that he hath done, whether it be good or bad. Knowing therefore the terror of the Lord, we persuade men*, 2 Corinthians 5:10-11.

The last two witnesses

In keeping with what we observed at the beginning of our last study, we now find that the subject matter of this chapter centres upon the city of Jerusalem at the time just prior to the return of Christ. I think that there can be little doubt about this. The most obvious indication of the location of the scenes of this chapter is given in verse 8. *And their dead bodies shall lie in the street of the great city, which spiritually is called Sodom and Egypt, where also our Lord was crucified.* But it is a Jerusalem as we do not know it today. It is a Jerusalem with a temple. *And there was given me a reed like unto a rod: and the angel stood, saying, Rise, and measure the temple of God, and the altar, and them that worship therein, verse* 1. Temple worship, long desired by orthodox Jews, is once again functioning. It must be noticed that this restoration has not altered the spiritual character of the city. It is still *the great city, which spiritually is called Sodom and Egypt, where also our Lord was crucified.* Jerusalem, it appears, has become a centre of world-wide interest. The events that take place there hold the attention of the world, verses 9-10. A comment by B.W. Newton in *Thoughts on the Apocalypse* is worth noting. 'In reading this chapter, therefore, we must imagine Jerusalem again restored to seeming dignity and greatness: its Temple re-built; its worship re-established; itself become a centre for the busy concourse of many nations; her own people resting under the shadow of the great chief of the Gentiles, who, for a little season, practises on them by his flatteries, and then suddenly grasps them for destruction. During the whole period of the smoothness and deceit of Antichrist, Christians and Christian testimony remain in Jerusalem. . . . But when the last period arrives, and the 1260 days of Antichrist's supremacy commence by the planting of the idol of the desolater, we find Christianity, not indeed extinguished in the earth, but withdrawn from Judah and Jerusalem, and Israel left to fall alike beneath the power of the great destroyer and the superadded afflictions of the wrath of God; *for then shall be great tribulation, such as was not since the beginning of the world to this time, no, nor ever shall be.* (Matthew 24:21). This, however, is the hour which God has selected for the mission of a new character of testimony into that most evil, yet beloved city. I will endow my two witnesses, and they shall prophesy a thousand two hundred and threescore days, clothed in sackcloth.'

The prophetic history of Israel is declared to be divided into *seventy weeks* or seventy periods of time. This is set down clearly in Daniel 9:25-28. *Know therefore and understand, that from the going forth of the commandment to restore and to build Jerusalem unto the Messiah the Prince shall be seven weeks, and threescore and two weeks: the street shall be built again, and the wall, even in troublous times. And after threescore and two weeks shall Messiah be cut off, but not for himself: and the people of the prince that shall come shall destroy the city and the sanctuary; and the end thereof shall be with a flood, and unto the end of the war desolations are determined. And he shall confirm the covenant with many for one week: and in the midst of the week he shall cause the sacrifice and the oblation to cease, and for the overspreading of abominations he shall make it desolate, even until the consummation, and that determined shall be poured upon the desolate.* We can easily calculate just how long those 69 weeks lasted for it clearly refers to the period from the commandment to rebuild Jerusalem until the Messiah was cut off. That covered a period of 483 years which is 69 multiplied by 7. Daniel then refers to another week during which a covenant with the Jews is confirmed but half way through that week the covenant shall be broken and the sacrifices and oblations made to cease. This period of a 'week', or seven years and particularly the events that will take place half way through that period, is frequently mentioned in Holy Scripture. We have a mention of it in verse 3 of this chapter. *And*

I will give power unto my two witnesses, and they shall prophesy a thousand two hundred and threescore days, clothed in sackcloth. That is a period of three and a half years. Their ministry shall end, we are told, just prior to the sounding of the seventh trumpet which is the signal that the Saviour is about to return, verses 12-15. Does this not determine for us just when the events of this chapter will take place? It is, as B. W. Newton said, that final three and a half years or *forty and two months* (verse 2) of this age which begin with the Antichrist's breaking of his covenant with Israel and his setting up the Abomination of Desolation in the Temple and declaring himself to be God. It is during these terrible final days that these two witnesses will testify.

I. THE PROPHECY OF THE TWO WITNESSES, VERSES 1-14.

These are literally two men, just as the Antichrist is literally one man. They are called witnesses in verse 3 and prophets in verse 10. Many have claimed that these two men are in fact Moses and Elijah returned to complete their ministry. The circumstances of the departure of these two men from the world are quoted in support of this proposition. The miracles that the two witnesses perform are also cited as evidence of them being Moses and Elijah, since there is a close parallel between that wrought by these two men and the miracles performed by Moses and Elijah. It should be remembered that John the Baptist, who was the forerunner of the Saviour at His first advent, ministered *in the spirit and power of Elias* (Luke 1:17). It may well be that these two men will minister in the spirit and power of Moses and Elijah. We cannot state with absolute certainty who they are, but we are strongly inclined to believe that Elijah will be one of them.

1. The character of their ministry.

They are men of standing. *These are the two olive trees, and the two candlesticks standing before the God of the earth*, verse 4. This is a direct reference to Zechariah 4: 2-3, 12-14. Though these two men are clothed in sackcloth (verse 3) they are nevertheless God's noblemen who shall *stand before* (in the presence of) the Lord of the whole earth.

It is with them as it is with God's saints generally. *Beloved, now are we the sons of God, and it doth not yet appear what we shall be: but we know that, when he shall appear, we shall be like him; for we shall see him as he is*, 1 John 3:2.

They are men of sorrow. They will go forth in a spirit of mourning. It will be a fullness of the spirit in which all the prophets, notably Jeremiah, ministered. It is that spirit to which Paul refers in Roman 9:1-5. *I say the truth in Christ, I lie not, my conscience also bearing me witness in the Holy Ghost, that I have great heaviness and continual sorrow in my heart. For I could wish that myself were accursed from Christ for my brethren, my kinsmen according to the flesh: who are Israelites; to whom pertaineth the adoption, and the glory, and the covenants, and the giving of the law, and the service of God, and the promises; whose are the fathers, and of whom as concerning the flesh Christ came, who is over all, God blessed for ever. Amen.* This was the distinguishing spirit of those spared from judgment in Ezekiel 9:4-6. *And the LORD said unto him, Go through the midst of the city, through the midst of Jerusalem, and set a mark upon the foreheads of the men that sigh and that cry for all the abominations that be done in the midst thereof. And to the others he said in mine hearing, Go ye after him through the city, and smite: let not your eye spare, neither have ye pity: slay utterly old and young, both maids, and little children, and women: but come not near any man upon whom is the mark; and begin at my sanctuary. Then they began at the ancient men which were before the house.*

It is that spirit which filled the blessed heart of our Saviour. *And when he was come near, he beheld the city, and wept over it, saying, If thou hadst known, even thou, at least in this thy day, the things which belong unto thy peace! but now they are hid from thine eyes. For the days shall come upon thee, that thine enemies shall cast a trench about thee, and compass thee round, and keep thee in on every side, and shall lay thee even with the ground, and thy children within thee; and they shall not leave in thee one stone upon another; because thou knewest not the time of thy visitation. And he went into the temple, and began to cast out them that sold therein, and them that bought*, Luke 19:41-45.

They are men of power. *I will give power unto my two witnesses,* verse 3. What power they shall exercise! Power to slay - *and if any man* *will hurt them, fire proceedeth out of their mouth, and devoureth their enemies: and if any man will hurt them, he must in this manner be killed*, verse 5. Power to shut heaven - *these have power to shut heaven, that it rain not in the days of their prophecy,* verse 6. Power over waters - *and have power over waters to turn them to blood.* Power to smite with plagues - *and to smite the earth with all plagues, as often as they will,* verse 6.

2. The rejection of their ministry. They will be resisted by those to whom they witness. Men will seek to hurt them, verse 5. The word *hurt* means *to act wrongfully against.* To suffer such has ever been the lot of God's people and God's servants. These two servants, however, will be able to strike back, something which God's suffering ones have not been able or even been permitted to do. But I say unto you, *That ye resist not evil: but whosoever shall smite thee on thy right cheek, turn to him the other also*, Matthew 5:39. Such an attitude is in keeping with the bearing of a patient and loving testimony with a view to winning souls to faith in Christ. However, the two witnesses are primarily ministers of judgment. They are harbingers of that great and terrible day when despisers and rejecters will suffer the consequences of their sin. All that is left to a people who reject the gospel of peace, as will be the case with Jerusalem, is judgment.

They are hated. *And when they shall have finished their testimony, the beast that ascendeth out of the bottomless pit shall make war against them, and shall overcome them, and kill them*, verse 7. Here is how all of God's people would be treated, were it not for the restraint God places upon the devil and his agencies. God has permitted that bitter hatred to break through at times. The occasions of the suffering of the people of God are numerous, but much less than would have been the case had not God subdued His enemies. Note that even then, the Antichrist, for he is *the beast that ascendeth out of the bottomless pit*, will not be able to strike against the two witnesses until *they shall have finished their testimony.*

They are considered tormentors. *And they that dwell upon the earth shall rejoice over them, and make merry, and shall send gifts one to another; because these two prophets tormented them that dwelt on the earth*, verse 10. The word *tormented* is the same word used by Peter to describe the feelings of Lot in Sodom. *For that righteous man dwelling among them, in seeing and hearing, vexed his righteous soul from day to day with their unlawful deeds*, 2 Peter 2:8. The vexation caused to the soul of Lot by the filthy living of the Sodomites is akin to what the world will feel under the ministry of the two witnesses. How contrary to man's nature are the holy things of God! Truly, *the flesh lusteth against the Spirit, and the Spirit against the flesh: and these are contrary the one to the other*, Galatians 5:17.

3. The vindication of their ministry. *And after three days and an half the Spirit of life from God entered into them, and they stood upon their feet; and great fear fell upon them which saw them*, verse 11. There is always an 'after' with God! Let this comfort every one of God's weary saints. The two witnesses had a resurrection. They were invited up to glory. Their enemies *beheld them* ascend up to heaven in a cloud. Dear Christian, so shall it be with all of God's dear children. There is a day of vindication. There is a day when the Lord shall own us as His own. He shall call us forth from the grave. He shall invite us to join Him in glory. And our enemies shall behold our vindication. *For the Lord himself shall descend from heaven with a shout, with the voice of the archangel, and with the trump of God: and the dead in Christ shall rise first: then we which are alive and remain shall be caught up together with them in the clouds, to meet the Lord in the air: and so shall we ever be with the Lord*, 1 Thessalonians 4:16-17.

The hour of the persecuted one's glory was the hour of the wicked city's judgment. *And the same hour was there a great earthquake, and the tenth part of the city fell, and in the earthquake were slain of men seven thousand: and the remnant were affrighted, and gave glory to the God of heaven*, verse 13. The glory given to God was not that of a humbled soul but rather a mere acknowledgment of the existence and power of God. It was the honour that Ahab gave to God after Elijah pronounced God's judgment against him, following his slaying of Naboth. *And it came to pass, when Ahab heard those words, that he rent his clothes, and put sackcloth upon his flesh, and fasted, and lay in sackcloth, and went softly.* See 1 Kings 21:17-27. Ahab was not graciously humbled in his heart but rather terrified and seeking to placate the anger of God.

There is a Christ-likeness seen in the two witnesses: in the period of their ministry - three and a half years; in the rejection they suffer; in the period under death - three days and a half; in their public resurrection; in their ascension in a cloud.

II. THE PROCLAMATION OF THE KINGDOM, VERSES 15-19.

While the earth was rejoicing over the death of the two witnesses, things were taking place in heaven. The time had come for the seventh trumpet to be blown and the end of the age to be proclaimed. The scene depicted by Daniel will most likely be taking place at this very time. *I saw in the night visions, and, behold, one like the Son of man came with the clouds of heaven, and came to the Ancient of days, and they brought him near before him. And there was given him dominion, and glory, and a kingdom, that all people, nations, and languages, should serve him: his dominion is an everlasting dominion, which shall not pass away, and his kingdom that which shall not be destroyed,* Daniel 7:13-14. Oh how foolish sinners are! What secret things are taking place even now, upon which no human eye may focus and because of that men assume they do not exist!

And the seventh angel sounded; and there were great voices in heaven, saying, The kingdoms of this world are become the kingdoms of our Lord, and of his Christ; and he shall reign for ever and ever, verse 15.

1. What a welcome is given this announcement! *And the four and twenty elders, which sat before God on their seats, fell upon their faces, and worshipped God, saying, We give thee thanks, O Lord God Almighty, which art, and wast, and art to come; because thou hast taken to thee thy great power, and hast reigned,* verses 16-17. Heaven, that place of perpetual worship, is aroused to greater heights of praise by the proclamation of the kingdom. It is a day in which the Lord God Almighty shall take to Himself His great power.

2. It is the time of great anger. Among the many feelings that will well up in the hearts of sinners: fear, dismay, consternation, there will be that of anger. To the end, man will be an implacable rebel to God. Whatever man may be forced to acknowledge of the power of God on that great and terrible day, he will remain estranged in his heart. His heart will ever remain a sea of raging anger against God. Cain's anger vented against his brother was really against God, as was Saul's anger against the early church. So it has ever been and so it shall ever be for the unregenerate sinner.

For the child of God, grace has doused that flame of rebellion. *For if, when we were enemies, we were reconciled to God by the death of his Son, much more, being reconciled, we shall be saved by his life. And you, that were sometime alienated and enemies in your mind by wicked works, yet now hath he reconciled*, Romans 5:10; Colossians 1:21.

3. It is a time of destruction. For those who destroy the earth, verse 18, destruction is coming. Since the beginning of time sinful man has, like a worm or moth in a garment, been destroying the earth. Man has corrupted everything that he has touched. Who can measure the moral destruction wrought upon the earth over the centuries? What of the physical corruption of the land, the rivers, the seas and oceans and the air tof which man has been guilty? He has managed to enter the realm of space within the last thirty years and already tens of thousands of pieces of junk litter the realm surrounding the earth. Man is a vandal in all his ways.

And the temple of God was opened in heaven, and there was seen in his temple the ark of his testament: and there were lightnings, and voices, and thunderings, and an earthquake, and great hail, verse 19. How ominous is an uncovered ark! The ark contained the law of God, the law broken and despised by sinful men. Here the ark is not sprinkled with Christ's blood of atonement by which the believing sinner is reconciled to God and enters into eternal peace. No! The ark is surrounded by those tokens of divine wrath displayed at Mount Sinai. *And there were lightnings, and voices, and thunderings, and an earthquake, and great hail.* Men shall one day give an account to God for every breach of that law. It is lightly esteemed today. Its exhortations and prohibitions are daily refused by individuals and by governments. But the day of account is coming. That defied law must be faced by men. While grace affords you an opportunity, *we pray you in Christ's stead, be ye reconciled to God*, 2 Corinthians 5:20.

Wonders, war and woe

T he title gives the main headings of this chapter. Again we are looking at events in Jerusalem during the period of Antichrist's power. There are a number of indications that this is so and we shall seek to deal with them as we progress through the chapter.

I. WONDERS IN HEAVEN

1. The first wonder is a woman. A woman is the Biblical symbol or sign of an ecclesiastical system. The particular features of the woman indicate whether it is a good or an evil system. The scarlet woman of chapter 17 has a golden cup of abominations and filthiness and she is bedecked with gold and precious stones and pearls. It is plain to see that this is no virtuous system. But here in chapter 12 the description indicates an entirely different character.

Clothed with the sun. She is adorned with the brightness of the Saviour's righteousness. He is the Sun of Righteousness, Malachi 4:2. All who are His by faith are partakers of His righteousness. *But of him are ye in Christ Jesus, who of God is made unto us wisdom, and righteousness, and sanctification, and redemption*, 1 Corinthians 1:30.

The moon is under her feet. The moon is the ruler of the night. *And God made two great lights; the greater light to rule the day, and the lesser light to rule the night*, Genesis 1:16. The woman is seen in a position of power over that which rules the night. That is the position to which every true child of God is brought as a result of conversion to Christ. *For sin shall not have dominion over you*, Romans 6:14. *Ye are all the children of light, and the children of the day: we are not of the night, nor of darkness*, 1 Thessalonians 5:5.

She has a crown of twelve stars. Twelve is the number of government and upon her head rests a crown of twelve stars. The church of Christ is destined for power. That is not evident at present but the Holy Scriptures do teach that the redeemed shall rule with Christ. *Do ye not know that the saints shall judge the world?* 1 Corinthians 6:2. What John saw here was heaven's perspective of the church of Christ. That crown is not yet visible here on earth. We are but strangers and pilgrims as of yet.

She is with child. There is a sense in which the church of Christ is the mother of us all. The symbol of child-bearing is a symbol associated with the winning of souls. Paul had this to say to the saints in Galatia: *My little children, of whom I travail in birth again until Christ be formed in you*, Galatians 4:19. Here is the language of child-bearing used of the apostle's efforts to see grace formed in the life of individuals. We all owe our salvation in part to the striving in prayer that the Holy Spirit induced in the hearts of some who loved us and who had a concern for our spiritual needs. Is it not a fact that a child-bearing church is one that Satan hates particularly? Those that are barren and dead are no threat to him.

To be specific, I believe we have a picture here of the church in Jerusalem driven out of the city by the devil's agent, the Antichrist. Satan has seen once before what an influence this church exerted when it was the centre of the great world-wide evangelistic crusade, in the first years of the apostolic age. His rage against it then succeeded only in spreading the gospel message everywhere. His slaying of Stephen resulted in Saul's conversion, and the cruel crusade that Saul had led only forced the gospel into other regions and spread the light of truth as a result. Satan does not intend doing that again. *The dragon stood before the woman which was ready to be delivered, for to devour her child as soon as it was born*, verse 4.

The Saviour had plainly indicated that there would be a sizable community of Bible-believers in Jerusalem in the last days. Indeed, He spoke directly to them when He said: *When ye therefore shall see the abomination of desolation, spoken of by Daniel the prophet, stand in the holy place, (whoso readeth, let him understand:) then let them which be in Judaea flee into the mountains: let him which is on the housetop not come down to take any thing out of his house: neither let him which is in the field return back to take his clothes. And woe unto them that are with child, and to them that give suck in those days! But pray ye that your flight be not in the winter, neither on the sabbath day: for then shall be great tribulation, such as was not since the beginning of the world to this time, no, nor ever shall be,* Matthew 24:15-21. The mountains referred to are the mountains that comprise the Judean wilderness and which lie just to the north-east of the city. I have no doubt that we have a prophetic picture in Revelation chapter 12 of those who will heed the Saviour's warning of Matthew 24:15-21, and who will flee to the Judean hills for shelter and to escape the rage of Antichrist.

2. The other wonder is a great red dragon. This is, of course, the devil. Chapter 20, verse 2 makes that plain. *The dragon, that old serpent, which is the Devil, and Satan.*

The description of his power. *And there appeared another wonder in heaven; and behold a great red dragon, having seven heads and ten horns, and seven crowns upon his heads,* verse 3. These symbols are explained for us. The ten horns refer to ten kingdoms. *And the ten horns which thou sawest are ten kings, which have received no kingdom as yet; but receive power as kings one hour with the beast,* 17:12. That the devil is depicted wearing the crowns upon his seven heads indicates that this scene takes place at a time when the devil exercises power over the government agencies within the ten kingdoms. There will be more about the seven heads in our next study. The crowns do not appear upon the ten horns until a fuller development of antichristianity has taken place and the ten kingdoms, depicted by the ten horns, give their power to the beast who shall then reign over the ten kingdoms in all the power of his master, the devil. The following scriptures clearly show that the Antichrist will be the devil's puppet. *Even him, whose coming is after the working of Satan with all power and signs and lying wonders,* 2 Thessalonians 2:9. *And I stood upon the sand of the sea, and saw a beast rise up out of the sea, having seven heads and ten horns, and upon his horns ten crowns, and upon his heads the name of blasphemy. And* *the beast which I saw was like unto a leopard, and his feet were as the feet of a bear, and his mouth as the mouth of a lion: and the dragon gave him his power, and his seat, and great authority,* Revelation 13:2. Although the Antichrist is seen wearing the crowns the real power rests with his master, the devil, and consequently it is he who is seen wearing the crowns in the passage under consideration.

The rage of the dragon. *And his tail drew the third part of the stars of heaven, and did cast them to the earth,* verse 4. The weapon of a dragon or a serpent is often its body or its tail. The boa-constrictor and the python are serpents that kill by crushing their victims with their tails or bodies. This act of striking at the stars of heaven is a brutal act. The word translated *drew* is used of the act of dragging a prisoner off to jail. Three out of the four other places where the Greek word appears indicate that it is an aggressive act. *As for Saul, he made havock of the church, entering into every house, and **haling** men and women committed them to prison,* Acts 8:3. *And there came thither certain Jews from Antioch and Iconium, who persuaded the people, and, having stoned Paul, **drew** him out of the city, supposing he had been dead,* Acts 14:19. *And when they found them not, they **drew** Jason and certain brethren unto the rulers of the city, crying, These that have turned the world upside down are come hither also,* Acts 17:6. The *stars* are Christians who, being prospectively described, are given the description that is used of them in their glorified state. Daniel's reference to this time indicates that it is the saints who are thus targeted by the devil and his hireling, the Antichrist. *And out of one of them came forth a little horn, which waxed exceeding great, toward the south, and toward the east, and toward the pleasant land. And it waxed great, even to the host of heaven; and it cast down some of the host and of the stars to the ground, and stamped upon them. And his power shall be mighty, but not by his own power: and he shall destroy wonderfully, and shall prosper, and practise, and shall destroy the mighty and the holy people,* Daniel 8:9-10, 24.

The purpose of Satan. *The dragon stood before the woman which was ready to be delivered, for to devour her child as soon as it was born. And she brought forth a man child, who was to rule all nations with a rod of iron: and her child was caught up unto God, and to his throne,* verses 4-5. How great will be the rage of the devil against all elements of the gospel, at that time when he feels that his ultimate purpose is

close to realisation! He will wickedly persist in believing that the utter
overthrow of all truth and all allegiance to Jehovah is within his grasp.
His persecuting fury will surely be at its zenith then.

The description of the child that is born denotes vigour and strength.
The church gives birth to overcomers who shall share the throne and
glory of God. Indeed to this end were we called by grace. *Whereunto
he called you by our gospel, to the obtaining of the glory of our Lord
Jesus Christ,* 2 Thessalonians 2:14. We shall *be preserved unto the
obtaining* of the glory of our Lord Jesus. That is what the phrase means.
The devil has ever attacked the church with a view to *destroying* her
offspring. It has ever been so, but it will be especially so in Jerusalem in
the final days of this age. As for ruling the nations with a rod of iron, is
that not what is promised to the overcomers in Thyatira? *And he that
overcometh, and keepeth my works unto the end, to him will I give power
over the nations: and he shall rule them with a rod of iron; as the vessels
of a potter shall they be broken to shivers: even as I received of my
Father,* chapter 2:26-27.

Protection from Satan. *And the woman fled into the wilderness,
where she hath a place prepared of God, that they should feed her there
a thousand two hundred and threescore days,* verse 6. *And to the woman
were given two wings of a great eagle, that she might fly into the wilderness, into her place, where she is nourished for a time, and times, and
half a time, from the face of the serpent,* verse 14. *And the earth helped
the woman, and the earth opened her mouth, and swallowed up the flood
which the dragon cast out of his mouth,* verse 16. This period of preservation is that of the second half of the seven-year period of Antichrist's
rule in Jerusalem. It is termed 1260 days in verse 6 and times, time and
half a time in verse 14. It begins with the setting up of the desolation of
abomination and ends with Christ's return in power and great glory. It
is that time when Christianity is banished from the dominions of
Antichrist. But God shall preserve His remnant. The means of preservation which the church has ever enjoyed is referred to in this passage.

Caught up to heaven, verse 5. This is the ultimate and final means
of preservation of God's people. Once there, they can never again be
molested or harmed.

Preserved in the wilderness, verse 6. It surely may be said that
the church was never more pure than when she was a lonely and rejected

outcast in the wilderness. We ought not to fear the place of the world's rejection for there it is that the church has often met with Christ and enjoyed the sweetest fellowship. *Who is this that cometh up from the wilderness, leaning upon her beloved?* Song of Solomon 8:5.

Preserved by flying away, verse 14. The eagle's wings symbolise prayer. *But they that wait upon the LORD shall renew their strength; they shall mount up with wings as eagles; they shall run, and not be weary; and they shall walk, and not faint,* Isaiah 40:31. The praying church shall be preserved from every attack of the devil.

Preserved by the earth's intervention, verse 16. How often God has caused the wrath of man to praise Him by turning the heart of an ungodly man to aid His people! *The king's heart is in the hand of the LORD, as the rivers of water: he turneth it whithersoever he will,* Proverbs 21:1. *But the LORD was with Joseph, and shewed him mercy, and gave him favour in the sight of the keeper of the prison,* Genesis 39:21. Many, as well as Joseph, have had this experience. No historic event is more illustrative of this truth than that referred to in 1 Samuel 22:3-4 when David sought shelter for his parents during the time he was cruelly pursued by Saul. *And David went thence to Mizpeh of Moab: and he said unto the king of Moab, Let my father and my mother, I pray thee, come forth, and be with you, till I know what God will do for me. And he brought them before the king of Moab: and they dwelt with him all the while that David was in the hold.* There is a reference to Moab in Isaiah 16:4 which may very well be fulfilled in the day of the Jerusalem saints' persecution. *Let mine outcasts dwell with thee, Moab; be thou a covert to them from the face of the spoiler: for the extortioner is at an end, the spoiler ceaseth, the oppressors are consumed out of the land.* Moab, being somewhat on the border of the territory that will be ruled by Antichrist, could well provide a place of escape for Christian refugees from Jerusalem.

Notice the devil's favourite method of attack. *And the serpent cast out of his mouth water as a flood after the woman, that he might cause her to be carried away of the flood,* verse 15. It reminds us of Isaiah 59:19. *When the enemy shall come in like a flood, the Spirit of the LORD shall lift up a standard against him.* The picture is vivid. It is a picture of the flood-like conditions which prevail today, for has not hell sent forth a flood of filth and corruption into the world with the specific purpose of drowning the people of God. Corrupting music, entertainment, literature both for leisure and education, the degrading behaviour of public figures such as the Prince and Princess of Wales - all constitute a flood which is particularly threatening to the young. This flood of iniquity is costing the Church of Christ a generation. Even in the best of congregations, fathers and mothers are finding it hard to persuade their older children to attend the house of God, let alone see them come to faith in Christ. I believe they are victims of the flood that all too often issues out of the television in the home. Many parents permit their children to have their own television sets in their room where they watch unsupervised. How can they be anything other than victims of the devil's flood?

II. WAR IN HEAVEN, VERSES 7-9.

This scene must of necessity refer to a period prior to the events that have just been depicted, when the devil attacked the church on earth. The exclusion of Satan and his angels from heaven must precede the attack upon the church on earth, with its particular emphasis upon the people of God in Jerusalem. Verse 12 supports this view. *Woe to the inhabiters of the earth and of the sea! for the devil is come down unto you, having great wrath, because he knoweth that he hath but a short time.*

1. The combatants in the war. *And there was war in heaven: Michael and his angels fought against the dragon; and the dragon fought and his angels*, verse 7. There are things going on of which we know very little, indeed nothing at all. We have already referred to the watching of angels over the affairs and persons of the elect of Christ. Here we see the heavenly host engaged in war against the devil. His being cast out of heaven is the beginning of his final and total defeat. The devil had been cast out of heaven before the world began when he first sinned. It was to this the Saviour referred when He said: *I beheld Satan as lightning fall from heaven*, Luke 10:18. Although he was cast down forever from his position of honour as the chief of God's heavenly beings, he was allowed to appear in heaven as an accuser of the people of God. *The accuser of our brethren is cast down, which accused them before our God day and night*, verse 10. It was as an accuser of Job that we read of Satan appearing among the angels of God in Job 1:6-12; 2:1-6. This evil advocate was answered in his accusations by our great *advocate with the Father, Jesus Christ the righteous*, 1 John 2:1.

The stages of his downfall may be traced in the book of the Revelation.

Cast out of heaven. Please note that in verse 8 it says *neither was their place found any more in heaven.* This event ends the licence that the devil exercised to appear in heaven as an accuser of the brethren. The word *place* (topos) literally means *a space marked off from the surrounding area.* This casting out takes place near to the end of the age, for we are told in verse 12; *he knoweth that he hath but a short time.* The word translated *short* (oligos) is translated by the word *little* in James 4:14. It tells us exactly how much time is being referred to. *Whereas ye know not what shall be on the morrow. For what is your life? It is even a vapour, that appeareth for a little time, and then vanisheth away.*

Bound in the bottomless pit. *And I saw an angel come down from heaven, having the key of the bottomless pit and a great chain in his hand. And he laid hold on the dragon, that old serpent, which is the Devil, and Satan, and bound him a thousand years,* 20:1-2. This takes place after the Saviour's return and at the commencement of His thousand-year reign.

Cast into the lake of fire. *And the devil that deceived them was cast into the lake of fire and brimstone, where the beast and the false prophet are, and shall be tormented day and night for ever and ever,* 20:10. Thus will the defeat of the devil be completed. This is the *everlasting fire, prepared for the devil and his angels* to which the Saviour referred in Matthew 25:41.

Sin results in a downward path even for the most clever. It will shut up heaven and will open up hell. It will end in everlasting misery, torment and shame.

2. This casting out of the devil signals the near return of Christ. *And I heard a loud voice saying in heaven, Now is come salvation, and strength, and the kingdom of our God, and the power of his Christ: for the accuser of our brethren is cast down, which accused them before our God day and night,* verse 10. *The kingdom of our God, and the power of his Christ* is signalled by this event. It is as if heaven were preparing for a new era, the day of Jesus Christ and His glory. Whatever access to heaven the devil had before, *their place,* as verse 8 puts it, is now at an end as preparations are made for the coming Kingdom of God. There remains only a *short time* until Christ comes to claim the earth and establish His kingdom.

3. The secret of the devil's defeat. *And they overcame him by the blood of the Lamb, and by the word of their testimony; and they loved not their lives unto the death,* verse 11. Satan is not all-powerful. He can be defeated. Satan and his angels can be defeated by either the holy angels or the saints of God only on the merits and basis of the Saviour's victory at the cross. The casting out of the devil from heaven by the holy angels and the overcoming of him on earth by believers is possible only on the basis of Calvary's triumph. This is what the first advent was all about. *Forasmuch then as the children are partakers of flesh and blood, he also himself likewise took part of the same; that through death he might destroy him that had the power of death, that is, the devil,* Hebrews 2:14. It was only in the might and authority of the name of the Lord Jesus that the angels, even Michael the archangel, could rebuke the devil. *Yet Michael the archangel, when contending with the devil he disputed about the body of Moses, durst not bring against him a railing accusation, but said, The Lord rebuke thee,* Jude 9. He who was cast out of heaven on the basis of the blood of Calvary's victory may be overthrown in our lives by the pleading of that same blood.

III. WOE TO THE EARTH, VERSE 12.

Therefore rejoice, ye heavens, and ye that dwell in them. Woe to the inhabiters of the earth and of the sea! for the devil is come down unto you, having great wrath, because he knoweth that he hath but a short time, verse 12.

1. Satan provoked. Satan being cast out of heaven provokes him to great wrath. Three things in particular provoke him.

His time is short. Though he *knows* he has only *a short time* before he faces certain defeat, still the devil goes on in his rebellion. Here is a picture of the functioning of a sinful nature. Nothing will alter or reform it. There is nothing within the sinner's nature that enables him to reason his ultimate destruction and the wisdom of repenting and seeking mercy.

Such a course of action is impossible to the totally depraved. Rejection of God and the hope of somehow defeating God ever burn within the depraved breast. That is why salvation is by grace alone. None of us who are saved ever concluded, as a result of the reasoning of our own hearts, that it would be wise to cease from sin and seek the Lord for mercy. We did reason so, but it was the result of grace renewing our hearts and wills that brought this about. *Wherefore, my beloved, as ye have always obeyed, not as in my presence only, but now much more in my absence, work out your own salvation with fear and trembling. For it is God which worketh in you both to will and to do of his good pleasure*, Philippians 2:12-13.

He is defeated by the church on earth through the blood of Christ. Satan must relive his defeat at the cross every time a child of God responds to his attack by pleading the blood of Christ in prayer. Little wonder he is provoked! We tread upon his broken head every time we pray and testify in the power of the blood of the Lamb.

The emergence of a strong church in Jerusalem is particularly vexing to the prince of darkness. For a lively church to be raised up in Jerusalem after the city has been in a state of great spiritual desolation for such a long period, and that at a time when the devil is hopeful of making it the centre of his God-denying empire, enrages him.

2. His rage is like a flood. *And the serpent cast out of his mouth water as a flood after the woman, that he might cause her to be carried away of the flood*, verse 15. As we have already commented on this verse, let it suffice to draw your attention to the satanic flood that will pollute the earth at this time of antichristianity. *And there was given unto him a mouth speaking great things and blasphemies*, 13:5. The reference is to the Antichrist. Daniel tells us more. *And he shall speak great words against the most High, and shall wear out the saints of the most High, and think to change times and laws: and they shall be given into his hand until a time and times and the dividing of time*, Daniel 7:25.

3. Believers will not be left without a refuge. Again, since we have commented on the provisions of God for His people in the midst of such satanic hatred, let us close this section with a reminder of the Saviour's promise. *When thou passest through the waters, I will be with thee; and through the rivers, they shall not overflow thee: when thou* *walkest through the fire, thou shalt not be burned; neither shall the flame kindle upon thee.   For I am the LORD thy God, the Holy One of Israel, thy Saviour*, Isaiah 43:2-3. It is the lot of God's people, as strangers and pilgrims, to pass through flood and fire. But they shall not destroy us. Neither shall they separate us from our God. *Who shall separate us from the love of Christ? shall tribulation, or distress, or persecution, or famine, or nakedness, or peril, or sword? As it is written, For thy sake we are killed all the day long; we are accounted as sheep for the slaughter. Nay, in all these things we are more than conquerors through him that loved us. For I am persuaded, that neither death, nor life, nor angels, nor principalities, nor powers, nor things present, nor things to come, nor height, nor depth, nor any other creature, shall be able to separate us from the love of God, which is in Christ Jesus our Lord*, Romans 8:35-39.

Let these words be our constant stay and support no matter what hell casts up in our pathway.

The beast and the false prophet
CHAPTER 13

The Holy Scripture contains frequent and full references to that personage who is variously titled. He is known as the Man of Sin; the Antichrist; the Son of Perdition; that Wicked One. One of the first references to him is found alongside the first reference to the Lord Jesus Christ. *And I will put enmity between thee and the woman, and between thy seed and her seed; it shall bruise thy head, and thou shalt bruise his heel*, Genesis 3:15. The Seed of the woman is the first prophetic reference to the Redeemer Who was to come. On the other hand, *thy seed,* the devil's seed, was undoubtedly a reference to all the spiritual offspring of the devil, but particularly a reference to that man who will, above all other evil-doers, prove to be the spawn of the devil.

Wicked men are called and considered to be the children of the devil. *The field is the world; the good seed are the children of the kingdom; but the tares are the children of the wicked one*, Matthew 13:38. *Ye are of your father the devil, and the lusts of your father ye will do. He was a murderer from the beginning, and abode not in the truth, because there is no truth in him. When he speaketh a lie, he speaketh of his own: for he is a liar, and the father of it*, John 8:44. *He that committeth sin is of the devil; for the devil sinneth from the beginning. For this purpose the Son of God was manifested, that he might destroy the works of the devil. . . . In this the children of God are manifest, and the children of the devil: whosoever doeth not righteousness is not of God, neither he that loveth not his brother*, 1 John 3:8, 10.

The foremost amongst sinning humanity is the subject of this chapter which divides into two parts. Verses 1-10 deal with the Antichrist and verses 11-18 deal with the False Prophet who promotes the worship of the Antichrist.

It would be appropriate to point out now that the visions given to John were not given in chronological order. In other words, what we see here in this chapter does not of necessity come before that revealed to him in chapter 17. In fact, the reverse is true. Chapter 17 presents us with a view of the Antichrist earlier in his career than that presented here in chapter 13. That is seen to be so when we consider the description of the heads of the Beast. *I saw a woman sit upon a scarlet coloured beast, full of names of blasphemy, having seven heads and ten horns,* 17:3. *I . . . . saw a beast rise up out of the sea, having seven heads and ten horns, and upon his horns ten crowns, and upon his heads the name of blasphemy*, 13:1. It is the same Beast but he is wearing ten crowns. He has come to power within the ten kingdoms of the old Roman Empire. We will deal with the matter of the ten crowns in a little more detail when we get to chapter 17. Suffice to know that we are here observing the Antichrist at the height of his wicked career.

One other note. The sea referred to in verse 1 is the *Great Sea* referred to in Numbers 34:6 or, as it is known to us today, the Mediterranean Sea. The word *Mediterranean* means *the middle of the earth*. It is indeed the sea at the middle of the earth. Benjamin Wills Newton rightly observed: 'If we take a map of the whole world, and mark by a line the boundaries of the Prophetic or Roman earth, in which the ten kingdoms are to be, they will appear little more than the coasts of the Mediterranean.' (*Thoughts on the Apocalypse.*)

This chapter contains the fullest and clearest description of Antichrist in Holy Scripture. It builds upon and enlarges the description given by Daniel. It is worthy of the closest scrutiny by God's people, especially as we see the time of Antichrist's manifestation approaching.

THE BEAST.

I.   The descriptive picture of the Beast.

And I stood upon the sand of the sea, and saw a beast rise up out of the sea, having seven heads and ten horns, and upon his horns ten crowns, and upon his heads the name of blasphemy. And the beast which I saw was like unto a leopard, and his feet were as the feet of a bear, and his mouth as the mouth of a lion: and the dragon gave him his power, and his seat, and great authority. . . . Here is wisdom. Let him that hath understanding count the number of the beast: for it is the number of a man; and his number is Six hundred threescore and six, verses 1-2, 18.

1. The location of Antichrist. He rises out of the Mediterranean Sea. This is the area of man's greatest achievements. From here came the explorers, the inventors, the artists and the musicians. Even that greatest and most spectacular of man's achievements in this century, the landing of men on the moon by the United States of America, had its European origins, in that it was the technology developed by Germany and her allies during the Second World War that provided the basic technology for the event. From that area, which has seen demonstrated so much of man's ingenuity, will come the man who is identified by the number 666. Six in scripture is associated with sinful man. A triple six must indicate sinful man at his zenith of development, just as a three-fold measurement will enable us to obtain the volume or cubic capacity of any object. This is the Antichrist who will stride on to the world's stage from the region washed by the Mediterranean Sea.

2. The likeness of the Antichrist. *And the beast which I saw was like unto a leopard, and his feet were as the feet of a bear, and his mouth as the mouth of a lion: and the dragon gave him his power, and his seat, and great authority,* verse 2.

Here is a being whose likeness incorporates all the descriptive terms employed by the Holy Spirit, when depicting the character of the four great world empires revealed to Daniel. *And four great beasts came up from the sea, diverse one from another. The first was like a lion, and had eagle's wings: I beheld till the wings thereof were plucked, and it was lifted up from the earth, and made stand upon the feet as a man, and a man's heart was given to it. And behold another beast, a second, like to a bear, and it raised up itself on one side, and it had three ribs in the mouth of it between the teeth of it: and they said thus unto it, Arise, devour much flesh. After this I beheld, and lo another, like a leopard, which had upon the back of it four wings of a fowl; the beast had also four heads; and dominion was given to it. After this I saw in the night visions, and behold a fourth beast, dreadful and terrible, and strong*

*exceedingly; and it had great iron teeth: it devoured and brake in pieces,
and stamped the residue with the feet of it: and it was diverse from all
the beasts that were before it; and it had ten horns,* Daniel 7:3-7. Here
are the Leopard of Greece, the Bear of Medo-Persia, the Lion of Babylon,
the dreadful terribleness of Rome all combining to create an unspeak-
ably wicked, cruel being, in whom will be concentrated the varieties of
carnal intellectual power and the diversities of outward greatness which
spasmodically were seen in some measure in the great world empires of
Babylon, Medo-Persia, Greece and Rome.

The Leopard of Greece is mentioned first. This is because the beauty
and culture that was Greece will be most prominent in the character of
Antichrist, thus making him carnally attractive to sensual minds. The
opulent luxury in which man loves to wallow was seen in the Grecian
empire as in few other of this world's dominions. That same desire after
such *sumptuous living* is rapidly emerging in our present generation. As
never before, it is a time of eating and drinking and making merry. The
Olympic Games of the summer of 1996 manifested man's delight in
such spectacular and theatrical events, when a world-wide audience of
many millions identified with the activities. The one who will promise
to provide freely such lavish merriment will be a most popular leader
indeed. Little notice will be taken of what is being sacrificed in order to
obtain such pleasure, for the leopard is not only beautiful and graceful.
It is cruel and savage. So doubtlessly will Antichrist be.

It is interesting to note that there is no mention of the leopard-like
qualities in the description given in chapter 17. This is because the
leopard-like features will develop only toward the apex of his career.

3. The lordship of the Antichrist. *A beast . . . having seven
heads and ten horns, and upon his horns ten crowns,* verse 1. The head
is the centre of intelligent thought; those functions of the mind by which
the actions of a person are controlled. As a symbol of political power it
must surely refer to the functions and operations of governmental power.
Seven heads suggest the complete control of all government functions,
seven being the number of completeness. Such power has not resided in
any person since Nebuchadnezzar, a king of such despotic powers
that even when he was mentally deranged by an act of God for a
period of seven years, none dared challenge his rulership. See Daniel
4:28-37.

A beast . . . having . . . ten horns, and upon his horns ten crowns.
Antichrist shall exercise this fullness of governmental power, this despotism within the territory of the ten kingdoms. To discover to which geographical territory this refers, we must go back again to Daniel's prophecies. In chapter 7, Daniel sees, in a vision, four great beasts arise from the *great sea*, the Mediterranean Sea. These beasts, fully described in verses 4-7, are declared to represent four great kings or kingdoms that shall arise out of the prophetic earth, verses 15-17. (See the comments made about *the earth* in 6:8 under the heading: **The pale horse.**) These four kingdoms are the Babylonian, the Medo-Persian, the Grecian and the Roman empires. This may be verified by a consideration of Daniel 2:36-40, where under the imagery of a great idol, these same four kingdoms are depicted, and it is clearly stated in verse 38 that Babylon was the first kingdom. Again, a study of Daniel 8:15-21 indicates that the second and third kingdoms were those of Medo-Persia and Greece. The last kingdom is that of Rome. It is represented by the two legs and ten toes of the feet of the idol of Daniel, chapter 2, upon which the *stone cut out without hands* will fall and thus destroy the image. This fourth kingdom came into being through its overthrow of the Grecian empire, yet it is still in existence at the time when Christ comes and establishes His millennial kingdom. *The stone that smote the image became a great mountain, and filled the whole earth.* This is the kingdom God shall establish at the glorious appearing of our Saviour, the Lord Jesus Christ. This smashing of the kingdoms takes place at the time of the *judgment being given to the saints of the most High* and the time of their possessing of the kingdom, Daniel 7:19-27.

So then, the kingdom that followed Greece will be in power when the Saviour returns, but not in the form it first appeared. When Rome first was established it had the strength of iron. It was the *legs of iron*, Daniel 2:33, 40. But it deteriorates into a mixture of iron and clay and is divided into ten toes. It is in this divided state that it shall re-appear upon the earth in the days just prior to the return of Christ.

The beast depicting Rome was described as having *ten horns*, Daniel 7:7. Up from among these horns sprang a little horn. That horn is pictured as having *eyes like the eyes of man, and a mouth speaking great things*. We are further told the *same horn made war with the saints, and prevailed against them; until the Ancient of days came, and judgment*

*was given to the saints of the most High; and the time came that the
saints possessed the kingdom,* Daniel 7:8, 21-22. The ten other horns
represent ten kings or kingdoms. *And the ten horns out of this kingdom
are ten kings that shall arise: and another shall rise after them; and he
shall be diverse from the first, and he shall subdue three kings. And he
shall speak great words against the most High, and shall wear out the
saints of the most High, and think to change times and laws: and they
shall be given into his hand until a time and times and the dividing of
time,* Daniel 7:24-25.

To summarise then, we have the Antichrist and the domain over
which he will exercise immediate and full power. *And the ten horns
which thou sawest are ten kings, which have received no kingdom as
yet; but receive power as kings one hour with the beast. These have one
mind, and shall give their power and strength unto the beast,* Revelation
17:12-13. He is the *little horn* who will speak great things against the
Almighty and make war with the saints. For a period of some seven
years, he will exercise power over the ten kingdoms that make up the
territory of the Roman Empire of old, and for the final three and a half
years of this period he will rule as the self-proclaimed god of all. The
territory ruled by the Roman Empire is easily established and the map
that we have provided displays that territory clearly.

4. The limitations of the Antichrist. *And power was given unto
him to continue forty and two months,* verse 5. The divine hand has
placed a limitation beyond which neither the devil or his agents may go.
As it was with the devil's attack upon Job, when there was a limit set
beyond which he could not go, so it will be with Antichrist. Though
God has removed restraint from the devil, He has not removed all
restraint. God's will and purpose for His people still is supreme and the
devil will not be permitted to hinder or frustrate in the slightest what
God has planned for His elect. Therefore, three and a half years will be
the length of time granted to the Antichrist. God's people will be able to
commence a count-down on his regime, once he sets up the abomination of desolation. That generation of believers will, like those who
took heed to the prophecy of Daniel in Daniel 9:25 and were therefore
able to calculate the time of the Messiah's first advent, be able to calculate
the time. *When these things begin to come to pass, then look up, and lift
up your heads; for your redemption draweth nigh,* Luke 21:28.

II. The deadly wound of the Beast.

And I saw one of his heads as it were wounded to death; and his deadly wound was healed: and all the world wondered after the beast, verse 3. When the Antichrist is arising to his full power, one of his heads has been wounded *to death* but healed again. I believe that this refers to a wounding of Antichrist in one of the agencies of his governmental power and a recovery of power that makes men to wonder all the more at him. But which agency of government? One of the chief agencies of government, even in our own system, is that of moral or religious affairs. We have, in Northern Ireland, a Department of Community Relations. This department is led by the man who is also the head of the Education Department. It is the task of the Community Relations department to promote ecumenism. This it does by assisting in every way that it can in the promotion of the ecclesiastical aspirations of the four main ecumenical denominations. To this end, the Department of Education is also employed. The promotion of ecumenism through the classrooms and the extra-curricular activities of the state schools is a common practice which has come to be accepted, or at least not vigorously opposed, even by many Christians whose children attend these schools.

Antichrist will be very much involved in the promotion of the false ideals of the whore of Babylon, which is today seen in embryo in the ecumenical union being sought between Rome, so-called Protestant churches and various other heathen religions. This will develop until there will be only one religious system recognised by men as the true system of religion, that of the Harlot of Babylon. In his early career, the Antichrist is seen assisting the whore. *I saw a woman sit upon a scarlet coloured beast, full of names of blasphemy, having seven heads and ten horns,* 17:3. Here the Antichrist is assisting the great whore and is obviously subservient to her wishes as any saddled animal is subservient to its rider. But when he comes to the fullness of his power, the Antichrist will destroy the whore of organised apostate religion. *And the ten horns which thou sawest upon the beast, these shall hate the whore, and shall make her desolate and naked, and shall eat her flesh, and burn her with fire. For God hath put in their hearts to fulfil his will, and to agree, and give their kingdom unto the beast, until the words of God shall be fulfilled,* 17:16-17. He shall then oppose and exalt *himself above all that is called God, or that is worshipped; so that he as God sitteth in the temple of God, shewing himself that he is God*, 2 Thessalonians 2:4. Such a declaration will prove to be a great shock to the whole social and political fabric of his kingdom, when all religious influences are suddenly swept away. As B. W. Newton rightly comments: 'Antichrist, when he destroys the harlot, purchases his place of solitary greatness by forfeiting one of the chief centres of his former influence; and therefore he may well be described as rising into his power with one of his government heads wounded as unto death.' (*Thoughts on the Apocalypse.*) His proclaiming himself as God will, of course, serve to heal any wounding that he may have suffered as a result of his destruction of the Harlot. The devil will have an alternative system ready to be substituted for that which is annihilated. It will be a system of utter blasphemy, for it will be a system based upon the total rejection of all that is of God and Antichrist will seek to take His place as the visible centre of all religion.

III. The devilish power of the Beast.

The dragon gave him his power, and his seat, and great authority. . . . And they worshipped the dragon which gave power unto the beast, verses 2 & 4. The programme of rebellion that the Beast will embark upon will require superhuman powers of mind and soul. Judas Iscariot had the idea of betraying Christ put into his heart by the devil (John 13:2), but then the devil himself had to enter into Judas in order to give the power needed to carry out the wicked task of betraying the Lord of Glory (John 13:7). So it will be with Antichrist. Such power is not given lightly. Before such power is given by the devil, there has to be a surrendering of mind and will and soul and body to the devil. Such a surrendered creature will the Antichrist be.

IV. The deceitful personality of the Beast.

He will be as a leopard, graceful and beautiful to behold outwardly but inwardly ravening and cruel. The words of Paul to the Corinthians remind us of the character of the one we are considering. *For such are false apostles, deceitful workers, transforming themselves into the apostles of Christ. And no marvel; for Satan himself is transformed into an angel of light. Therefore it is no great thing if his ministers also be transformed as the ministers of righteousness; whose end shall be according to their works*, 2 Corinthians 11:13-15. Daniel tells us of the tactics the Antichrist will employ in coming to power. *He shall come in peaceably, and obtain the kingdom by flatteries*, Daniel 11:21. The word *peaceably* literally means *with prosperity*. It is a tactic not unknown to politicians in the United Kingdom and in other nations! The word *flatteries* is elsewhere translated by the word *slippery*. (See Psalm 35:6 & Jeremiah 23:12.) Never will men have been so deceived by a leader as will those who give allegiance to the Beast. His coming will be *after the working of Satan with all power and signs and lying wonders, and with all deceivableness of unrighteousness in them that perish; because they received not the love of the truth, that they might be saved*, 2 Thessalonians 2:9-10.

V. The diabolical blasphemies of the Beast.

And there was given unto him a mouth speaking great things and blasphemies; and power was given unto him to continue forty and two months. And he opened his mouth in blasphemy against God, to blaspheme his name, and his tabernacle, and them that dwell in heaven, verses 5-6. This is an echo of the words of the vision given to Daniel. *I considered the horns, and, behold, there came up among them another little horn, before whom there were three of the first horns plucked up by the roots: and, behold, in this horn were eyes like the eyes of man, and a mouth speaking great things. . . . And he shall speak great words against the most High, and shall wear out the saints of the most High, and think to change times and laws: and they shall be given into his hand until a time and times and the dividing of time*, Daniel 7:8, 25. These *great words* are words of blasphemy. They shall be spoken *against the most High*. The fool has always *said in his heart, There is no God*, Psalm 14 :1; 53:1. But the Beast shall publicly, loudly, brazenly deny that there is a God. He shall go further and proclaim himself as God. *He as God sitteth in the temple of God, shewing himself that he is God*, 2 Thessalonians 2:4. That is the ultimate blasphemy.

VI. The determined rejecters of the Beast.

And all that dwell upon the earth shall worship him, whose names are not written in the book of life of the Lamb slain from the foundation of the world, verse 8. There is an exception to the *all* who worship.

1. They are a minority. While all the world will be made intoxicated by the allurements of the whore (17:2) and then shall worship the Beast and chant: *Who is like unto the beast? who is able to make war with him?* there will be a tiny remnant which shall stoutly refuse to conform, irrespective of the price they must pay for such faithfulness to Christ.

2. They belong to Christ. Their names are in His book. They are those for whom He died. They have been redeemed by His blood.

3. They are true believers. They are the same people referred to in Rev 12:17 as those who keep *the commandments of God, and have the testimony of Jesus Christ.* and who keep *the commandments of God, and the faith of Jesus,* 14:12. It is unscriptural to claim that the Church of Christ will be raptured away from the earth during the days of Antichrist as some claim. It is not until Christ comes in glorious power that the saints will be resurrected and with the living saints ascend to meet their returning Lord.

4. They will with patience endure these afflictions. *He that leadeth into captivity shall go into captivity: he that killeth with the sword must be killed with the sword. Here is the patience and the faith of the saints,* verse 10. It will be a sore trial and endurance for the saints not to react by war in response to the Antichrist's declaration of war on them. But the cause of Christ is neither defended nor advanced by the sword. Instead, faith in the ultimate victory of Christ will promote patient submission to captivity or whatever other affliction Providence has ordained. The warning that the one who takes up the sword shall perish by the sword is a repeat of the warning given to Peter when he attempted briefly to defend the Saviour by the sword. *Then said Jesus unto him, Put up again thy sword into his place: for all they that take the sword shall perish with the sword,* Matthew 26:52.

THE FALSE PROPHET.

And he called unto him the twelve, and began to send them forth by two and two, Mark 6:7. Such was the Saviour's practice. Thus will the devil do also, for with the appearance of the false Christ will come also the appearance of the False Prophet.

I. The source of the False Prophet. *And I beheld another beast coming up out of the earth*, verse 11. As already noted, the word translated earth (*ge*) may also be translated *land*. Indeed, it is so translated in its first occurrence. *And thou Bethlehem, in the land (ge) of Juda, art not the least among the princes of Juda: for out of thee shall come a Governor, that shall rule my people Israel*, Matthew 2:6. I am inclined to believe that the false prophet will be linked to Israel. It would seem to fit in with the blasphemous regime of the Antichrist and the devil's scheme generally, if the spokesman of antichristianity were one of the chosen race. After all, the devil set his pattern when he recruited Judas Iscariot from Christ's band of professed followers.

2. The sham of the False Prophet. He was *like a lamb* but *spake as a dragon*, verse 11. There will be a contradiction between his appearances and his actions.

How important are our words! They tell us what we are really like. *O generation of vipers, how can ye, being evil, speak good things? for out of the abundance of the heart the mouth speaketh*, Matthew 12:34. *A good man out of the good treasure of his heart bringeth forth that which is good; and an evil man out of the evil treasure of his heart bringeth forth that which is evil: for of the abundance of the heart his mouth speaketh*, Luke 6:45. It is by our words that we shall be judged one day. *But I say unto you, That every idle word that men shall speak, they shall give account thereof in the day of judgment. For by thy words thou shalt be justified, and by thy words thou shalt be condemned*, Matthew 12:36-37. Let us not be of those who say one thing but do another.

It is by a preacher's words that we judge his theology. *To the law and to the testimony: if they speak not according to this word, it is because there is no light in them*, Isaiah 8:20. *But though we, or an angel from heaven, preach any other gospel unto you than that which we have preached unto you, let him be accursed. As we said before, so say I now again, If any man preach any other gospel unto you than that ye have received, let him be accursed*, Galatians 1:8-9. No science is so exact as that of theology. No science holds such disastrous consequences for the one who errs as does theology. Let us not count our expressing of divine truth as of little importance.

The False Prophet is, of course, a pattern for all false prophets. *Beware of false prophets, which come to you in sheep's clothing, but inwardly they are ravening wolves*, Matthew 7:15. The wolf masquerading as a sheep is the most dangerous creature on the earth. We here in Northern Ireland have learned that to our cost. All the bombs and all the bullets expended by terrorists have not inflicted the harm that the sheep-like false prophets of ecumenism have inflicted over the last three decades. Eternity will bear this out.

   3. The signs of the False Prophet. *And he doeth great wonders, so that he maketh fire come down from heaven on the earth in the sight of men, and deceiveth them that dwell on the earth by the means of those miracles which he had power to do in the sight of the beast; saying to them that dwell on the earth, that they should make an image to the beast, which had the wound by a sword, and did live. And he had power to give life unto the image of the beast, that the image of the beast should both speak, and cause that as many as would not worship the image of the beast should be killed*, verses 13-15. Men foolishly think that signs are the definitive proof of the heavenly origin of a man and his ministry. *Then certain of the scribes and of the Pharisees answered, saying, Master, we would see a sign from thee. But he answered and said unto them, An evil and adulterous generation seeketh after a sign; and there shall no sign be given to it, but the sign of the prophet Jonas*, Matthew 12:38-39. *For the Jews require a sign, and the Greeks seek after wisdom*, 1 Corinthians 1:22. Those who seek signs, and see them as incontestable proof of the authenticity of an individual's heavenly credentials, shall have them aplenty from the False Prophet. He will bring down fire from heaven, verse 13. The word *heaven* does not refer to God's dwelling place but rather to the expanse of the sky above our heads. Let none be surprised at this, since the devil has the power to do such. Was not this power evident in the days of Job's trial? *While he was yet speaking, there came also another, and said, The fire of God is fallen from heaven, and hath burned up the sheep, and the servants, and consumed them; and I only am escaped alone to tell thee*, Job 1:16. The messenger presumptuously assumed that the fire came from God. This is precisely what the inhabitants of the world will believe when they see this miracle. They will believe that the power of God is behind such a thing. What will blinded men make of the False Prophet having the *power to give life unto the image of the beast, that the image of the beast should both speak, and cause that as many as would not worship the image of the* *beast should be killed*, verse 15? It will be both spectacular and terrifying and, doubtless, very convincing for those bereft of all gospel light.

4. The success of the False Prophet. The consequences of these displays of supernatural power will be that the False Prophet will persuade those whose names are not written in the Book of Life to worship the Antichrist, verses 8 & 12. The world, or at least that part over which the Antichrist will exercise direct control, will worship him. No exceptions will be tolerated. *As many as would not worship the image of the beast should be killed*, verse 15. This will be the decree of the False Prophet, but what men decree is not always what is done. Nebuchadnezzar decreed something similar, but Shadrach, Meshach, and Abednego were delivered. Jezebel sought to slay all the prophets of the Lord, but Elijah and seven thousand others survived. We have already seen how that God shall preserve the seed of the woman from the rage of the devil, 12:6, 14, 16, and I have no doubt that, even in the heat of the Antichrist's rage against God and His saints, that preservation will be continued. *I will build my church; and the gates of hell shall not prevail against it*, Matthew 16:18. The word of the Lord shall stand.

5. The seal of the False Prophet. *And he causeth all, both small and great, rich and poor, free and bond, to receive a mark in their right hand, or in their foreheads: and that no man might buy or sell, save he that had the mark, or the name of the beast, or the number of his name*, verses 16-17. Conversion to Antichrist is an induction into slavery. With Christ a sinner is set free. *If the Son therefore shall make you free, ye shall be free indeed*, John 8:36. The very opposite is the case with Antichrist.

His mark will be required before any business may be transacted. Something of this attitude prevailed during the crisis over the BSE disease in cattle in the United Kingdom. The European Union refused the United Kingdom the right to sell its beef products anywhere in the world until it gave permission! This is the spirit of Antichrist at work.

It is a seal that spells damnation. *And the third angel followed them, saying with a loud voice, If any man worship the beast and his image, and receive his mark in his forehead, or in his hand, the same shall drink of the wine of the wrath of God, which is poured out without mixture into the cup of his indignation; and he shall be tormented with* *fire and brimstone in the presence of the holy angels, and in the presence of the Lamb,* Revelation 14:9-10. Before a man give consideration to his earthly prosperity, let him first consider the words of the Lord Jesus Christ on this subject. *For what shall it profit a man, if he shall gain the whole world, and lose his own soul?* Mark 8:36.

In all, is not the regime of the Antichrist the very antithesis of the Kingdom of God? The heavenly kingdom is marked by holiness, 1 Peter 1:14-15. It enriches its citizens with eternal and spiritual treasures, 1 Corinthians 8:9, and it seals its citizens with a blessed seal of sweet assurance of final glory, Ephesians 1:13-14; Colossians 1:27.

I counsel you to hasten, and by faith and repentance seek a place in the heavenly and holy and happy kingdom of the Blessed Redeemer, the Lord Jesus Christ.

The Lamb standing on Mount Sion and other latter day scenes
CHAPTER 14

I. THE LAMB AND THE GLORY OF HIS SAINTS, VERSES 1-5.

The method of teaching employed by the Lord involves a repeating of the truth, setting it forth in its various aspects and reiterating it so that it is imparted to the mind of the pupil. As it is throughout the Bible, so it may be seen in the book of the Revelation. This principle is explained by Isaiah: *for precept must be upon precept, precept upon precept; line upon line, line upon line; here a little, and there a little*, Isaiah 28:10. The idea seems to be that of the builder with his bricks and mortar gradually assembling a wall, as row after row is placed upon another. So God assembles a knowledge of His Truth in the hearts and minds of His people.

Chapter 14 carefully reiterates the main truths that have already been touched upon. It starts with the truth of Christ's triumphant return. Before dealing with the darker aspects of the events that will take place at the end, the Lord reminds us of the all-glorious end of all things - the victory of the Lamb.

And I looked, and, lo, a Lamb stood on the mount Sion, and with him an hundred forty and four thousand, having his Father's name written in their foreheads, verse 1.

What a contrast the opening scene of this chapter is to the one we have just completed! It should be noted that the Holy Spirit takes John from a view of the Antichrist and the False Prophet to a view of the Lord Jesus. Today, we are experiencing the rise of the spirit of antichristianity. The increasing ungodliness is a depressing environment for the child of God. Let us counter the devil's assaults upon our mind and spirit by *looking unto Jesus the author and finisher of our faith*, Hebrews 12:2.

The Lamb, not Antichrist and his minions, stands astride the world in this chapter. The time of His triumph has come.

The accomplishments of our Redeemer and Mediator may be measured by all the actions in which we see Him engaged.

Walking – His ministry amongst men. *How God anointed Jesus of Nazareth with the Holy Ghost and with power: who went about doing good, and healing all that were oppressed of the devil; for God was with him,* Acts 10:38.

Hanging – His atoning sacrifice upon the cross. *And we are witnesses of all things which he did both in the land of the Jews, and in Jerusalem; whom they slew and hanged on a tree,* Acts 10:39.

Lying – His three days in the tomb. *Now in the place where he was crucified there was a garden; and in the garden a new sepulchre, wherein was never man yet laid. There laid they Jesus therefore because of the Jews' preparation day; for the sepulchre was nigh at hand,* John 19:41-42.

Sitting – Waiting for the ingathering of His elect. *The LORD said unto my Lord, Sit thou at my right hand, until I make thine enemies thy footstool,* Psalm 110:1. *But this man, after he had offered one sacrifice for sins for ever, sat down on the right hand of God; from henceforth expecting till his enemies be made his footstool,* Hebrews 10:12-13.

Standing – Victorious over His enemies.

'The purpose of the Lamb in again visiting the earth is to bring into it, and finally to establish in it, the glory and the holiness and the happiness of heaven. He has finished the work of atonement, and has sat down on the throne of the majesty in the heavens; but we wait for His return, in order that we may behold what the full manifested results of redemption are to be.' – B. W. Newton.

Rightly did John Newton, preacher and hymnwriter, pen the words:-

Glorious things of thee are spoken,
Zion, city of our God!
He, Whose Word cannot be broken,
Formed thee for His own abode.

What great things are spoken of Zion! *And it shall come to pass in the last days, that the mountain of the LORD'S house shall be established in the top of the mountains, and shall be exalted above the hills; and all nations shall flow unto it. And many people shall go and say, Come ye, and let us go up to the mountain of the LORD, to the house of the God of Jacob; and he will teach us of his ways, and we will walk in his paths: for out of Zion shall go forth the law, and the word of the LORD from Jerusalem. And he shall judge among the nations, and shall rebuke many people: and they shall beat their swords into plowshares, and their spears into pruninghooks: nation shall not lift up sword against nation, neither shall they learn war any more. O house of Jacob, come ye, and let us walk in the light of the LORD*, Isaiah 2:2-5. It is to become the capital of the Messiah's kingdom and to it shall all nations be gathered.

The greatness of Zion consists in that heavenly glory which will there be manifest before men's eyes. It was seen before at Mount Sinai, at the head of the marching ranks of migrating Israel, and also above the tabernacle. These were occasions when the divine glory was seen upon the earth, but it was witnessed by a small number in comparison to the multitudes of the earth. But a day is coming when heaven shall be opened above Mount Zion and, as the Saviour promised, in John 1:51, *Verily, verily, I say unto you, Hereafter ye shall see heaven open, and the angels of God ascending and descending upon the Son of man.*

Here is the fulfilment of the Father's promised victory over His Son's opponents. *Yet have I set my king upon my holy hill of Zion,* Psalm 2:6.

1. His saints are with Him in His glory on Zion. *A Lamb stood on the mount Sion, and with him an hundred forty and four thousand,* verse 1. I believe the number 144,000 is a mystical number that refers to the numberless multitude of the redeemed who will accompany the Saviour when He returns. 12x12x1000 suggests a vast number and so it is with regard to Christ's elect. They are *a great multitude, which no man could number, of all nations, and kindreds, and people, and tongues,*

Revelation 7:9. It is similar in import to the phrase used in chapter 5 verse 11. *And I beheld, and I heard the voice of many angels round about the throne and the beasts and the elders: and the number of them was ten thousand times ten thousand, and thousands of thousands.*

That these are the glorified saints may be seen from the phrase: *these are they which follow the Lamb whithersoever he goeth*, verse 4. The child of God on earth today cannot follow the Lamb wherever He goes. This was the sad truth the disciples had to bear as the Saviour ascended to His Father. *Little children, yet a little while I am with you. Ye shall seek me: and as I said unto the Jews, Whither I go, ye cannot come; so now I say to you. . . . Simon Peter said unto him, Lord, whither goest thou? Jesus answered him, Whither I go, thou canst not follow me now; but thou shalt follow me afterwards*, John 13:33, 36. Only those who are glorified with Christ can follow Him *whithersoever he goeth.*

Those who had honoured Christ are now honoured by Him. They who had borne the cross now wear a crown. How faithful is the Master we serve!

These are they which were not defiled with women; for they are virgins, verse 4. The utter perfection of the saints is seen here. Such is the declaring of them righteous through the cleansing blood of Christ that they are as if they had never sinned. They are virgin pure. There were occasions when the menfolk of Israel were required for the sake of ceremonial cleanness to remain separated from their wives. *And Moses went down from the mount unto the people, and sanctified the people; and they washed their clothes. And he said unto the people, Be ready against the third day: come not at your wives. And it came to pass on the third day in the morning, that there were thunders and lightnings, and a thick cloud upon the mount, and the voice of the trumpet exceeding loud; so that all the people that was in the camp trembled. And Moses brought forth the people out of the camp to meet with God; and they stood at the nether part of the mount. And mount Sinai was altogether on a smoke, because the LORD descended upon it in fire: and the smoke thereof ascended as the smoke of a furnace, and the whole mount quaked greatly. And when the voice of the trumpet sounded long, and waxed louder and louder, Moses spake, and God answered him by a voice. And the LORD came down upon mount Sinai, on the top of the mount: and the LORD called Moses up to the top of the mount; and Moses went up,* Exodus 19:14-20. It is not Sinai but Zion that the Lord has descended upon and His people are marked, not by ceremonial but by actual spiritual, virginal purity.

Having his Father's name written in their foreheads, verse 1. What a contrast this multitude makes with earth's throngs as set forth in the previous chapter! They have their heavenly Father's name in their foreheads rather than the mark of the Antichrist. They have the new song of redemption on their lips rather than the chant of blasphemy. (Compare 14:2-3 with 13:4.) They present a marked contrast in character. (Compare 14:4-5 with 17:2.)

II. THE PREACHING OF THE EVERLASTING GOSPEL.

And I saw another angel fly in the midst of heaven, having the everlasting gospel to preach unto them that dwell on the earth, and to every nation, and kindred, and tongue, and people, saying with a loud voice, Fear God, and give glory to him; for the hour of his judgment is come: and worship him that made heaven, and earth, and the sea, and the fountains of waters, verses 6-7.

The work of preaching the gospel will continue right to the end, though Antichrist will make every effort to crush it out in the dominion over which he exercises control. The message preached is termed *the everlasting gospel.* This is no new gospel but the same eternal message that has been proclaimed to men since Adam's transgression. There is no other gospel. It is called the everlasting Gospel for a number of reasons.

1. It is the message of the everlasting God. *And Abraham planted a grove in Beersheba, and called there on the name of the LORD, the everlasting God,* Genesis 21:33. *Blessed be the LORD God of Israel from everlasting, and to everlasting. Amen, and Amen,* Psalm 41:13. *Before the mountains were brought forth, or ever thou hadst formed the earth and the world, even from everlasting to everlasting, thou art God,* Psalm 90:2. *Thy throne is established of old: thou art from everlasting,* Psalm 93:2. In days such as these, when we see a decline in the number of professing Christians and a departure on the part of the main denominations from the truth of God, let us cling to the truth of the eternal nature of our God and His word. *For all flesh is as grass, and all the glory of man as the flower of grass. The grass withereth, and the flower thereof falleth away: but the word of the Lord endureth for ever. And this is the word which by the gospel is preached unto you,* 1 Peter 1:24-25.

2. It is the message of everlasting salvation. *But Israel shall be saved in the LORD with an everlasting salvation: ye shall not be ashamed nor confounded world without end,* Isaiah 45:17. *For God so loved the world, that he gave his only begotten Son, that whosoever believeth in him should not perish, but have everlasting life,* John 3:16. The life we enjoy, dear Christian, will last as long as God endures. We are partakers of His life.

3. It is a message that imparts everlasting joy. *Therefore the redeemed of the LORD shall return, and come with singing unto Zion; and everlasting joy shall be upon their head: they shall obtain gladness and joy; and sorrow and mourning shall flee away,* Isaiah 51:11. *Whom having not seen, ye love; in whom, though now ye see him not, yet believing, ye rejoice with joy unspeakable and full of glory,* 1 Peter 1:8. This is the portion of those who believe but see not Christ. What will that joy be when we see Him face to face!

4. It is a message of deliverance from everlasting wrath. *The sinners in Zion are afraid; fearfulness hath surprised the hypocrites. Who among us shall dwell with the devouring fire? who among us shall dwell with everlasting burnings?* Isaiah 33:14. *Who shall be punished with everlasting destruction from the presence of the Lord, and from the glory of his power,* 2 Thessalonians 1:9. *And to wait for his Son from heaven, whom he raised from the dead, even Jesus, which delivered us from the wrath to come,* 1 Thessalonians 1:10. An eternity after the damning of sinners, there shall still be wrath to come, as much to come as ever there was. From this dreadful hell the gospel delivers us, hallelujah!

This message is for all. It is to be preached *unto them that dwell on the earth, and to every nation, and kindred, and tongue, and people,* verse 6. It is a call to fear and worship the Creator, as His hour of judgment is near. The angel proclaims *with a loud voice, Fear God, and give glory to him; for the hour of his judgment is come: and worship him that made heaven, and earth, and the sea, and the fountains of waters,* verse 7.

He Who made you requires you to heed this call today.

III. THE DOOM OF BABYLON DECLARED.

And there followed another angel, saying, Babylon is fallen, is fallen, that great city, because she made all nations drink of the wine of the wrath of her fornication, verse 8. Here is the fall of the city that men have yet to build, and, when they have it built, will believe to be imperishable.

1. The greatness of Babylon. The word *great* is a translation of the Greek word *megas* from which we get the prefix *mega,* as in megastore or megastar. This is a city which will dwarf in magnificence and earthly glory all other cities. It will incorporate every exquisite design and carnal desire of earthly man. We shall have more to say about Babylon when we reach chapter 18.

2. The fall of Babylon. This is the same word as that used when the fall of the devil is referred to in chapter 9, verse one. It was a forced fall rather than a voluntary one. It is a fall into judgment.

3. The reason for Babylon's fall. *Because she made all nations drink of the wine of the wrath of her fornication*, verse 8. Sin is ever followed by judgment. *Be not deceived; God is not mocked: for whatsoever a man soweth, that shall he also reap*, Galatians 6:7. What is true for individuals is true for cities and systems.

IV. THE CONSEQUENCES OF WORSHIPPING THE BEAST.

And the third angel followed them, saying with a loud voice, If any man worship the beast and his image, and receive his mark in his forehead, or in his hand, the same shall drink of the wine of the wrath of God, which is poured out without mixture into the cup of his indignation; and he shall be tormented with fire and brimstone in the presence of the holy angels, and in the presence of the Lamb: and the smoke of their torment ascendeth up for ever and ever: and they have no rest day nor night, who worship the beast and his image, and whosoever receiveth the mark of his name. Here is the patience of the saints: here are they that keep the commandments of God, and the faith of Jesus, verses 9-12.

1. All false worship is condemned. There are those who would tell us that it does not matter how or what you worship as long as you are sincere. Such is clearly a lie of the devil in the light of this verse. ALL worship of false gods will bring damnation. What the Saviour said to the devil ought to be carefully noted by all in this ecumenical, multi-faith world. *Then saith Jesus unto him, Get thee hence, Satan: for it is written, Thou shalt worship the Lord thy God, and him only shalt thou serve*, Matthew 4:10.

2. Roman Catholicism is not the Beast. It has to be noted that those who would find in Roman Catholicism a fulfilment of the prophecies related to the Beast must have difficulty with this verse. If the pope or the system of Romanism is the Beast, then all who have at any time given allegiance to it are most certainly damned. *The same shall drink of the wine of the wrath of God, which is poured out without mixture into the cup of his indignation; and he shall be tormented with fire and brimstone in the presence of the holy angels, and in the presence of the Lamb,* verse 10. There can be no mistaking of this matter. Consequently, there can never be any one saved out of Romanism, if it be the Antichrist, and those who have claimed that they have been saved by the grace of God out of its darkness are, at best, sadly mistaken or, at worst, devilish deceivers. I do not believe that the pope or popes or the system of Romanism is the Beast, the Antichrist. I believe that popery is antichristian. I believe that, as the Westminster Confession of Faith puts it, the pope is 'that Antichrist . . . that exalteth himself in the Church against Christ,' that is the pope is the principal antichrist within Christendom. He is not the sole antichrist within the world. The Dalai Lama, to mention just one, is an antichrist, since he claims that he is divine and ought to receive the worship that is due to God alone. But the Beast, referred to in verse 9, is not yet revealed. We shall discuss in more detail the matter of Romanism and its failure to meet the descriptions of the Beast, as set down in Holy Scripture, when we get to chapter 17.

3. The dreadful truth of eternal punishment. *The same shall drink of the wine of the wrath of God . . . and he shall be tormented with fire and brimstone in the presence of the holy angels, and in the presence of the Lamb: and the smoke of their torment ascendeth up for ever and ever: and they have no rest day nor night,* verses 10-11. Eternal damnation is a rejected truth on the part of most denominations today. Following the approval of a report by the Church of England General Synod, in which damnation is declared to be annihilation, a popular newspaper carried an account of the matter under the headline: 'Rejoice! They've done away with hell.' We are not to formulate our faith by what the Church of England decides or what the writers in the popular press may say. Rather, we are to build upon the Word of God *which liveth and abideth for ever*, 1 Peter 1:23. While the believer will drink of the living fountains of water (7:17), the unbeliever will *drink of the wine of the wrath of God* (verse 10). While the believer will sing the new song of triumph (verse 30), the smoke of the torment of the unbeliever will ascend upward for ever and ever (verse 11). Let sinful men tremble and fear and cast themselves upon the mercy of God set forth in the gospel of Christ.

4. These truths aid patience. *Here is the patience of the saints: here are they that keep the commandments of God, and the faith of Jesus*, verse 12. Nothing tests the patience of the saints and serves to undermine holiness like the apparent escape from punishment by evil doers. Assurance of future retribution makes present-day injustices bearable. The whole of Psalm 37 is dedicated to the expounding of this truth. It ought to be read often by fretting saints.

V. THE BLESSED REST AND REWARD OF THE DEAD IN CHRIST.

And I heard a voice from heaven saying unto me, Write, Blessed are the dead which die in the Lord from henceforth: Yea, saith the Spirit, that they may rest from their labours; and their works do follow them, verse 13. To die in Christ is a most blessed thing. It is to die forgiven. It is to die reconciled to God. It is to die with an assurance of heaven.

1. It indicates a gracious change of status. Sinners are born estranged from God. It takes an act of God's power and mercy to place a sinner in Christ. *That at that time ye were without Christ, being aliens from the commonwealth of Israel, and strangers from the covenants of promise, having no hope, and without God in the world: but now in Christ Jesus ye who sometimes were far off are made nigh by the blood of Christ*, Ephesians 2:12-13. The sinner cut off from God by his sin is reconciled and adopted into the family of God. He becomes a new creature in Christ, with a new life, a new hope and a new home in glory. When death comes, he dies *in Christ,* safe and secure for all eternity.

2. Rest and reward await the child of God. The word *henceforth* denotes a moment of commencement when Christians will enter upon their rest and reward. As there is an end to every day; as there is an end to every night, so shall there be an end of this earthly pilgrimage and we shall enter into rest and enjoy whatever rewards our kind and generous Master will apportion us.

VI. THE REAPING OF THE HARVEST.

Verses 14 through to 20 deal with the harvest of the earth. The Saviour is seen coming with a sharp sickle. *And I looked, and behold a white cloud, and upon the cloud one sat like unto the Son of man, having on his head a golden crown, and in his hand a sharp sickle*, verse 14. The cloud and the crown indicate that it is the Saviour's second advent that is pictured here. Among the many things, that will take place at that time, is the harvest. Note that He carries a *sharp* sickle. None shall stand before its edge. Please recall the despairing cry of the wicked as recorded in chapter 6:17. *The great day of his wrath is come; and who shall be able to stand?* Who indeed?

This is the harvest of the professing church. It is the time referred to in Matthew 7:22-23. It is the harvest referred to in Matthew 13:24-30. Then the sheep will be separated from the goats and the wheat from the tares.

It is also the time for judgment in the Antichrist's kingdom. What a judgment awaits the Man of Sin and those who follow him! When he and his armies are cast into the winepress of God's wrath and trampled beneath those *feet of brass,* then great shall be the slaughter. *And the winepress was trodden without the city, and blood came out of the winepress, even unto the horse bridles, by the space of a thousand and six hundred furlongs*, verse 20. It is to this judgment that Joel refers in his prophecy. *Let the heathen be wakened, and come up to the valley of Jehoshaphat: for there will I sit to judge all the heathen round about. Put ye in the sickle, for the harvest is ripe: come, get you down; for the press is full, the fats overflow; for their wickedness is great. Multitudes, multitudes in the valley of decision: for the day of the LORD is near in the valley of decision. The sun and the moon shall be darkened, and the stars shall withdraw their shining. The LORD also shall roar out of Zion, and utter his voice from Jerusalem; and the heavens and the earth shall shake: but the LORD will be the hope of his people, and the strength of the children of Israel,* Joel 3:12-16.

So ends this chapter which, in outline form, has given us a resumé of the events that will mark the end of this age.

The vials of wrath, part one
CHAPTERS 15 AND 16

The chapters 15 and 16 should be read and considered as one. We shall deal with chapter 15 as an introduction to the events of chapter 16.

We have come very close to the end, with the pouring out of the seven vials of wrath. It might be appropriate to consider at this juncture the pattern formed by the seven seals, the seven trumpets and the seven vials of wrath. Back in chapter 6, verses 1 and 2, we had the first seal opened. It depicted the return of Christ as Conqueror. It also began the sequence of instruction given to John about the events that will take place, chiefly within the Antichrist's kingdom, as the time of the Saviour's return in power and glory draws near. *And when he had opened the seventh seal, there was silence in heaven about the space of half an hour*, chapter 8:1. It was said, in commenting on that portion, that it was the awful stillness that preceded a great battle. And indeed the battle of the ages was drawing very near when Christ would go forth to engage and conquer His enemies and reign in glory.

It was during the period of the seventh seal that the seven trumpets were sounded. The first trumpet initiated a series of increasing judgments upon the earth. The last trumpet brought the announcement: *The kingdoms of this world are become the kingdoms of our Lord, and of his Christ; and he shall reign for ever and ever*, chapter 11:15.

The seven vials of wrath are poured out during the period of the seventh trumpet. The final vial is followed by the announcement: *And the seventh angel poured out his vial into the air; and there came a great voice out of the temple of heaven, from the throne, saying, It is done*, chapter 16:17. There then follow the events and occurrences which signal the glorious return of Christ.

Thus as we progress through the seals, the trumpets and the vials, we are observing in ever-increasing detail the events that take place just prior to the Saviour's return. During the period of the trumpets we zoom in, as it were, upon the period of the seventh seal and during the period of the seven vials we zoom in on the period of the seventh trumpet.

In this chapter 15, we read of much that reminds us of the period of the exodus out of Egypt. Of course, the characteristics of every great period of evil and every infamous person will come together and be manifested in the age and person of the Antichrist. The cruelty and hatred of Pharaoh will be seen once again. Thus we have before us God sending plagues upon His enemies as He did in Egypt. It will be a day in which a downtrodden people will gain a notable victory over the greatest king on the face of the earth. We have a reference to Moses in the song that is sung by the saints who have gotten the victory over the beast in chapter 15:2-3. The events during Israel's exodus from Egypt under Moses were foreshadowings of the great day of Antichrist and the victory that God's downtrodden ones will enjoy over him.

In considering this chapter 15 as an introduction to the pouring out of the vials of wrath, please note:-

I.   GOD WILL ANSWER THE REBELLIOUS CHALLENGE OF MEN.

1.   One of the greatest challenges men can offer to God is to attack His people. *He suffered no man to do them wrong: yea, he reproved kings for their sakes; saying, Touch not mine anointed, and do my prophets no harm*, Psalm 105:14-15.

That challenge Antichrist will issue in an unprecedented way. *And it was given unto him to make war with the saints, and to overcome them: and power was given him over all kindreds, and tongues, and nations . . . And he had power to give life unto the image of the beast, that the image of the beast should both speak, and cause that as many as would not worship the image of the beast should be killed,* Revelation 13:7, 15.

2. What men mistake as God ignoring their sins is, in fact, the time taken for God to fill up the vials of wrath. God may not answer man's sin immediately but He will answer it in His time. *And he said unto Abram, Know of a surety that thy seed shall be a stranger in a land that is not theirs, and shall serve them; and they shall afflict them four hundred years; and also that nation, whom they shall serve, will I judge: and afterward shall they come out with great substance. And thou shalt go to thy fathers in peace; thou shalt be buried in a good old age. But in the fourth generation they shall come hither again: for the iniquity of the Amorites is not yet full,* Genesis 15:13-16. I repeat, the Lord will not ignore sin, especially sins against the people redeemed by the blood of His dear Son. *Thou tellest my wanderings: put thou my tears into thy bottle: are they not in thy book?* Psalm 56:8. God keeps a record of every tear that the enemy has caused to be shed and will demand an account for it from them.

3. The answer of God will come when sinful men feel themselves to be at their strongest. Pharaoh, Goliath, Haman and Belshazzar are but some of the demonstrations of this truth. Antichrist's destruction will be the final demonstration. The more men forget God, the nearer they are to His judgment. *Because sentence against an evil work is not executed speedily, therefore the heart of the sons of men is fully set in them to do evil,* Ecclesiastes 8:11. This pertains to individuals and nations. *The wicked shall be turned into hell, and all the nations that forget God,* Psalm 9:17.

Sinner, beware of the delusion from which Israel suffered in the days of Jeremiah. *Behold, ye trust in lying words, that cannot profit. Will ye steal, murder, and commit adultery, and swear falsely, and burn incense unto Baal, and walk after other gods whom ye know not; and come and stand before me in this house, which is called by my name, and say, We are delivered to do all these abominations?* Jeremiah 7:8-10. The people foolishly believed themselves free to sin against God. They feared no retribution. There are many who know the truth of God as it has been taught to them but they take no heed. It is as if they feel that they have a dispensation from the Lord to break His laws and reject His Son and still go to heaven. Such is a wicked and disastrous delusion from which, if grace does not rescue your soul, you will awaken in hell.

II. GOD'S PEOPLE WILL SING OVER THEIR ENEMIES.

Singing has ever followed the victory of one people over another. But the triumphant song of the people of God will be the last and loudest and longest of all victory songs.

God's people have often sung in triumph during the hard years of pilgrimage, for the Lord it is Who *giveth songs in the night,* Job 35:10. *And David spake unto the LORD the words of this song in the day that the LORD had delivered him out of the hand of all his enemies, and out of the hand of Saul,* 2 Samuel 22:1. Often have the saints of God joined in singing the psalms of David, as we have entered into his joy of victory.

But the victorious saints have a song to sing that will surpass all of our former victory songs. *And they sing the song of Moses the servant of God, and the song of the Lamb, saying, Great and marvellous are thy works, Lord God Almighty; just and true are thy ways, thou King of saints,* 15:3. The sufferings they endured under Antichrist will be forgotten and will the saints not say with Paul, *Our light affliction, which is but for a moment, worketh for us a far more exceeding and eternal weight of glory?* 2 Corinthians 4:17.

1. Note where they sing. It is before the throne of God. Here is the place where true singing may take place. Here is where joy will be at its fullest. The redeemed sinner has entered into the fullness of redemption when he stands before the throne of God. Whenever there has been a sense of God's throne and the atmosphere of that throne amongst God's people, what singing has been the result! Revival singing is throneroom singing. May God give us again such times of sweet worship and rejoicing!

2. Note what they stand on as they sing. *And I saw as it were a sea of glass mingled with fire: and them that had gotten the victory over the beast, and over his image, and over his mark, and over the number of his name, stand on the sea of glass, having the harps of God,* verse 2. The sea of glass in chapter 4:6 is described in the words *a sea of glass like unto crystal.* Here it is *a sea of glass mingled with fire.* In the former, the emphasis was upon the purity of heaven. Now fire is mingled with that purity which means only one thing - wrath. The saints, who stand upon this sea of glass mingled with fire, sing indeed of judgment, verse 4. They are like Israel of old as they walked through the Red Sea. They were immune from all judgment. But the waters of the Red Sea became the instrument of destruction for Pharaoh and his host. From the very place, in which the saints in glory stand, will issue forth the vials of wrath upon Antichrist's domains.

3. Note with what they sing. It is with *the harps of God.* We often heard that we must not take these harps as being literal. If they are not literal harps, just what are they? If the harps are not literal, what else must we take as being allegorical? Various instruments were employed in the worship of God on earth by divine order. We cannot imagine that heaven will have no music and surely none is more sweet than the music of the harp.

The music employed in the worship of God is very distinct from that of the world. Many wish to modernise the tunes and words of the old hymns. They cry out against the old tunes and the old psalms. They would have us sing tunes that are but echoes of those played at the dance hall and disco. The 'Country and Western' fans would be delighted with the tunes that some would introduce to the house of God. When the Church and the world are singing the one tune you can be sure that the Church has strayed and is backslidden.

4. Note what they sing. *And they sing the song of Moses the servant of God, and the song of the Lamb*, verse 3. It is a combination of the song of triumph sung at the first passover and the song glorying in the last passover. How we shall understand and enjoy much more fully the victories of former generations of God's saints! Truly their victories will be our victories. Indeed, in truth, there is only one timeless victory in which all the saints have participated. As in every great battle, one regiment differed in its battle experiences from another, one soldier differed in his experiences from another, but all shared in the same battle, in the same victory, so it will be in glory. Moses' victory will be our victory. David's victory will be our victory. Luther's, Calvin's, Knox's, the martyrs' and covenanters' victories are all our victories. All are separate but intimately linked aspects of the one great victory of the Lord Jesus Christ over all His enemies and foes. These who sang here *had gotten the victory over the beast, and over his image, and over his mark, and over the number of his name.* Perhaps you ask: How was that victory gained? How can I share in the victory of God's people? The answer is simple. *For whatsoever is born of God overcometh the world: and this is the victory that overcometh the world, even our faith,* 1 John 5:4. The new birth by which we enter into the life of victory over sin, the world and the devil and all his works, is the experience of all those who believe on the Lord Jesus Christ. Heed the directions of the apostle Paul right now! *Believe on the Lord Jesus Christ, and thou shalt be saved,* Acts 16:31.

III. IN A TIME OF JUDGMENT, ALL OTHER TEMPLE ACTIVITIES ARE DISCONTINUED.

And after that I looked, and, behold, the temple of the tabernacle of the testimony in heaven was opened . . . And the temple was filled with smoke from the glory of God, and from his power; and no man was able to enter into the temple, till the seven plagues of the seven angels were fulfilled, 15:5, 8.

There is a lesson here for us all. While the judgments are being poured out upon Antichrist's kingdom we are told that no man was able to enter the temple which John saw in heaven. Judgment always brings a suspension of mercy. The words of the prophet Habakkuk remind us that there is a moratorium on mercy; it is forgotten for a time, in the midst of judgment. *O LORD . . . in wrath remember mercy,* Habakkuk 3:2. When sin entered the camp of Israel through the transgression of Achan, Joshua was reprimanded for praying when the need of the hour was a purging out of the offensive thing that had brought God's judgment upon Israel (Joshua 7).

1. This truth has an application for every Christian. Sin will bring a suspension of our enjoyments of many of the blessings of the Lord. *If I regard iniquity in my heart, the Lord will not hear me,* Psalm 66:18. We could multiply verses to demonstrate this truth. But I think we all have felt in our hearts the power of this truth.

2. There is a lesson here for every parent. It is useless to expect God's blessing upon your home while there is tolerated within your home that which is offensive to God, that which ought to be judged and put away by the head of the house. It is vain to plead for blessing while sin is harboured and our families engage in that which is sinful. God will not overlook our wrong-doings. *Thou art of purer eyes than to behold evil, and canst not look on iniquity*, Habakkuk 1:13. Many are chasing mercy from their doors by giving a lodging place to sin and worldliness. Let us heed the lesson of the shut temple.

3. Church leaders should likewise take note. Sin must not be ignored simply to avoid offending some within the congregation. There will be no access to God until that matter is dealt with. The Saviour set us the example. *And they come to Jerusalem: and Jesus went into the temple, and began to cast out them that sold and bought in the temple, and overthrew the tables of the moneychangers, and the seats of them that sold doves*, Mark 11:15. Where sin is tolerated no blessing can be expected. The most merciful thing that can be done in a case of sin springing up in the life of a believer is for that person to be told lovingly but clearly that he cannot continue to enjoy the benefits of fellowship in the house of God until he ceases from sin. That is what is required in Galatians 6:1. *Brethren, if a man be overtaken in a fault, ye which are spiritual, restore such an one in the spirit of meekness; considering thyself, lest thou also be tempted.*

There is a great difference between the presence of sin and sin being tolerated. Sin may be present amongst a people without the people being aware of it. When that is the case the guilt is the offender's alone. But once the offence becomes known then action must be taken. It must not be ignored and tolerated for the sake of avoiding division. That can result only in God being offended. The tolerating of sin makes the tolerator as guilty as the perpetrator.

There is a need at this time among many of the congregations of God's people for all thought of harmony and peace and concord to take second place to a consideration of purity and obedience to God's Holy Word. It is a time for that work for which Jeremiah was commissioned. *Then the LORD put forth his hand, and touched my mouth. And the LORD said unto me, Behold, I have put my words in thy mouth. See, I have this day set thee over the nations and over the kingdoms, to root out, and to pull down, and to destroy, and to throw down, to build, and to plant*, Jeremiah 1:9-10. Until the judging of sin and worldliness takes place there will be a suspending of the blessing of God upon those guilty of offence. *If my people, which are called by my name, shall humble themselves, and pray, and seek my face, and turn from their wicked ways; then will I hear from heaven, and will forgive their sin, and will heal their land,* 2 Chronicles 7:14.

The vials of wrath, part two
CHAPTERS 15 AND 16

O ur study of chapter 15 serves as an introduction to chapter 16, for it is in this chapter that we have the substantial account of the vials being poured out upon the earth.

These judgments come from God. *And I heard a great voice out of the temple saying to the seven angels, Go your ways, and pour out the vials of the wrath of God upon the earth*, verse 1. It is the time when God's wrath is filled up to overflowing and spills over, as it were, as a foretaste of what will come in all its fullness in a very short time. There is an end of God's patience and forbearance. There is a time when the delusion under which most men labour - that there is no wrath or judgment - will be shattered and shattered utterly, *when the wrath of God is revealed from heaven against all ungodliness and unrighteousness of men, who hold the truth in unrighteousness*, Romans 1:18. There is mercy seen in the pouring out of the vials of wrath for they serve as yet another warning to rebellious man.

I.   THE TIME OF THESE JUDGMENTS.

There are a number of markers which clearly tell us when these vials will be poured out.

1. It is in the latter half of Antichrist's reign. *And the first went, and poured out his vial upon the earth; and there fell a noisome and grievous sore upon the men which had the mark of the beast, and upon* *them which worshipped his image*, verse 2. As stated before, the reign of Antichrist will last seven years, but it is only during the last 1260 days or 42 months, or the time, times and half a time, that he will be manifestly revealed as the Antichrist of Holy Scripture, when he erects the *Abomination of Desolation*, the image of himself that the False Prophet will require all to worship, in the rebuilt temple at Jerusalem and declare himself God. *Let no man deceive you by any means: for that day shall not come, except there come a falling away first, and that man of sin be revealed, the son of perdition; who opposeth and exalteth himself above all that is called God, or that is worshipped; so that he as God sitteth in the temple of God, shewing himself that he is God*, 2 Thessalonians 2:3-4. Another of the requirements of the False Prophet, is that all men in the Beast's dominion receive a mark upon their foreheads or on their right hand (13:16-17). It is a mark of damnation. *And the third angel followed them, saying with a loud voice, If any man worship the beast and his image, and receive his mark in his forehead, or in his hand, the same shall drink of the wine of the wrath of God, which is poured out without mixture into the cup of his indignation; and he shall be tormented with fire and brimstone in the presence of the holy angels, and in the presence of the Lamb*, 14:9-10. So for the first vial to be poured out upon those who have the mark of the beast and who worship his image, it must be poured out during the latter part of his seven-year reign.

2. The vials coincide with the time of the gathering of the armies of Antichrist to Armageddon. *And the sixth angel poured out his vial upon the great river Euphrates; and the water thereof was dried up, that the way of the kings of the east might be prepared. And I saw three unclean spirits like frogs come out of the mouth of the dragon, and out of the mouth of the beast, and out of the mouth of the false prophet. For they are the spirits of devils, working miracles, which go forth unto the kings of the earth and of the whole world, to gather them to the battle of that great day of God Almighty. Behold, I come as a thief. Blessed is he that watcheth, and keepeth his garments, lest he walk naked, and they see his shame. And he gathered them together into a place called in the Hebrew tongue Armageddon*, Revelation 16:12-16. Perhaps it should be emphasised that there is no 'Battle of Armageddon' as is so often referred to. Armageddon is but a very large flat area centred upon the town of Megiddo, approximately sixty miles north of Jerusalem. The place is but a mustering area for Antichrist's armies. From there he travels to Jerusalem and is crushed in the Valley of Jehoshaphat as the Saviour returns in judgment. This is *the battle of that great day of God Almighty.* Chapters 2 and 3 of Joel contain details of this event.

The river Euphrates is the strength of Babylon. Its drying up by an act of judgment removes a substantial defence from Antichrist's city and makes an attack upon his stronghold possible for *the kings of* (or from) *the east.* We are told in Daniel that Antichrist is campaigning in Egypt when this attack is made upon his capital city. *He shall stretch forth his hand also upon the countries: and the land of Egypt shall not escape. But he shall have power over the treasures of gold and of silver, and over all the precious things of Egypt: and the Libyans and the Ethiopians shall be at his steps. But tidings out of the east and out of the north shall trouble him: therefore he shall go forth with great fury to destroy, and utterly to make away many. And he shall plant the tabernacles of his palace between the seas in the glorious holy mountain; yet he shall come to his end, and none shall help him,* Daniel 11:42-45. The *tidings out of the east and out of the north* that trouble Antichrist are of the attack referred to in Revelation 16:12.

The kings of the east are identified for us by the prophets Isaiah and Jeremiah. *A sound of battle is in the land, and of great destruction. How is the hammer of the whole earth cut asunder and broken! how is Babylon become a desolation among the nations! I have laid a snare for thee, and thou art also taken, O Babylon, and thou wast not aware: thou art found, and also caught, because thou hast striven against the LORD. The LORD hath opened his armoury, and hath brought forth the weapons of his indignation: for this is the work of the Lord GOD of hosts in the land of the Chaldeans,* Jeremiah 50:21-25.

Set ye up a standard in the land, blow the trumpet among the nations, prepare the nations against her, call together against her the kingdoms of Ararat, Minni, and Ashchenaz; appoint a captain against her; cause the horses to come up as the rough caterpillers. Prepare against her the nations with the kings of the Medes, the captains thereof, and all the rulers thereof, and all the land of his dominion. And the land shall tremble and sorrow: for every purpose of the LORD shall be performed against Babylon, to make the land of Babylon a desolation without an inhabitant. The mighty men of Babylon have forborn to fight, they have remained in their holds: their might hath failed; they became as women: they have burned her dwellingplaces; her bars are broken. One post shall run to meet another, and one messenger to meet another, to shew the king of Babylon that his city is taken at one end, and that the passages are stopped, and the reeds they have burned with fire, and the men of war are affrighted. For thus saith the LORD of hosts, the God of Israel; The daughter of Babylon is like a threshingfloor, it is time to thresh her: yet a little while, and the time of her harvest shall come, Jeremiah 51:27-33.

In a rage, the Beast sets out for Babylon but, by the secret providence of God, turns his anger against Israel and gathers the ten kings of his dominions and their armies to Armageddon from which he launches an attack upon Jerusalem. This results in the Lord consuming him *with the spirit of his mouth*, and destroying him *with the brightness of his coming*, 2 Thessalonians 2:8.

Thus we are privileged to view and examine God's blueprints of war against His enemies. So certain is the outcome that even the enemies may read of the plan which shall bring about their destruction and yet fail to take cognizance of it.

3. The seventh vial clearly indicates a time very close to the end of the age. *And the seventh angel poured out his vial into the air; and there came a great voice out of the temple of heaven, from the throne, saying, It is done. And there were voices, and thunders, and lightnings; and there was a great earthquake, such as was not since men were upon the earth, so mighty an earthquake, and so great. And the great city was divided into three parts, and the cities of the nations fell: and great Babylon came in remembrance before God, to give unto her the cup of the wine of the fierceness of his wrath. And every island fled away, and the mountains were not found. And there fell upon men a great hail out of heaven, every stone about the weight of a talent: and men blasphemed God because of the plague of the hail; for the plague thereof was exceeding great,* verses 17-21. *'It is done.'* The purpose of God with regard to the Antichrist is finally coming to a close. The sins of Babylon have come up in remembrance before God. It is time to give the *cup of the wine of the fierceness of his wrath* to His enemies. This is at the time of the final vial.

II. THESE PLAGUES AND JUDGMENTS WILL HAVE A LITERAL FULFILMENT.

The plagues are as literal as were the plagues upon Egypt, prior to Israel's great deliverance from Pharaoh. The noisome and grievous sores that will befall those with the mark of the beast; the sea and the fountains of water becoming as the blood of a dead man; men scorched with fire; the plague of darkness; the earthquake such as will never have been witnessed before and the great hail - all will take place literally. By them the people of God will be able to tell of the approaching return of Christ. As the angels of judgment that brought news of deliverance for Lot, so the pouring out of the vials will herald for the children of God the approach of their redemption. It is to them that the words of verse 15 are addressed. *Behold, I come as a thief. Blessed is he that watcheth, and keepeth his garments, lest he walk naked, and they see his shame.* We must keep our garments, maintain our testimony and so avoid shaming the Lord and His gospel before our enemies. This is the mark of the true child of God in any age but especially in the age of antichristianity. *Pure religion and undefiled before God and the Father is this, To visit the fatherless and widows in their affliction, and to keep himself unspotted from the world*, James 1:27.

III. MEN SHALL YET SEE THAT GOD HAS NOT CHANGED.

Some of the greatest blasphemies have been uttered by theological modernists and liberals. They have mocked the idea that the God portrayed in the Old Testament is anything other than a figment of an overheated and superstitious brain. Only recently, leading Church of England theologians denounced the idea of hellfire and damnation and accused those who preached it of psychologically damaging their hearers! What a lesson these scoffers have to learn about the Word of God and the God of the Word!

The scenes set before us in Revelation chapter 16 are straight out of the Old Testament. This earth shall see again the power of the God of Moses and Joshua and Gideon and Elijah. Here are scenes out of Exodus and Numbers and Deuteronomy and Joshua and Judges. As the scoffing scepticism of Pharaoh, *Who is the LORD, that I should obey his voice?*

(Exodus 5:2) was answered clearly by the Lord, so shall it be again.

And the LORD spake unto Moses, Say unto Aaron, Take thy rod, and stretch out thine hand upon the waters of Egypt, upon their streams, upon their rivers, and upon their ponds, and upon all their pools of water, that they may become blood; and that there may be blood throughout all the land of Egypt, both in vessels of wood, and in vessels of stone, Exodus 7:19. *And the LORD said unto Moses and unto Aaron, Take to you handfuls of ashes of the furnace, and let Moses sprinkle it toward the heaven in the sight of Pharaoh. And it shall become small dust in all the land of Egypt, and shall be a boil breaking forth with blains upon man, and upon beast, throughout all the land of Egypt. And they took ashes of the furnace, and stood before Pharaoh; and Moses sprinkled it up toward heaven; and it became a boil breaking forth with blains upon man, and upon beast. And the magicians could not stand before Moses because of the boils; for the boil was upon the magicians, and upon all the Egyptians,* Exodus 9:8-11.

As the magicians of Egypt were confounded by the judgments of Jehovah, so it will be with the unbelieving *ecumenical magicians* of this age when God pours forth His wrath.

IV. EXPERIENCING GOD'S JUDGMENTS DOES NOT CONVERT SINNERS.

Men shall feel God's wrath and know that their sins have angered God, but it will not change their hearts or their ways. *And the fourth angel poured out his vial upon the sun; and power was given unto him to scorch men with fire. And men were scorched with great heat, and blasphemed the name of God, which hath power over these plagues: and they repented not to give him glory. And the fifth angel poured out his vial upon the seat of the beast; and his kingdom was full of darkness; and they gnawed their tongues for pain, and blasphemed the God of heaven because of their pains and their sores, and repented not of their deeds,* verses 8-11. They repented not. Repentance is not the easy matter that men perceive it to be. Repentance is not something men can produce of their own will. Repentance is a work of God's free grace. 'Repentance unto life is an evangelical grace, the doctrine whereof is to be preached by every minister of the gospel, as well as that of faith in Christ. By it a sinner, out of the sight and sense, not only of the danger, but also of the filthiness and odiousness of his sins, as contrary to the holy nature and righteous law of God, and upon the apprehension of his mercy in Christ to such as are penitent, so grieves for and hates his sins, as to turn from them all unto God, purposing and endeavouring to walk with him in all the ways of his commandments.' (Westminster Confession of Faith, chapter 15, paragraphs 2 and 3.) If you know nothing of true repentance, then rely not on the idea that at some future time, when you deem it prudent, you can turn and repent and escape coming judgment. It is time now to seek the Lord and ask for the spirit of repentance.

V.   THESE MOST TERRIBLE JUDGMENTS ARE JUST AND RIGHTEOUS.

And the seven angels came out of the temple, having the seven plagues, clothed in pure and white linen, and having their breasts girded with golden girdles, 15:6. *And I heard the angel of the waters say, Thou art righteous, O Lord, which art, and wast, and shalt be, because thou hast judged thus. For they have shed the blood of saints and prophets, and thou hast given them blood to drink; for they are worthy. And I heard another out of the altar say, Even so, Lord God Almighty, true and righteous are thy judgments,* 16:5-7.

The reason men charge God with injustice, whenever they think of judgment, is because they have little or no perception of the wickedness of sin and the awful holiness of God. The offence that sin is against the holiness of God thoroughly and entirely deserves what judgment God metes out. How often we have heard comments about the punishment that should follow the abuse and murder of some little child, examples of which are taking place with increasing frequency. Few people would object to the guilty one being judiciously killed, even though the death penalty is not available in the United Kingdom. Why are they in agreement with such a severe penalty? It is because their perception of the heinousness of the crime and the helpless innocence of the little victim is such that they consider the greatest punishment would still be just in such a case.

Even so is it with God's judgments. Were men able to discern the outrageously evil nature of sin and the utterly pure and innocent character of the One sinned against, then they would cry with the angels: *Thou art righteous, O Lord, which art, and wast, and shalt be, because thou hast judged thus,* 16:5.

It ought to be remembered that the saints of God in heaven will see these judgments as an answer to their cries. *And they cried with a loud voice, saying, How long, O Lord, holy and true, dost thou not judge and avenge our blood on them that dwell on the earth?* Revelation 6:10.

VI. IN ALL THIS, GOD IS WORKING OUT HIS ETERNAL PURPOSE.

It was just so with Pharaoh. *For the scripture saith unto Pharaoh, Even for this same purpose have I raised thee up, that I might shew my power in thee, and that my name might be declared throughout all the earth,* Romans 9:17. So shall it be with Antichrist. He will be brought to Armageddon and then to the Valley of Jehoshaphat, just as Pharaoh was brought into the heart of the Red Sea. There God shall work His destruction of man's rebellion.

Man's wickedness and rebellion do not trouble or threaten the eternal throne of Jehovah. Rather, *He that sitteth in the heavens shall laugh: the Lord shall have them in derision. Then shall he speak unto them in his wrath, and vex them in his sore displeasure,* Psalm 2:4-5.

Even the evil spirits must submit to His will. *And they were all amazed, insomuch that they questioned among themselves, saying, What thing is this? what new doctrine is this? for with authority commandeth he even the unclean spirits, and they do obey him,* Mark 1:27.

Dear child of God, this book was written for your comfort and blessing. Nothing can advance these like a clear understanding of the sovereignty of God and the irresistible nature of His will and purpose.

> *God is my everlasting King;*
> *God is my strength, and I will sing;*
> *His power upholds my feeble frame,*
> *And I'm victorious through His name.*

> *Devils retreat when He appears;*
> *Then I arise above my fears,*
> *And every fiery dart repel,*
> *And vanquish all the force of hell.*

Through the Redeemer's precious blood,
I feel the mighty power of God;
Through the rich aid divinely given,
I rise from earth, and soar to heaven.

Now, Lord, thy wondrous power exert,
And every ransomed soul support;
Give us fresh strength to wing our way
To regions of eternal day.

There may we praise the great I AM,
And shout the victories of the Lamb;
Raise every chorus to His blood,
And triumph in the power of God.

The great whore of Babylon
CHAPTER 17

W e move back to a time previous to that which we have been studying, when we come to chapter 17. I must stress that in relation to time, the events of chapter 17 take place before the events of chapters 13 to 16.

Often in conversation, a person speaking to us will make a reference to a matter, a person or an event. Because we know very little about the topic, we may interrupt and ask for more information, since it is necessary for this to be given to us if we are rightly to understand further references and comments made on this subject. This, in a way, is what is happening with this reverting to a previous time in the history of the Beast and his rise to power.

Chapter 17 ends where chapter 13 begins. From a position of subservience in chapter 17, the Beast rises to one of complete domination in chapter 13. At the time of this chapter 17, there is a greater power than that of the Beast evident in the Roman or prophetic earth: *the great whore that sitteth upon many waters*, verse 1. We may share in the invitation extended to John the apostle, and see and consider the judgment of this great phenomenon.

I. THE APOSTLE CONSIDERING THE MOTHER OF HARLOTS.

And there came one of the seven angels which had the seven vials, and talked with me, saying unto me, Come hither; I will shew unto thee the judgment of the great whore that sitteth upon many waters: with whom the kings of the earth have committed fornication, and the inhabitants of the earth have been made drunk with the wine of her fornication. So he carried me away in the spirit into the wilderness: and I saw a woman sit upon a scarlet coloured beast, full of names of blasphemy, having seven heads and ten horns, verses 1-3.

1. John was taken into the wilderness to view the Mother of Harlots. In Holy Scripture, the wilderness is often the place of separation and of communion with God and the place of the revealing of His will and purpose.

It was so for Moses. *Now Moses kept the flock of Jethro his father in law, the priest of Midian: and he led the flock to the backside of the desert, and came to the mountain of God, even to Horeb. And the angel of the LORD appeared unto him in a flame of fire out of the midst of a bush: and he looked, and, behold, the bush burned with fire, and the bush was not consumed,* Exodus 3:1-2. It was there that the Lord revealed to Moses His purpose to deliver His people from Egypt. In that very same wilderness, Israel was given the holy law of God and taught His precepts and distinguished from all other nations by the experience of these privileges. *And what one nation in the earth is like thy people, even like Israel, whom God went to redeem for a people to himself, and to make him a name, and to do for you great things and terrible, for thy land, before thy people, which thou redeemedst to thee from Egypt, from the nations and their gods?* 2 Samuel 7:23. It was in the wilderness that these privileges were realised.

In the New Testament, it was in the wilderness that John the Baptist was prepared for and also carried out his ministry. *Now in the fifteenth year of the reign of Tiberius Caesar, Pontius Pilate being governor of Judaea, and Herod being tetrarch of Galilee, and his brother Philip tetrarch of Ituraea and of the region of Trachonitis, and Lysanias the tetrarch of Abilene, Annas and Caiaphas being the high priests, the word of God came unto John the son of Zacharias in the wilderness,* Luke 3:1-2. More importantly, the wilderness was a place of fellowship with His Heavenly Father for the Lord Jesus Christ. *And he withdrew himself into the wilderness, and prayed,* Luke 5:16. Such was a common practice for our Saviour.

The purpose of the angel taking John into the wilderness in order to view the Harlot is, I believe, to stress that a clear picture of the Harlot can be had only by those who view her from the position of separation to and fellowship with the Lord. It is a natural requirement to have to withdraw some distance from a large object, in this instance a city (verse 18), if we are to obtain a proper and full view of it. Those who are part of this Harlot system, who live in the suburbs, as it were, of this city (and here we are talking about believers) cannot see the full extent of her wicked character. That is why we have, today, many believers still in denominations that are openly and blatantly corrupt and apostate. They dwell within the city and cannot see it, as does the one who withdraws from it and obtains an overall picture of the corruption and sin within. The answer to the question asked so often by perplexed believers about those who remain in apostate denominations: 'Why can they not see that they should separate?' is simply this: they cannot see it as does the separated believer. They do not consider it to be as wicked as it really is. This is no excuse. It is merely an explanation for their sinful disobedience of God's call to separate from that which is unclean. Recently, we had a very few members of the Church of England separate from that long apostate organisation because of the ordination of woman. Why did they not act when the doctrine of the atonement was denied by leading churchmen? Or when the deity of Christ was questioned? Or the inspiration of the Holy Scriptures was rejected? Or when sodomy was condoned? Or when union with Rome was described as the purpose and will of God for His people? The answer is they could not see the corruption of the system of which they were a part while they remained within it. We cannot avoid the suspicion that in the end, they reacted only when they perceived that the sanctity of their sacred priestly role had been violated. It appears to have been more an action in defence of a sacerdotal shibboleth than a response to an assault upon the holy standards of God.

The need today for the witness of the separated remnant against the apostasy of ecumenism is greater than ever. Let our voices be heard loud and clear crying out against this wickedness.

2. John was in the spirit when he was shown the Harlot. Is this not like Ezekiel's experience when God showed to him the apostasy of Jerusalem for which it was soon to be judged? *And he put forth the form of an hand, and took me by a lock of mine head; and the spirit lifted me up between the earth and the heaven, and brought me in the visions of God to Jerusalem, to the door of the inner gate that looketh toward the* *north; where was the seat of the image of jealousy, which provoketh to jealousy. . . . Then he said unto me, Hast thou seen this, O son of man? Is it a light thing to the house of Judah that they commit the abominations which they commit here? for they have filled the land with violence, and have returned to provoke me to anger: and, lo, they put the branch to their nose. Therefore will I also deal in fury: mine eye shall not spare, neither will I have pity: and though they cry in mine ears with a loud voice, yet will I not hear them,* Ezekiel 8:3, 17-18.

The separated, spiritual man ALONE will perceive and recognise the wickedness of the Harlot. Let us beware of drinking of her cup that makes the nations drunk, for then we will be deceived and deluded and become a partaker of her plagues.

3. John was shown the judgment of the Harlot. *Come hither; I will shew unto thee the judgment of the great whore that sitteth upon many waters,* verse 1. Whatever she may rise to become, her judgment is sure. Of this every believer should be assured. The word *judgment* means *damnation.* There will be times when it will be nigh impossible to imagine this mighty system being destroyed. It is then that the child of God must cling to God's Word. The Harlot is damned.

II. THE IDENTITY OF THE HARLOT.

A woman, in Holy Scripture, is the symbol of a moral system. I think I need refer only to the Church of Jesus Christ, that system of truth and righteousness established by Christ, for it is commonly likened unto a woman. *Who is she that looketh forth as the morning, fair as the moon, clear as the sun, and terrible as an army with banners?* Song of Solomon 6:10. *And there came unto me one of the seven angels which had the seven vials full of the seven last plagues, and talked with me, saying, Come hither, I will shew thee the bride, the Lamb's wife,* Revelation 21:9. Here are but two of the many examples of the Church of Christ being likened to a woman.

The woman in this chapter differs from the Bride of Christ in that she is an immoral woman, a great whore, a mother of harlots. She is an immoral system. She is the false bride, the apostate church. *And upon her forehead was a name written, MYSTERY, BABYLON THE GREAT, THE MOTHER OF HARLOTS AND ABOMINATIONS OF THE EARTH,* verse 5. Fornication is the stock and trade of this woman. Spiritual fornication is idolatry, a turning from the true God to worship other gods, as an unfaithful wife turns from her husband to seek to other men. This what she is and the Lord would have His people understand this. To us is revealed the mystery of this woman. She will not appear to us as she does to the beguiled worldling. To the sinner, the kingdom of God is a mystery. *He answered and said unto them, Because it is given unto you to know the mysteries of the kingdom of heaven, but to them it is not given,* Matthew 13:11. To the sinner, godliness is a mystery. *And without controversy great is the mystery of godliness,* 1 Timothy 3:16. And likewise, the true nature of this evil system will be a mystery. But it ought not to be so for the child of God.

Here is the mysterious spirit of iniquity, that even in Paul's time was at work (2 Thessalonians 2:7), nearing its final manifestation. It is the spirit of Babylonianism that has been hidden, mingled and disguised, but secretly advancing amidst the various societies of men. Its thread may be traced through the actions of Cain, Nimrod, the idolatry of the Canaanite tribes, the apostasy of Israel, the great kingdoms of Babylon, Persia, Greece and Rome, its gradual emergence and centring in Roman Catholicism and, latterly, the great apostasy of the last days embracing Roman Catholicism, ecumenical Protestantism and all other false religions. The woman is not its full and final manifestation. No! She is destroyed. But Babylonianism is not destroyed. The final and full manifestation of Babylonianism will be seen in the Antichrist and it will continue until he is destroyed. As the roots of a plant, growing and spreading beneath the surface, put forth a stem which in turn puts forth leaves and then, finally, a bud which opens into a flower and so the whole process of growth, begun and carried on at first hidden beneath the surface of the soil, reaches its climax - even so will it be with the mystery of iniquity.

There have ever been God's truth and the devil's lie operating in this world. There have been the true and the counterfeit, the Christ and the antichrists, the true prophet and the false prophet, the Holy Spirit and the spirit of antichrist, the gospel and another gospel. Cain followed a false way of redemption when he offered up the fruit of the ground. Abel, on the other hand, was of the truth and offered the lamb in accordance with God's Word. There are still the Cainites and the

Abelites in the world today. We belong to one or the other. We are part of Christ's Church and under His redeeming blood, or we are part of the false system symbolised here by the Harlot.

The chief manifestation of the spirit of the Harlot today is undoubtedly the ecumenical movement. It is true that it may be seen in the religions of the Moslems, the Sikhs and the innumerable other false religions that litter the earth. But it is CHIEFLY seen in the ecumenical movement with its union of idolatrous Roman Catholicism and apostate Protestantism. The ecumenical movement is growing in its uncleanness and filthiness as' it absorbs every wickedness that emerges from the bowels of hell. The other false religions will eventually link up with the ecumenical movement and be absorbed. That is evident from the moves that are already taking place in that direction, with talks under way between various leading pagan groupings and the ecumenical church leaders and negotiators. This whore is the *Mother of Harlots* and her unclean daughters will all return home one day and that reunion will be centred in Babylon, the ancient home of man's defiance of God.

1. The Harlot is a city. *And the woman which thou sawest is that great city, which reigneth over the kings of the earth,* verse 18. The great city of man has ever been the city of Babylon. That was the city Nimrod and his followers started to build but were forced to abandon when God intervened. *And the beginning of his kingdom was Babel, and Erech, and Accad, and Calneh, in the land of Shinar. . . . . So the LORD scattered them abroad from thence upon the face of all the earth: and they left off to build the city. Therefore is the name of it called Babel; because the LORD did there confound the language of all the earth: and from thence did the LORD scatter them abroad upon the face of all the earth,* Genesis 10;10, 11:8-9. They *left off* with the intention of returning one day and recommencing their building of the city. Babylon became the centre of Nebuchadnezzar's world empire. It is but a small town at present. It was in the news not so long ago when it was bombed by the allies during the war fought to drive Saddam Hussein's Iraqi forces out of Kuwait in 1991. However, it will become a world centre according to Holy Scripture and it will firstly gain notoriety as the seat of the Harlot. Zechariah was shown the *woman which was wickedness,* the same woman that is seen here in this chapter, being brought to the land of Shinar or Babylon, and there placed upon a site prepared for her and established, Zechariah 5:5-11. Here in this chapter we see her established.

2. This city rules over men. *And he saith unto me, The waters which thou sawest, where the whore sitteth, are peoples, and multitudes, and nations, and tongues,* verse 15. She rules over them by the power of the *wine of her fornication,* verse 2. How often have control and advantage been gained over individuals by first getting them drunk. The sordid story of Lot and his daughters, who played the harlot, is but one example of this infamous way of obtaining a wicked objective. So will it be with this Harlot. Even today, when the Harlot has still not come to the zenith of her power, she controls the minds and hearts of millions.

The struggle in Northern Ireland is one against the mind-blinding powers of ecumenism and popery. Those who support terrorism consider themselves to have the support of the Harlot system, and indeed they do. Despite the oft-repeated apparent denunciations of terrorism by Rome, her priests, nuns and monks are among the most fervent supporters of the Irish Republican Army, the IRA. It must surely be noted that whenever the IRA has suffered some major military set-back, such as has happened following a successful ambushing of an IRA group about to launch a murder bid, the first to denounce the security forces for their actions is the Cardinal or his spokesman. Demands are made as to why the IRA members were not arrested rather than shot. This has happened again and again. Ulster loyalists consider themselves to be fighting for their political freedoms and for their very lives against the advance of the forces of Irish republicanism, the IRA and its allies. But despite this plain siding with the terrorist by Romanism, many of Northern Ireland's loyalists still cling to those denominations that daily demonstrate their common cause with popery. Week by week, the ministers of these denominations urge their congregations to yield themselves up to the arms of ecumenical union with Rome.

How can this be? The answer is that nominal Protestants are largely drugged and made drunk with the wine of ecumenism. They persistently sup at the cup of lies and falsehoods and each sip makes them less able to discern what is right and best for them. In the 1960s, when the dangers of ecumenism were first pointed out to them, there was a recoiling in horror and many thousands left the ecumenical churches under the campaigning ministry of Dr. Ian Paisley and others. But ecumenism counter-attacked and redoubled its efforts in order to control its people. It has to be admitted that today they have very much regained control of their flock. Protestants are now far less fearful of Rome and less influenced by warnings against Rome than they were thirty years ago. During the widely publicised dispute, in July 1996, over the rights of Orangemen to walk to church down a main road that skirts some Roman Catholic homes, many Orangemen raised no objections to the local member of Parliament, a prominent Orangeman, holding talks about the route to be taken with ecumenical leaders including the Roman Catholic Cardinal, Cahal Daly, who has proved himself to be an ally of the Irish Republican attempt to overthrow democracy in Northern Ireland. This mind-numbing stupor has been induced by the daily intake of ecumenism from the radio, the television, the newspapers, the church services and the state school classrooms. We are all aware of the effects of a chloroform-soaked handkerchief over the mouth of an individual. At first there is quite a violent struggle but this quickly subsides as the drug takes effect. The struggles die away and are replaced by quiet compliance. Such is a suitable and accurate picture of what is happening in Northern Ireland. The body politic of Northern Ireland's Protestantism jerks spasmodically in resistance to what is taking place, but overall there is a sinking down into compliance and surrender.

The same folly is seen at work in mainland Britain. There is a commonly and widely held perception that Britain's national freedom and identity are increasingly being taken away by the European Union. Legislation governing every aspect of life, from what we may call our pies and confectionery to whether or not we may chastise our children in accordance with God's Word and common sense, is regularly being enforced upon us. But still the people stick with the EU. The answer is found in the same intoxicating brew that is behind the violation of Northern Ireland. Leaders of Church and State preach up the virtues of European union. It will be the cure-all of all social and thereby moral ills. War will cease and a period of universal peace is guaranteed. This is the heady concoction that has Britain drunkenly staggering down the road to national surrender with only the occasional whimpering protest or feeble attempt to turn back.

This intoxication will increase more and more, as the Harlot, which today is seen only in the spirit that is at work in the various false religions in the world, takes on a definite, corporate identity and is enthroned as the mistress of the domain of Antichrist. Presently, Roman Catholicism calls herself the Mistress of the Nations but that is far from a reality in most cases. She does not even control such states as Italy where her presence is very much in the majority. But Romanism is not the final or full manifestation of the Mother of Harlots. When the amalgamations and unions have all taken place, then will come the final manifestation and the Harlot will ride the beast in triumph for a time.

3. The Harlot sits upon seven mountains. *And here is the mind which hath wisdom. The seven heads are seven mountains, on which the woman sitteth*, verse 9. Wisdom is indeed needed to understand the meaning of these words. The woman is a moral system that is centred in a city so that the system and city are viewed as one. When the woman is said to sit on seven mountains, does that mean that the city associated with this woman is literally built upon seven mountains? I do not believe it does. The Harlot is said to be seated on *many waters*, verse 1; on *the beast*, verse 3; upon *seven mountains*, verse 9. Now none would say that this woman will literally be builded upon waters or upon the head of the beast. Why, therefore should the mountains be considered as the literal site for the foundations of this city? We must seek to show consistency of interpretation when seeking to understand Holy Scripture.

The seven heads, which are said to be seven mountains in verse 9, are the same seven heads referred to in verse 3. *A scarlet coloured beast, full of names of blasphemy, having seven heads and ten horns.* The Beast is a man (see 13:8) and therefore the seven heads signify some aspect of his character or being. Seven literal mountains cannot be a part of his being or his character.

These seven heads are mentioned five times in the book of the Revelation. We will look at them chronologically according to the sequence of time.

Chapter 12:3. *And there appeared another wonder in heaven; and behold a great red dragon, having seven heads and ten horns, and seven crowns upon his heads.* The ten horns have been identified as referring to the ten kingdoms, or more particularly their kings (17:12), that will rule the old Roman earth whenever the era of the Antichrist dawns. Here the devil is seen with these horns. The period referred to in Revelation chapter 12 is prior to the emergence of the Antichrist as the supreme ruler and exerciser of power in these kingdoms. He will assume that supremacy when these kings *have one mind, and shall give their power and strength unto the beast,* 17:13.

So then, in chapter 12, the devil is seen with the ten horns, or exercising the power or strength of the ten kings of the Roman earth. He is also said to have *seven heads with seven crowns upon his heads.* We move a little nearer to understanding what these seven heads refer to by understanding what the ten horns refer to.

Chapter 17:3, 7, 9. *A scarlet coloured beast, full of names of blasphemy, having seven heads and ten horns. . . . I will tell thee the mystery of the woman, and of the beast that carrieth her, which hath the seven heads and ten horns. . . The seven heads are seven mountains, on which the woman sitteth.*

In chapter 17, we have moved on from the time alluded to in chapter 12. Things have happened in the Roman or prophetic earth. The devil's scheme has advanced. The day of the revelation of the Son of Perdition, the Antichrist, is now nearer. The power and strength of the ten kingdoms are now transferred to the Beast, the Antichrist. He now is described as having the ten horns. He is also depicted as having seven heads, but the Harlot sits upon those heads. The emblematic significance of *sitting* in Holy Scripture is *to enter into the enjoyment of that upon which one sits or sits down to.* Two illustrations will suffice to show this to be so. The first use of the word *sit* in the Old Testament is found in Genesis 27:19. *And Jacob said unto his father, I am Esau thy firstborn; I have done according as thou badest me: arise, I pray thee, sit and eat of my venison, that thy soul may bless me.* The invitation to Isaac to *sit and eat* the venison Jacob had prepared him was an invitation to partake of the meat and enjoy it. The first use of the word *sit* in the New Testament is in Matthew 8:11. *And I say unto you, That many shall come from the east and west, and shall sit down with Abraham, and Isaac, and Jacob, in the kingdom of heaven.* To sit down with Abraham, Isaac and Jacob in the kingdom of heaven is to enter into the blessings they presently experience, to enjoy the kingdom to the full. Therefore, when we read of the Harlot *sitting on the seven heads* of the Antichrist it means that at that period in his career, whatever those seven heads symbolise, she, the Harlot, and not the Antichrist, is enjoying the benefits of the symbols. Remember that the Harlot is said to sit upon many waters, verse 1. We are told in verse 15 what this means. *And he saith unto me, The waters which thou sawest, where the whore sitteth, are peoples, and multitudes, and nations, and tongues.* To sit must mean to enjoy the exercising of the rule over, to dominate. This is again borne out in verse 18. *And the woman which thou sawest is that great city, which reigneth over the kings of the earth.*

Chapter 13:1. *And I stood upon the sand of the sea, and saw a beast rise up out of the sea, having seven heads and ten horns, and upon his horns ten crowns, and upon his heads the name of blasphemy.* This chapter depicts the Antichrist at the zenith of his power. He rules supreme. In sequence of time, the events of this chapter come after those specified in chapter 17. What now of the seven heads? There is now no Harlot sitting on them. Whatever they are emblems of, the Antichrist is not required to share them or permit another to enjoy them. What then do they mean?

We have a further clue in the fact that whatever they symbolise, seven mountains symbolise it also, for it seems, from verse 9 of chapter 17, that the two symbols are interchangeable. *The seven heads are seven mountains.* What then may be said to be symbolised in Holy Scripture both by heads and by mountains? In a physical sense, the head refers to that place of control and government within the body. The word is used so of Christ with regard to the church and of husbands with regard to the wives. *For the husband is the head of the wife, even as Christ is the head of the church,* Ephesians 5:23. The head contains those elements by which the body is governed, the decision-making apparatus as it were. In a political sense, the *head of a government* is the one who embodies the decision-making power of government. He may well delegate certain aspects of the decision-making authority to *heads of departments or ministries.* It is in this picture or image that I believe that we have the answer to what the seven heads are. In the Roman world, things will develop so that more and more the decision-making apparatus of government will pass into the hands of the devil and cease to be influenced by Christians or considerations of Biblical morality. Do we not see this happening now with decisions about Sabbath-trading, abortion, sodomy, divorce, capital punishment and the education of children? Decisions affecting such matters are being taken without the least reference to God or His Word. The devil is more and more controlling governments' decision making and policy direction. This is going to continue until he rules supreme in these matters and the government of the Roman earth will be utterly godless. Then the devil will transfer such power to his servant, the Antichrist. At the first, the exercise of this power will be very much under the control of the Harlot, the system of moral apostasy. Again we see a foreshadowing of this in the influence that ecumenical clerics and bodies exercise within the realm of decision making. Cardinals and archbishops are consulted by governments and few governments within the European Union would deliberately fly in the face of the thinking of the Vatican or one of its ecumenical satellites. The trends that have taken place over the last fifty years are going to continue to their logical conclusion, when apostasy has ousted Biblical truth completely from the nations' thinking and the Harlot will sit supreme within the circle of governance within the nations.

Does this interpretation of the symbolic meaning of *heads* fit in with it being interchanged with *mountains*? For if heads and mountains cannot carry the same symbolic meaning, then our interpretation is wrong.

The strongest and most obvious link that we have between legislative power and a mountain is the fact that God chose to legislate to Israel from Mount Sinai. From its peaks the moral law still rules us today. Again, it was on a mount that the Saviour expounded that law as it affected His people. Again, Isaiah the prophet, speaking of the future reign of Christ on the earth, spoke of mount Zion being the legislative centre of the Saviour's millennial kingdom. *And it shall come to pass in the last days, that the mountain of the LORD'S house shall be established in the top of the mountains, and shall be exalted above the hills; and all nations shall flow unto it. And many people shall go and say, Come ye, and let us go up to the mountain of the LORD, to the house of the God of Jacob; and he will teach us of his ways, and we will walk in his paths: for out of Zion shall go forth the law, and the word of the LORD from Jerusalem,* Isaiah 2:1-3. I think, therefore, that our interpretation stands up.

The woman sitting upon the seven heads or seven mountains is a picture of the dominant position over all matters of government that apostate religion will have, in the early stages of the Antichrist's kingdom, before he destroys her, that is all religion, and declares himself God. In his rise to full power, the Antichrist will assume full control over all aspects of government. The influence of the Harlot will be destroyed within his kingdom and he will rule supreme. He will control all: what men buy and what men sell (13:16-17). Above all, he will control whom men worship, decreeing that none may be worshipped but he himself (2 Thessalonians 2:4; Revelation 13:15).

III. THE PATRONAGE OF THE HARLOT.

We have spent some time considering the subservience of the Antichrist to the Harlot in the early stages of his career. There is another side to that coin.

1. The Harlot is conveyed by the Beast. She benefits greatly from his power for she *rides the beast.* In other words she is conveyed to a position of prominence by the Antichrist. It will suit his purposes to further her interests for a season. Again, we see a foreshadowing of this co-operation in the preference shown to apostasy and its minions today. In many instances, church leaders lead that which has only a paper exist-ence. In England particularly, the archbishops and bishops wield great power, but the percentage of the nation that adheres to them is microscopic! This preferring of the religion of antichristianity will continue until the Beast, the embodiment of apostate political power, elevates to prominence, and conveys along by his power, the system of spiritual harlotry.

2. She will be destroyed by her patron one day. *And the ten horns which thou sawest upon the beast, these shall hate the whore, and shall make her desolate and naked, and shall eat her flesh, and burn her with fire. For God hath put in their hearts to fulfil his will, and to agree, and give their kingdom unto the beast, until the words of God shall be fulfilled,* verses 16-17. These horns are the kings who give allegiance to the Beast. It shows his control over them that they willingly destroy that which before they adored. *I will shew unto thee the judgment of the great whore that sitteth upon many waters: with whom the kings of the earth have committed fornication, and the inhabitants of the earth have been made drunk with the wine of her fornication,* verses 1-2.

3. The Lord rules in the nations of men. We have already touched upon this, but please note that above the kings of the Roman earth, above the Antichrist, above the devil sits the Almighty, the Ruler of heaven and earth. *God hath put in their hearts to fulfil his will, and to agree, and give their kingdom unto the beast, until the words of God shall be fulfilled.* God worketh all things after the counsel of His own good pleasure. He can bring to an end the defiance of evil and employ evil's own hand against itself. Not for the first time has a Haman built a gallows upon which he himself is hung! Such is the sovereign overruling providence of our God. See it, Christian, and rejoice!

As we ponder these matters regarding the power of the Harlot and the power of the Antichrist and the power of the devil that this world will see in the last days, let us not forget the transient, fleeting and deceitful character of all that springs from this earth. Even John was, for a time, powerfully influenced by the alluring sight of this worldly pomp and beauty. *And I saw the woman drunken with the blood of the saints, and with the blood of the martyrs of Jesus: and when I saw her, I wondered with great admiration. And the angel said unto me, Wherefore didst thou marvel?* Revelation 17:6-7. There is that within us all which is inclined to marvel at and to admire worldly grandeur. We must guard against it for as this age progresses, there will emerge a display of worldly ostentation unparalleled in all of earth's history. This woman was *arrayed in purple and scarlet colour, and decked with gold and precious stones and pearls, having a golden cup in her hand,* verse 4. What grandeur, what glory, what splendour is here depicted by this costly apparel! It is only when you look into the golden cup that she is proffering to the lips of the nations that the character of this evil thing becomes clear, for it is *full of abominations and filthiness of her fornication.*

For all that is in the world, the lust of the flesh, and the lust of the eyes, and the pride of life, is not of the Father, but is of the world. And the world passeth away, and the lust thereof: but he that doeth the will of God abideth for ever, 1 John 2:16-17. May we by grace be enabled ever to keep this truth in mind.

Grief and gladness
CHAPTER 18

There is a distinction between the Babylon of chapter 17 and the Babylon of chapter 18. In chapter 17 we have the system of Babylon which had been at work amongst the nations of men, virtually since the beginning of time. That system of wickedness will be centred in the city of Babylon, first in the incorporated union of false religions that is symbolised by the Great Whore and then, when she is destroyed by the Antichrist, residing in him.

The Babylon of chapter 18 is the great city of Babylon, which rebellious man *left off to build* (Genesis 11:8), but which will be built to become the capital of Antichrist and antichristianity. It is here that the spirit of iniquity, or lawlessness and wickedness, will be given a base. *This is wickedness. And he cast it into the midst of the ephah; and he cast the weight of lead upon the mouth thereof. Then lifted I up mine eyes, and looked, and, behold, there came out two women, and the wind was in their wings; for they had wings like the wings of a stork: and they lifted up the ephah between the earth and the heaven. Then said I to the angel that talked with me, Whither do these bear the ephah? And he said unto me, To build it an house in the land of Shinar: and it shall be established, and set there upon her own base*, Zechariah 5:8-11. In this chapter we have the judgment of God falling on and destroying the base upon which this wickedness has been established.

Again, let it be noted that there is an emphasis upon the *destruction* of this evil city which will appear so glorious in the eyes of wicked men.

This same emphasis was seen in the vision of the great Harlot in chapter 17. God would have His people ever to bear in mind the end of these things. He who can see the evil maggot in the core of the apple will not be persuaded to bite the fruit, no matter how red and luscious its skin may appear. So it is with the magnificence that will pervade the world, particularly the Roman or prophetic earth, in the final days of this age. In its heart is an evil that will bring down God's wrath upon it.

This chapter contains much grief, verses 9-19. But it also contains much gladness, verse 20. How diverse are the ways of unbelievers and believers. That which makes the one lament with bitter grief makes the other to rejoice with great gladness. I might say to all, that you are known by what makes you happy and what makes you sad. Is your rejoicing with that of the saints or with that of wicked men? *I was glad when they said unto me, Let us go into the house of the LORD*, Psalm 122:1. Is the company of the people of God and your accompanying them to the house of God what makes you happy or do you delight in the company of the wicked? *Blessed is the man that walketh not in the counsel of the ungodly, nor standeth in the way of sinners, nor sitteth in the seat of the scornful. But his delight is in the law of the LORD; and in his law doth he meditate day and night*, Psalm 1:1-2.

What a contrast is presented to us in verses 15 and 20! *The merchants of these things, which were made rich by her, shall stand afar off for the fear of her torment, weeping and wailing*, verse 15. *Rejoice over her, thou heaven, and ye holy apostles and prophets; for God hath avenged you on her*, verse 20. The laughter of sin has turned into the wailing of sorrow for the sinner. For the saints, *weeping may endure for a night, but joy cometh in the morning*, Psalm 30:5. The morning of eternal joy is dawning for the people of God and the destruction of Babylon is one of the first brightening tints lighting up the eastern sky. The Sun of Righteousness is about to rise with healing and blessing in His rays.

I.   BABYLON'S CHARACTER AND CONDEMNATION.

Here we have heaven's view of Babylon. For a time it may have seemed that her activities were of no interest to heaven. So must it also have appeared to Sodom and Gomorrah. But nothing goes on unnoticed by God. He may, in mercy to sinners, patiently bear with their sinning, but there comes a time when their evil will be taken account of. Just so was it with Babylon *for her sins have reached unto heaven, and God hath remembered her iniquities*, verse 5. The word *reached* is a translation of a word which is elsewhere translated *follow*. It is the word that is used of the actions of a disciple following the Lord Jesus. Thus it is translated on the first occasion that it appears in the New Testament. *And they straightway left their nets, and followed him*, Matthew 4:20. Just as the steps of a disciple will always follow behind the Saviour, so sin's steps will always bring it before God for judgment. When we are told that God remembered the sins of Babylon, it is not that God had forgotten her sins and then suddenly recalled them. No! It refers to the sins of Babylon coming into the mind of God for the time to judge her had come. As we bring to the front of our minds and act upon an arrangement when the appointed time comes round, so it will be one day with the Lord and the sins of Babylon.

Note what we are told of the sinfulness of this evil city.

1. She is the centre of deception. *And the light of a candle shall shine no more at all in thee; and the voice of the bridegroom and of the bride shall be heard no more at all in thee: for thy merchants were the great men of the earth; for by thy sorceries were all nations deceived*, verse 23. The spirit of deception will pervade Babylon. The city will be its own chief victim. *How much she hath glorified herself, and lived deliciously, so much torment and sorrow give her: for she saith in her heart, I sit a queen, and am no widow, and shall see no sorrow*, 18:7. Isaiah refers to this feature of the Babylon of his day and, prophetically, he is indicating that it is an attribute of her character which will still be with her when she re-emerges in the last days. *And thou saidst, I shall be a lady for ever: so that thou didst not lay these things to thy heart, neither didst remember the latter end of it. Therefore hear now this, thou that art given to pleasures, that dwellest carelessly, that sayest in thine heart, I am, and none else beside me; I shall not sit as a widow, neither shall I know the loss of children*, Isaiah 47:7-8.

How deceitful is pride! How destructive is pride! *Pride goeth before destruction, and an haughty spirit before a fall*, Proverbs 16:18. Pride and deception can end only in tears and misery. For this reason we urge upon sinners to repent of their sins and rebellion against God. No matter how secure they feel today, God shall yet bring them into judgment.

Be not deceived; God is not mocked: for whatsoever a man soweth, that shall he also reap, Galatians 6:7.

The means employed by Babylon to deceive the nations was sorceries. As already noted (9:20-21), the word is a translation of the Greek word *pharmakeia.* It refers to the administering of drugs. This is presently becoming a world-wide scourge. The use of drugs will become the chief means of deceiving the nations during the heyday of Babylon. Those who call, among them some members of parliament, for the legalising of drugs give us a portent of that day.

2. She is a centre of deliciousness. *For all nations have drunk of the wine of the wrath of her fornication, and the kings of the earth have committed fornication with her, and the merchants of the earth are waxed rich through the abundance of her delicacies,* verse 3. *How much she hath glorified herself, and lived deliciously, so much torment and sorrow give her: for she saith in her heart, I sit a queen, and am no widow, and shall see no sorrow,* verse 7. The words *delicacies* and *deliciously* are closely allied, being from the same root, and refer to an overflowing and wanton luxuriousness. This is the sumptuous opulence of the ancient heathen courts all flowing together in lascivious abandonment and reaching beyond the small favoured circle of courtiers and attendants, who alone were the participants in ancient times, to the broader mass of merchants and traders who operate out of this great commercial metropolis.

These merchants have *waxed rich,* verse 3. The wealth so often promised by other political regimes has become a reality within the commercial empire centred upon this city.

3. She is a centre of depravity. *For all nations have drunk of the wine of the wrath of her fornication, and the kings of the earth have committed fornication with her . . . For her sins have reached unto heaven, and God hath remembered her iniquities. . . . And the merchants of the earth shall weep and mourn over her; for no man buyeth their merchandise any more: the merchandise of gold, and silver, and precious stones . . . and slaves, and souls of men. . . . And in her was found the blood of prophets, and of saints, and of all that were slain upon the earth,* verses 3, 5, 11-13, 24. These quotations from these verses show something of the corruptions found within the city of Babylon. All that the gospel, by its enlightening power, has banished from among those nations, that came under its influence, has returned under Babylon. Even trading in slaves has returned in Babylon. For those who feel that such is impossible, let them just consider the fact that slavery is presently tolerated in all the larger cities of the United Kingdom in the form of prostitution where men solicit and control the selling of women and take the larger portion of the ill-gotten profits. Slavery has never completely been overthrown, even in the most advanced countries. In Babylon, it will become just another enterprise to exploit.

There is only one method of avoiding contamination by Babylonianism. *And I heard another voice from heaven, saying, Come out of her, my people, that ye be not partakers of her sins, and that ye receive not of her plagues,* verse 4. It is amazing that there should be found in the midst of this sinful city any that are numbered amongst the people of God. Yet God sees them there and calls them out. That is where He would have them. It never has been God's will that His people be found in the midst of sin. Let this be as a rebuke to those who claim that the Lord would have them remain in a position of influence within the ecumenical apostasy that they might serve Him there. Insiders do nothing to hinder the advance of apostasy or advance the cause of truth. It influences them, rather than the reverse. To remain in can result only in the partaking of her sins and receiving her plagues. Far from acting as a restraint, believers who remain within the apostasy are being dragged toward judgment.

II. BABYLON'S DOWNFALL AND DESTRUCTION.

And after these things I saw another angel come down from heaven, having great power; and the earth was lightened with his glory. And he cried mightily with a strong voice, saying, Babylon the great is fallen, is fallen, and is become the habitation of devils, and the hold of every foul spirit, and a cage of every unclean and hateful bird, verses 1-2.

1. It comes about just before the return of Christ. There is a brief period between the destruction of the city and the return of Christ. It is within this brief interval that the wailing and mourning by the merchants will take place. The prophet Isaiah, among others, spoke of this destruction. *And Babylon, the glory of kingdoms, the beauty of the*

Chaldees' excellency, shall be as when God overthrew Sodom and Gomorrah. It shall never be inhabited, neither shall it be dwelt in from generation to generation: neither shall the Arabian pitch tent there; neither shall the shepherds make their fold there. But wild beasts of the desert shall lie there; and their houses shall be full of doleful creatures; and owls shall dwell there, and satyrs shall dance there. And the wild beasts of the islands shall cry in their desolate houses, and dragons in their pleasant palaces: and her time is near to come, and her days shall not be prolonged, Isaiah 13:19-22.

2. It will be accomplished by armies from the east. We have already noted this in chapter 16, verse 12. The last but one of the vials of wrath is poured out upon the river Euphrates and, by this judgment, a way (the word means *a road by which to travel*) is made for a number of kingdoms that lie to the east of Babylon to launch an attack upon the city. We note again that the prophecy of Jeremiah provides us with a detailed account of the nations involved. *Set ye up a standard in the land, blow the trumpet among the nations, prepare the nations against her, call together against her the kingdoms of Ararat, Minni, and Ashchenaz; appoint a captain against her; cause the horses to come up as the rough caterpillers. Prepare against her the nations with the kings of the Medes, the captains thereof, and all the rulers thereof, and all the land of his dominion. And the land shall tremble and sorrow: for every purpose of the LORD shall be performed against Babylon, to make the land of Babylon a desolation without an inhabitant. The mighty men of Babylon have forborn to fight, they have remained in their holds: their might hath failed; they became as women: they have burned her dwellingplaces; her bars are broken,* Jeremiah 51:27-30. The Antichrist will not be in his capital. Hence the reference to messengers bringing him the report of the destruction of his city. *One post shall run to meet another, and one messenger to meet another, to shew the king of Babylon that his city is taken at one end,* Jeremiah 51:31. As we have already seen (16:12-16), Daniel 11:44 indicates that he will be in Egypt when the attack upon Babylon takes place.

3. It will be utter and complete. *She shall be utterly burned with fire: for strong is the Lord God who judgeth her,* verse 8. *And a mighty angel took up a stone like a great millstone, and cast it into the sea, saying, Thus with violence shall that great city Babylon be thrown down,* *and shall be found no more at all. And the voice of harpers, and musicians, and of pipers, and trumpeters, shall be heard no more at all in thee; and no craftsman, of whatsoever craft he be, shall be found any more in thee; and the sound of a millstone shall be heard no more at all in thee; and the light of a candle shall shine no more at all in thee; and the voice of the bridegroom and of the bride shall be heard no more at all in thee: for thy merchants were the great men of the earth; for by thy sorceries were all nations deceived,* verses 21-23. She has fallen in the past only to rise again. This time there will be no resurrection for this city of iniquity.

4. It will be sudden and unexpected. *Therefore shall her plagues come in one day,* verse 8. *Alas, alas, that great city Babylon, that mighty city! for in one hour is thy judgment come,* verse 10. *Alas, alas, that great city, wherein were made rich all that had ships in the sea by reason of her costliness! for in one hour is she made desolate,* verse 19. In one day, in one hour, with the swiftness of a millstone sinking into the depths of the sea, so shall Babylon's destruction come. As it was with Sodom and Gomorrah so shall it be with their end-time counterpart.

The end of the old ~ the beginning of the new

In this chapter, one dispensation ends and another begins. The divisions of the chapter are these. Verses 1-4 - Heaven's joy over Babylon's judgment. Verses 5-10 - the marriage supper of the Lamb announced. Verses 11-16 - Christ going forth with the armies of heaven. Verses 17-21 - the defeat of the army of Antichrist.

We have already noted how that the joy of heaven at the fall of Babylon contrasts sharply with the weeping and wailing of Babylon's merchants (18:15). Heaven's joy centres upon the judgment and vengeance of God upon His enemies. *And after these things I heard a great voice of much people in heaven, saying, Alleluia; Salvation, and glory, and honour, and power, unto the Lord our God: for true and righteous are his judgments: for he hath judged the great whore, which did corrupt the earth with her fornication, and hath avenged the blood of his servants at her hand,* 19:1-2. Such a concept of God and the joy of the saints are beyond the comprehension of unregenerate men. For the child of God, the righteous judgments of God and the fulfilling of His law are a source of joy, just as the breaking and defying of God's law was a source of grief and brokenness. *Rivers of waters run down mine eyes, because they keep not thy law,* Psalm 119:136.

The ascending smoke of Babylon's torments mingle with the rising songs of joy of heaven's citizens! *And again they said, Alleluia. And her smoke rose up for ever and ever,* Revelation 19:3. It must be said that the true child of God can rejoice only in the defeat of the spirit of rebellion and lawlessness, the spirit of Antichrist. All the sorrows of the child of God during his earthly pilgrimage may be traced to that spirit. The picture of the sighing, crying believer, in the midst of Jerusalem's apostasy in Ezekiel 9:4, is representative of the saints of all ages whenever they were confronted by man's apostasy. The falling down in worship of the four and twenty elders (representatives of the Church of Christ in both the Old and New Testament ages) following the fall of Babylon (verse 4) and their crying out *Amen; Alleluia* serve to underscore the delight of the redeemed at the casting down of that which opposed everything that was holy and was of God in the earth.

The crushing of Babylon, and then of Antichrist and his armies, is an indication of the character of the Saviour's glorious reign. Rebellion is going to be put down by the sword and the earth will be ruled by Christ's rod of iron.

I. THE GLORIFICATION OF THE SAINTS.

There is an abridged reference made to the saints' glory in verses 5-10. Closely following the judgment of the city of Babylon, the old age ends and *the day of the Lord* begins.

It begins with a marriage feast and rightly so. The Bride of Christ has been brought into glorious union with her Beloved and the heavenly nuptials have begun. The bride has made herself ready. This day has occupied her thoughts for a very long time. On occasions she has despaired of the day ever dawning. *How long, O Lord, holy and true, dost thou not judge and avenge our blood on them that dwell on the earth?* is not just the cry of the martyred souls under the altar. Every generation of believers, indeed every believer has, at times, uttered this lament.

The waiting has been long, but now it is over. The marriage is come. The bride is arrayed in the most costly garments ever donned. *And to her was granted that she should be arrayed in fine linen, clean and white: for the fine linen is the righteousness of saints*, verse 8. These garments cost the blood of God's dear Son, for their beauty and glory is a result of their being washed and made white in the blood of the Lamb. *The king's daughter is all glorious within: her clothing is of wrought gold. She shall be brought unto the king in raiment of needlework: the virgins her companions that follow her shall be brought unto thee*, Psalm 45:13-14.

There will be those who present themselves at this supper who are unfitted. *And when the king came in to see the guests, he saw there a man which had not on a wedding garment: and he saith unto him, Friend, how camest thou in hither not having a wedding garment? And he was speechless. Then said the king to the servants, Bind him hand and foot, and take him away, and cast him into outer darkness; there shall be weeping and gnashing of teeth. For many are called, but few are chosen*, Matthew 22:11-14. The professing church will be purged by the Saviour at the beginning of the Day of the Lord and those who have merely an empty profession and are not really clothed in His righteousness will be cast into outer darkness. This is the same event, though under a different imagery, as that depicted in Matthew 7:21-23. *Not every one that saith unto me, Lord, Lord, shall enter into the kingdom of heaven; but he that doeth the will of my Father which is in heaven. Many will say to me in that day, Lord, Lord, have we not prophesied in thy name? and in thy name have cast out devils? and in thy name done many wonderful works? And then will I profess unto them, I never knew you: depart from me, ye that work iniquity.* It is brought before us again in Matthew 25:31-46 in even greater detail.

And he saith unto me, Write, Blessed are they which are called unto the marriage supper of the Lamb. And he saith unto me, These are the true sayings of God, verse 9. The blessedness of the saints is not detailed. That is dealt with later in chapter 21, and when we come to that portion we will look at it more closely.

Our unfittedness in the flesh to comprehend and cope with heavenly things is manifested in the actions of John before the angel. *And I fell at his feet to worship him. And he said unto me, See thou do it not: I am thy fellowservant, and of thy brethren that have the testimony of Jesus: worship God: for the testimony of Jesus is the spirit of prophecy*, verse 10. This was the first of two occasions on which John attempted to worship the angel. This man of God who at that time was endued with the Holy Spirit, nevertheless, was overwhelmed by what he saw and acted most foolishly. How glorious is that world which lies beyond our sight, but to which all who are washed in the Saviour's blood are going!

II. THE SAVIOUR GOING FORTH TO JUDGE ANTICHRIST, VERSES 11-21.

The Saviour is depicted as being *clothed with a vesture dipped in blood*, verse 13. This is an emblem well suited to show us the purpose of His coming. It is a day of vengeance and crushing judgment for His enemies. He is depicted as being blood-stained before His encounter with Antichrist to emphasise the character of the mission He is on.

1. The defiance of God by Antichrist. *And I saw the beast, and the kings of the earth, and their armies, gathered together to make war against him that sat on the horse, and against his army,* verse 19. How like Pharaoh he is, as he defiantly flies in the face of the Lord Jesus coming in glory, by preparing to make war with Him. *And Pharaoh said, Who is the LORD, that I should obey his voice to let Israel go? I know not the LORD, neither will I let Israel go,* Exodus 5:2. *And the Egyptians pursued, and went in after them to the midst of the sea, even all Pharaoh's horses, his chariots, and his horsemen. And it came to pass, that in the morning watch the LORD looked unto the host of the Egyptians through the pillar of fire and of the cloud, and troubled the host of the Egyptians, and took off their chariot wheels, that they drave them heavily: so that the Egyptians said, Let us flee from the face of Israel; for the LORD fighteth for them against the Egyptians. And the LORD said unto Moses, Stretch out thine hand over the sea, that the waters may come again upon the Egyptians, upon their chariots, and upon their horsemen. And Moses stretched forth his hand over the sea, and the sea returned to his strength when the morning appeared; and the Egyptians fled against it; and the LORD overthrew the Egyptians in the midst of the sea,* Exodus 14:23-27.

The defiance of the Antichrist is greater than that of Pharaoh since he will defy the Lord in His visible glory, while Pharaoh defied the Lord veiled in the symbol of that glory, the pillar of cloud. The Antichrist will indeed be man at his most defiant of God.

Like the king of Egypt and his army of long ago, the armies of Antichrist end up as food for creatures. Pharaoh became food for the fish of the sea while the Antichrist's armies will feed the fowls of the air. *And I saw an angel standing in the sun; and he cried with a loud voice, saying to all the fowls that fly in the midst of heaven, Come and gather yourselves together unto the supper of the great God; that ye may eat the flesh of kings, and the flesh of captains, and the flesh of mighty men, and the flesh of horses, and of them that sit on them, and the flesh of all men, both free and bond, both small and great,* verses 17-18. *And all the fowls were filled with their flesh,* verse 21.

Remember also the fate of boasting Goliath! *And the Philistine said to David, Come to me, and I will give thy flesh unto the fowls of the air, and to the beasts of the field. Then said David to the Philistine, Thou comest to me with a sword, and with a spear, and with a shield: but I come to thee in the name of the LORD of hosts, the God of the armies of Israel, whom thou hast defied. This day will the LORD deliver thee into mine hand; and I will smite thee, and take thine head from thee; and I will give the carcases of the host of the Philistines this day unto the fowls of the air, and to the wild beasts of the earth; that all the earth may know that there is a God in Israel. And all this assembly shall know that the LORD saveth not with sword and spear: for the battle is the LORD'S, and he will give you into our hands,* 1 Samuel 17:44-47.

2. The damnation of Antichrist. While his armies were eaten by the fowls, that was not the fate of the false prophet and the Antichrist. *And the beast was taken, and with him the false prophet that wrought miracles before him, with which he deceived them that had received the mark of the beast, and them that worshipped his image. These both were cast alive into a lake of fire burning with brimstone,* verse 20. They are the first to be condemned to the lake of fire. This fate will await the rest of the ungodly until the judgment of the great white throne, which follows the resurrection of the unjust at the end of the thousand-year reign of Christ. *But the rest of the dead lived not again until the thousand years were finished,* 20:5. They will then be judged and cast into the lake of fire.

3. The defiant spirit of the Antichrist displayed by sinners. It happens every time a sinner rejects the gospel call to repentance and obedience. The sinner who hears the gospel call is guilty of the same spirit of defiance as will be seen in the Antichrist on this dread day before us. The sinner hears of the sin and shame of which Israel was guilty in rejecting and crucifying the Lord Jesus Christ as he listens to the gospel message, but still allies himself with that sin and strikes against the Son of God. This makes his sin greater than Israel's to the same degree as will the sin of Antichrist exceed that of Pharaoh.

III. CHRIST FOLLOWED BY THE ARMIES OF HEAVEN.

And I saw heaven opened, and behold a white horse; and he that sat upon him was called Faithful and True, and in righteousness he doth judge and make war, verse 11. The horse is often used as a symbol of earthly power. It is entirely suitable, therefore, that the Saviour is seen riding a horse as He comes forth to subdue the earth.

1. Note the Saviour's titles.

Faithful and True. No name is more fitting for the Saviour than this, and no day is more fitted for Him to bear it than the day of His appearing. The mocker may have sneered: *Where is the promise of his coming?* But we are of like faith to Mary, of whom it is said: *Blessed is she that believed: for there shall be a performance of those things which were told her from the Lord*, Luke 1:45. The day of the Lord's return will prove Him faithful to His promise. *In my Father's house are many mansions: if it were not so, I would have told you. I go to prepare a place for you. And if I go and prepare a place for you, I will come again, and receive you unto myself; that where I am, there ye may be also*, John 14:2-3.

A name written, that no man knew, but he himself. When Manoah asked after the name of the Angel of the Lord he was told, *Why askest thou thus after my name, seeing it is secret?* Judges 13:18. There is an unknowable name which belongs to God alone. This title reminds us that the One for Whom we wait expectantly is the eternal God.

The Word of God. He is the Living Word of God. *God, who at sundry times and in divers manners spake in time past unto the fathers by the prophets, hath in these last days spoken unto us by his Son, whom he hath appointed heir of all things, by whom also he made the worlds*, Hebrews 1:1-2.

KING OF KINGS, AND LORD OF LORDS. What little regard is paid to that title today! His name is a byword and a curse upon the lips of men and women and children. But all the world will one day see the glory of the One before Whom they must stand. Happy on that day will be those who can look back upon a day when they bowed before Him and in true repentance said:

King of my life I crown Thee now,
Thine shall the glory be.

2. Note the Saviour's crowns. *On his head were many crowns,* verse 12. Antichrist may wear his ten crowns for a short season, but Christ shall wear His many crowns for ever, as He descends the skies to claim dominion over His earth and its nations.

3. Note the Saviour's weapons. *And out of his mouth goeth a sharp sword, that with it he should smite the nations: and he shall rule them with a rod of iron: and he treadeth the winepress of the fierceness and wrath of Almighty God,* verse 15. With the sword He shall conquer and with the rod He shall rule. The nations shall be brought under His rule during the early years of the millennial reign. It was of this period the psalmist spoke. *Say among the heathen that the LORD reigneth: the world also shall be established that it shall not be moved: he shall judge the people righteously. Let the heavens rejoice, and let the earth be glad; let the sea roar, and the fulness thereof. Let the field be joyful, and all that is therein: then shall all the trees of the wood rejoice before the LORD: for he cometh, for he cometh to judge the earth: he shall judge the world with righteousness, and the people with his truth,* Psalm 96:10-13.

The Old Testament is filled with references to this period of the earth's history. It is entirely understandable that the Old Testament should be the repository of views on the millennium. It will be a day of exaltation for Israel. *Blessed be the Lord God of Israel; for he hath visited and redeemed his people, and hath raised up an horn of salvation for us in the house of his servant David; as he spake by the mouth of his holy prophets, which have been since the world began: that we should be saved from our enemies, and from the hand of all that hate us; to perform the mercy promised to our fathers, and to remember his holy covenant; the oath which he sware to our father Abraham, that he would grant unto us, that we being delivered out of the hand of our enemies might serve him without fear, in holiness and righteousness before him, all the days of our life,* Luke 1:68-75.

What glories God has promised to place upon Israel during this period! *For Zion's sake will I not hold my peace, and for Jerusalem's sake I will not rest, until the righteousness thereof go forth as brightness, and the salvation thereof as a lamp that burneth. And the Gentiles shall see thy righteousness, and all kings thy glory: and thou shalt be called by a new name, which the mouth of the LORD shall name. Thou shalt also be a crown of glory in the hand of the LORD, and a royal diadem in the hand of thy God. Thou shalt no more be termed Forsaken; neither shall thy land any more be termed Desolate: but thou shalt be called Hephzibah, and thy land Beulah: for the LORD delighteth in thee, and thy land shall be married. For as a young man marrieth a virgin, so shall thy sons marry thee: and as the bridegroom rejoiceth over the bride, so shall thy God rejoice over thee. I have set watchmen upon thy walls, O Jerusalem, which shall never hold their peace day nor night: ye that make mention of the LORD, keep not silence, and give him no rest, till he establish, and till he make Jerusalem a praise in the earth,* Isaiah 62:1-7.

In the book of the Revelation the millennial reign is given but a brief mention as we are carried onward toward that for which Peter looked. *Nevertheless we, according to his promise, look for new heavens and a new earth, wherein dwelleth righteousness*, 2 Peter 3:13. That is the final objective of our God and Saviour.

Resurrection, renovation and retribution
CHAPTER 20

I n our studies, we have followed the chapter divisions in our Bible. We should, of course, know that these divisions were not part of the inspired text but were devised by one, Robert Stephens, around 1551, for the convenience of readers. While the chapter and verse divisions are not perfect, it has served Bible readers well throughout the centuries since it was introduced. But there are occasions when the divisions can be misleading. Often when we start a new chapter we unconsciously feel that we are entering upon a new subject. That is not always the case. Sometimes the chapter division is unnatural and cuts off a section from where it rightly belongs. An improvement to the divisions here at the end of the book of the Revelation, that we have at present in our Bibles, was suggested by Benjamin Wills Newton in his book: *Thoughts on the Apocalypse*. We believe that there is merit in his suggestion. We believe it makes it easier to see the progression from one subject to another and so avoid the confusing of one visionary subject with another. He suggested the following chapter divisions and we leave them with you to see how they help your understanding of the final chapters of this wonderful book.

The present 19:1-10 would become the new chapter 19.

The present 19:11-21:8. would become the new chapter 20.

The present 21:9-22:5 would become the new chapter 21.

The present 22:6-to the end would become the new chapter 22.

The present chapter 20 is divided into four sections.

I.   THE FALL OF SATAN.

*And I saw an angel come down from heaven, having the key of the
bottomless pit and a great chain in his hand. And he laid hold on the
dragon, that old serpent, which is the Devil, and Satan, and bound him
a thousand years, and cast him into the bottomless pit, and shut him up,
and set a seal upon him, that he should deceive the nations no more, till
the thousand years should be fulfilled: and after that he must be loosed
a little season*, verses 1-3.

The earth can have no rest until the devil is dealt with. It was a
great deliverance to be rid of the evil influence of the Antichrist and the
False Prophet, but that is like cutting nettles off at the root. They will
surely grow again. They must be cut down root and all. The devil is
substantially the root of this world's rebellion. That has been so since
the hour that he provoked Eve to doubt the mercy and goodness of God.
Earth's history has been basically a catalogue of the devil's scheming
triumphs. If it is to know any peace that root must be dealt with. That is
what the Lord Jesus plans to do during the millennial reign.

1. Satan is subject to the Lord.   Never let this be forgotten. At
the hour of the devil's greatest display of rebellious power Christ takes
him and subdues him for a thousand years.

2. Satan's titles display his evil character.   As the DRAGON he
displayed his fierceness; as the OLD SERPENT he displayed his crafty
subtlety; as the DEVIL he acted as the accuser of the people of God; as
SATAN he was ever the adversary.

3. During the thousand-year reign his deceptions will cease.   In
all his actions, the devil sought to deceive. Often his fierce threats were
just that - threats only. He could not do all he threatened to do. Thus he
intimidated and deceived many a poor sinner. He ever claimed for himself
greater powers than he actually enjoyed and beguiled all who listened.
But all his deceiving will cease during the time that he is bound.

II.   THE FIRST RESURRECTION.

*And I saw thrones, and they sat upon them, and judgment was given
unto them: and I saw the souls of them that were beheaded for the*

witness of Jesus, and for the word of God, and which had not worshipped the beast, neither his image, neither had received his mark upon their foreheads, or in their hands; and they lived and reigned with Christ a thousand years. But the rest of the dead lived not again until the thousand years were finished. This is the first resurrection. Blessed and holy is he that hath part in the first resurrection: on such the second death hath no power, but they shall be priests of God and of Christ, and shall reign with him a thousand years, verses 4-6.

1. There are two resurrections. That is made most plain here in these verses. There were some dead who lived not again until the thousand years were finished. Just who the participants in this first resurrection are may be seen from these verses. *I saw the souls of them that were beheaded for the witness of Jesus, and for the word of God, and which had not worshipped the beast, neither his image, neither had received his mark upon their foreheads, or in their hands; and they lived and reigned with Christ a thousand years.* This resurrection is a literal bodily resurrection rather than a spiritual resurrection, as some would claim, and is yet future since it involves those who served Christ during the period of the Antichrist's great power, the last three and a half years of this age.

2. This is a blessed resurrection. *Blessed and holy is he that hath part in the first resurrection.* Not for them the lake of fire, verse 14, but rather the throne of Christ.

3. It is a time of sharing in Christ's glory and power. *They shall be priests of God and of Christ, and shall reign with him a thousand years*, verse 6. The earth will be under a new holy regime. This is the time of which Paul spoke when he said: *Do ye not know that the saints shall judge the world? Know ye not that we shall judge angels?* 1 Corinthians 6:2-3.

It is the privilege of every child of God to know kingly power and priestly fellowship during this earthly pilgrimage. By the grace of God we have been delivered from the dominion of sin and raised to life in Christ. *That like as Christ was raised up from the dead by the glory of the Father, even so we also should walk in newness of life*, Romans 6:4. It is an overcoming life, a life of victory. *For sin shall not have dominion over you*, Romans 6:14. We have been made nigh to God, reconciled by the blood of Christ. *But now in Christ Jesus ye who sometimes were far off are made nigh by the blood of Christ*, Ephesians 2:13. But during our earthly pilgrimage it was a *spiritual* kingship that we enjoyed. Often our outward circumstances were those of beggars and outcasts. Even great and godly men such as the apostles, who enjoyed such spiritual blessings and power, nevertheless were heard to say: *We are made as the filth of the world, and are the offscouring of all things unto this day*, 1 Corinthians 4:13.

During Christ's reign this will change. The earth, as the unbelieving brothers of Joseph, will be brought to the feet of the true believer in Christ. It was to this time that the saints of old looked and spoke of it prophetically. *O clap your hands, all ye people; shout unto God with the voice of triumph. For the LORD most high is terrible; he is a great King over all the earth. He shall subdue the people under us, and the nations under our feet. He shall choose our inheritance for us, the excellency of Jacob whom he loved. Selah. God is gone up with a shout, the LORD with the sound of a trumpet. Sing praises to God, sing praises: sing praises unto our King, sing praises. For God is the King of all the earth: sing ye praises with understanding. God reigneth over the heathen: God sitteth upon the throne of his holiness. The princes of the people are gathered together, even the people of the God of Abraham: for the shields of the earth belong unto God: he is greatly exalted*, Psalm 47:1-9.

The word that Isaiah the son of Amoz saw concerning Judah and Jerusalem. And it shall come to pass in the last days, that the mountain of the LORD'S house shall be established in the top of the mountains, and shall be exalted above the hills; and all nations shall flow unto it. And many people shall go and say, Come ye, and let us go up to the mountain of the LORD, to the house of the God of Jacob; and he will teach us of his ways, and we will walk in his paths: for out of Zion shall go forth the law, and the word of the LORD from Jerusalem. And he shall judge among the nations, and shall rebuke many people: and they shall beat their swords into plowshares, and their spears into pruninghooks: nation shall not lift up sword against nation, neither shall they learn war any more. O house of Jacob, come ye, and let us walk in the light of the LORD, Isaiah 2:1-5.

III. THE FINAL CONFLICT.

And when the thousand years are expired, Satan shall be loosed out of his prison, and shall go out to deceive the nations which are in the four quarters of the earth, Gog and Magog, to gather them together to battle: the number of whom is as the sand of the sea. And they went up on the breadth of the earth, and compassed the camp of the saints about, and the beloved city: and fire came down from God out of heaven, and devoured them. And the devil that deceived them was cast into the lake of fire and brimstone, where the beast and the false prophet are, and shall be tormented day and night for ever and ever, verses 7-10.

1. Imprisonment has not changed the devil. He is still a deceiver and still holds to the evil hope of defeating God.

2. Note the source of war and strife amongst men. Contrary to what many say, the religion of Christ is not the cause of war but the rebellious nature of man, stirred and aroused by the devil. He is the chief instigator of war. The earth has enjoyed peace for one thousand years but, within a brief period of Satan's release, there are those deceived and led into battle against the Lord. The target of the devil is the beloved city, the millennial Jerusalem, the camp of the saints. Here again, as ever before in earth's ages, the devil rages against the people of Christ. They are hated of him for the Saviour's sake. As it was during the period of their earthly witness, so it is again. *The world hath hated them, because they are not of the world, even as I am not of the world,* John 17:14.

During Christ's thousand-year reign, a vast ingathering of souls will take place. It is the time referred to by the Old Testament prophets, Isaiah and Zechariah in particular.

We can trace the sequence of events in the writings of these two prophets. In the writings of Zechariah, in chapter 14, we read of **the coming of Christ to deliver Jerusalem** from the armies of Antichrist which have gathered to destroy the holy city forever. What familiar words are found in that chapter! *Then shall the LORD go forth, and fight against those nations, as when he fought in the day of battle. And his feet shall stand in that day upon the mount of Olives, which is before Jerusalem on the east, and the mount of Olives shall cleave in the midst* *thereof toward the east and toward the west, and there shall be a very great valley; and half of the mountain shall remove toward the north, and half of it toward the south. . . . . and the LORD my God shall come, and all the saints with thee*, verses 3-5.

The reign of Christ is established. *And the LORD shall be king over all the earth: in that day shall there be one LORD, and his name one*, verse 9. Isaiah speaks of this time. *He shall smite the earth with the rod of his mouth, and with the breath of his lips shall he slay the wicked. And righteousness shall be the girdle of his loins, and faithfulness the girdle of his reins. The wolf also shall dwell with the lamb, and the leopard shall lie down with the kid; and the calf and the young lion and the fatling together; and a little child shall lead them. And the cow and the bear shall feed; their young ones shall lie down together: and the lion shall eat straw like the ox. And the sucking child shall play on the hole of the asp, and the weaned child shall put his hand on the cockatrice' den. They shall not hurt nor destroy in all my holy mountain: for the earth shall be full of the knowledge of the LORD, as the waters cover the sea*, Isaiah 11:4-9.

Jerusalem shall become the centre of the worship of Jehovah. *And it shall come to pass, that every one that is left of all the nations which came against Jerusalem shall even go up from year to year to worship the King, the LORD of hosts, and to keep the feast of tabernacles. And it shall be, that whoso will not come up of all the families of the earth unto Jerusalem to worship the King, the LORD of hosts, even upon them shall be no rain. And if the family of Egypt go not up, and come not, that have no rain; there shall be the plague, wherewith the LORD will smite the heathen that come not up to keep the feast of tabernacles. This shall be the punishment of Egypt, and the punishment of all nations that come not up to keep the feast of tabernacles. In that day shall there be upon the bells of the horses, HOLINESS UNTO THE LORD; and the pots in the LORD'S house shall be like the bowls before the altar. Yea, every pot in Jerusalem and in Judah shall be holiness unto the LORD of hosts: and all they that sacrifice shall come and take of them, and seethe therein: and in that day there shall be no more the Canaanite in the house of the LORD of hosts*, Zechariah 14:16-21.

It is clear from these latter verses, that there are remnants left of the nations that gave allegiance to Antichrist and that of these remnants there will be those who will come with the other nations flocking to Jerusalem to worship the Lord. It is also clear that there will be those who will not submit to Christ and, in consequence, He will smite them with plagues and drought (verses 17-19).

Though the earth has been under the direct rule of Christ and many nations have been brought to faith in the Saviour during His reign, not all men will be saved. The easing of the Saviour's restraint upon the devil soon shows that this is so. This may seem strange to some. But is it really? What of Capernaum of which it was said: *And thou, Capernaum, which art exalted unto heaven, shalt be brought down to hell: for if the mighty works, which have been done in thee, had been done in Sodom, it would have remained until this day*, Matthew 11:23. Did not Israel in the days of the Saviour's ministry enjoy unprecedented privileges under His ministry? Did not John write: *And there are also many other things which Jesus did, the which, if they should be written every one, I suppose that even the world itself could not contain the books that should be written. Amen*, John 21:25. And yet how few repented! Rather, they rebelled and became guilty of the greatest crime of all. *Him, being delivered by the determinate counsel and foreknowledge of God, ye have taken, and by wicked hands have crucified and slain*, Acts 2:23. This is a greater crime than that attempted by the unregenerate at the end of the millennial reign of Christ.

It is noteworthy, that the ancient kingdom of Magog is specifically mentioned. This kingdom is mentioned in Ezekiel 38 and 39. I believe that these chapters in Ezekiel refer to an attack upon Israel by Gog and Magog in the early part of the millennial kingdom. Their attack is described as being against *the land that is brought back from the sword, and is gathered out of many people, against the mountains of Israel, which have been always waste: but it is brought forth out of the nations, and they shall dwell safely all of them*, Ezekiel 38:8. Such rest, such bringing *back from the sword*, will be experienced by Israel only after the Saviour's return. Again, the judgment that falls upon Gog and Magog is not that described in our study portion for the latter is final and eternal. They are devoured, (eaten up) by the fire of God. The Lord says that, in response to the attack upon Israel recorded in Ezekiel 39:2, *I will turn thee back, and leave but the sixth part of thee*. Furthermore, the attack in Revelation 20:9 is not just upon the land of Israel or a mere targeting of the nation of Israel. Rather, it is an attack upon the camp of the saints, the beloved city. Finally, though Gog and Magog are mentioned, they seem to be allied with a vast multitude from the four quarters of the earth.

The mention of Gog and Magog reminds us that the ancient seats of opposition to Christ remain, though suppressed, during the reign of Christ. They ignite again in rebellion when the opportunity arises. It is the final rising of men against Christ and marks the end of the old earth.

3. The devil's rebellion will be short-lived. *And the devil that deceived them was cast into the lake of fire and brimstone, where the beast and the false prophet are, and shall be tormented day and night for ever and ever*, verse 10. Whereas, in the past, the devil was permitted of God to continue in rebellion and often trample the saints under his feet, that day is over forever. The place that was prepared for the devil and his angels now welcomes its chief occupant. It has to be noted by those who deny the eternal nature of the punishment awaiting sinners, those who claim that the ungodly will be annihilated, that after one thousand years the Beast and the False Prophet are still in the lake of fire. They have not been consumed. They have not ceased to be. So begins the endless torment of the tormenter of men and the chief rebel against God.

IV. THE FATE OF SINNERS.

And I saw a great white throne, and him that sat on it, from whose face the earth and the heaven fled away; and there was found no place for them. And I saw the dead, small and great, stand before God; and the books were opened: and another book was opened, which is the book of life: and the dead were judged out of those things which were written in the books, according to their works. And the sea gave up the dead which were in it; and death and hell delivered up the dead which were in them: and they were judged every man according to their works. And death and hell were cast into the lake of fire. This is the second death. And whosoever was not found written in the book of life was cast into the lake of fire, verses 11-15. It is *the day of wrath and revelation of the righteous judgment of God*, Romans 2:5.

1. The great white throne. The throne is great because of the greatness of the One Who is seated upon it; because of the greatness of the decisions taken on it; because of the multitudes that will assemble before it. It is white because of the purity and righteousness of its judgments.

2. The great Judge. He is the Son of God to Whom the Father *hath committed all judgment* (John 5:22), and before Whom *the earth and the heavens fled away; and there was found no place for them.*

This the day of which Peter speaks. *But the heavens and the earth, which are now, by the same word are kept in store, reserved unto fire against the day of judgment and perdition of ungodly men,* 2 Peter 3:7. Peter tells us more. *But the day of the Lord will come as a thief in the night; in the which the heavens shall pass away with a great noise, and the elements shall melt with fervent heat, the earth also and the works that are therein shall be burned up. Seeing then that all these things shall be dissolved, what manner of persons ought ye to be in all holy conversation and godliness, looking for and hasting unto the coming of the day of God, wherein the heavens being on fire shall be dissolved, and the elements shall melt with fervent heat? Nevertheless we, according to his promise, look for new heavens and a new earth, wherein dwelleth righteousness. Wherefore, beloved, seeing that ye look for such things, be diligent that ye may be found of him in peace, without spot, and blameless,* 2 Peter 3:10-14. The great day of judgment marks the end of the old earth and the beginning of the new.

3. The dreadful judgments. It will be according to their works. A record of the works of the ungodly is being kept. While the Christian can say, *Thou hast cast all my sins behind thy back,* Isaiah 38:17, the sins of the ungodly are duly recorded and the books will be opened on that day to the utter condemnation of the wicked. The evidence will be there. The combined witness of the three persons of the Godhead will corroborate all that is recorded. The fate of the sinner is sealed.

4. The dreadful sentence. They who shared in Satan's rebellion will share in his eternal damnation. *And whosoever was not found written in the book of life was cast into the lake of fire,* verse 15. O my friend, is your name written in the book of life? Have you ever even considered this matter? Proof of your name being written in the Lamb's book of life will be written in your life. There is a duplicate, as it were, of that record written down in your daily actions. Those who have their names in the Lamb's book of life manifest the life of the Lamb in their daily activities. *Therefore if any man be in Christ, he is a new creature: old things are passed away; behold, all things are become new,* 2 Corinthians 5:17. Here is the evidence, the sure grounds of assurance, that your soul is saved and that the portion of the wicked will not be yours.

Many of those sentenced on this dread day will have heard the gospel. They will have heard the best of preachers proclaim it. Those who stood amidst the congregations of Moses, Elijah, Isaiah and Jeremiah, of Daniel, John the Baptist, the apostles and the reformers, even of the Lord Jesus Himself shall stand condemned on that day. They will be damned because they did not believe the gospel and trust in Christ for salvation. Will there be those there who have read these words in this book? Most certainly so, if you have not yet repented and believed.

John said that he saw a great white throne. We ought to live in the view of that throne. How resistant is the sinner to that view! He does not wish his mind to be elevated from the earth to consider such dreadful and troubling matters. It ought not to be so with the child of God. A right view, a constant view of this great throne will have a profound effect upon our living, upon our witnessing to our families and friends. It was to this throne Paul alluded when he set a solemn charge before Timothy shortly before the apostle suffered a martyr's death. *I charge thee therefore before God, and the Lord Jesus Christ, who shall judge the quick and the dead at his appearing and his kingdom; preach the word; be instant in season, out of season; reprove, rebuke, exhort with all longsuffering and doctrine,* 2 Timothy 4:1-2.

May it be our daily desire and determination to see all we meet warned to flee from wrath to come!

A new heavens and a new earth and the new Jerusalem
CHAPTER 21: 1-8

The setting up of the great white throne marked the termination of the old creation. As already noted, the reference to the earth and the heaven fleeing away is to be seen as that event to which Peter referred in his second epistle. *But the day of the Lord will come as a thief in the night; in the which the heavens shall pass away with a great noise, and the elements shall melt with fervent heat, the earth also and the works that are therein shall be burned up,* 2 Peter 3:10. Consequently, the opening verses of chapter 21 describe for us the new creation.

Nothing can inject hope and provide comfort for despondent believers like the consideration of the eternal abode of the glorified saints. What a distressing sight this world is today for the child of God! *And there shall be signs in the sun, and in the moon, and in the stars; and upon the earth distress of nations, with perplexity; the sea and the waves roaring; men's hearts failing them for fear, and for looking after those things which are coming on the earth: for the powers of heaven shall be shaken. And then shall they see the Son of man coming in a cloud with power and great glory. And when these things begin to come to pass, then look up, and lift up your heads; for your redemption draweth nigh,* Luke 21:25-28. Lies are replacing truth, especially with regard to spiritual matters. In the worship of the nations, Antichrist is replacing Christ as the one worshipped. The whole of creation is groaning ever more loudly.

*The whole creation groaneth and travaileth in pain together until now.
And not only they, but ourselves also, which have the firstfruits of the
Spirit, even we ourselves groan within ourselves, waiting for the adop-
tion, to wit, the redemption of our body,* Romans 8:22-23.

In the midst of such growing signs of dissolution, let us look up and
consider what God has planned and that which He will most assuredly
bring about for His people. Remember, this vision is also part of *the
things which must shortly come to pass,* chapter 1:1.

I.   THE REGENERATION OF THE EARTH AND
THE HEAVENS.

*And I saw a new heaven and a new earth: for the first heaven and
the first earth were passed away; and there was no more sea,* verse 1.
This is that promised restitution of which all the prophets spoke. *Whom
the heaven must receive until the times of restitution of all things, which
God hath spoken by the mouth of all his holy prophets since the world
began,* Acts 3:21.

The word *new* means *fresh, unused.* The flood in Noah's day
provided a partial renovation of the earth. There were changes brought
in at that time which altered the whole climatic and environmental state
of the earth. But it did not destroy the fabric of creation. So it shall be
again. A purging by fire is naturally more thorough than that by water,
but the fabric of creation shall not cease to be. The words *passed away*
may be understood more clearly when we remember that they are the
same words used to describe what took place at the regeneration of our
souls. *Therefore if any man be in Christ, he is a new creature: old things
are passed away; behold, all things are become new,* 2 Corinthians 5:17.
While we underwent a great change, we remained the same beings.

1. That which characterises this earth will pass away. *And God
shall wipe away all tears from their eyes; and there shall be no more
death, neither sorrow, nor crying, neither shall there be any more pain:
for the former things are passed away,* verse 4. Pain, sorrow, crying,
tears, death - this is the lot of all men on this earth. There is not a
dwelling, be it palace or hovel, that is immune from these experiences.
Neither money nor status can shield us from their touch. But there is
none of these things in God's new earth. *And he that sat upon the throne*

said, Behold, I make all things new. And he said unto me, Write: for
these words are true and faithful, verse 5.

2. The wiping away of these things will be by the hand of God.
Sin is the root cause of all misery and it is only as forgiveness of sins is
found through the blood of Christ that there can be a removal of the
consequences of sin. *And, behold, they brought to him a man sick of the*
palsy, lying on a bed: and Jesus seeing their faith said unto the sick of
the palsy; Son, be of good cheer; thy sins be forgiven thee, Matthew 9:2.
Good cheer can be the lot only of those whose sins are forgiven.

3. There will be no sea on the new earth. The sea is ever associated with separation and sorrow. No part of the world has felt more of
the pain of parting, as the emigrant set sail across the ocean, than has
Ulster. Many, many of her sons and daughters have left her shores for
foreign lands, leaving behind grieving loved ones.

The sea is linked in Holy Scripture with the wickedness of man.
But the wicked are like the troubled sea, when it cannot rest, whose
waters cast up mire and dirt, Isaiah 57:20. The restlessness of its surface
is so like the restless stirrings of sinful men, while its casting up, through
its storms, of all manner of dirt symbolises the corruptions that men's
sinful desires have produced in society. All that is finished and done
away with in God's new earth. God is now in the midst and the earth
has been cleansed and made ready for His abiding amongst His redeemed
ones.

II. THE NEW JERUSALEM.

And I John saw the holy city, new Jerusalem, coming down from
God out of heaven, prepared as a bride adorned for her husband. And I
heard a great voice out of heaven saying, Behold, the tabernacle of God
is with men, and he will dwell with them, and they shall be his people,
and God himself shall be with them, and be their God, verses 2-3.

1. It is the place long desired. In using his name in the fashion
that he did, John surely implied that he was the subject of a great privilege.
Indeed he was. To have seen the things that he did, made him a very
privileged person indeed. But John seems to show a special measure of
excitement on seeing the new Jerusalem. Little wonder, for is this not
what God's people have been taught by the Holy Spirit to look for since

the beginning of time? It was said of Abraham, the father of the faithful, that *he looked for a city which hath foundations, whose builder and maker is God*, Hebrews 11:10. For that city all of God's people have looked. *But now they desire a better country, that is, an heavenly: wherefore God is not ashamed to be called their God: for he hath prepared for them a city. For here have we no continuing city, but we seek one to come*, Hebrews 11:16, 13:14.

2. The city descends out of heaven. It is a creation of God. The old city of Jerusalem was cursed by man's sin. *The great city, which spiritually is called Sodom and Egypt, where also our Lord was crucified*, 11:8. It was the city where Christ was rejected. The new Jerusalem will be the place where God shall dwell, verse 3.

The Saviour referred to the new Jerusalem when He said: *In my Father's house are many mansions: if it were not so, I would have told you. I go to prepare a place for you. And if I go and prepare a place for you, I will come again, and receive you unto myself; that where I am, there ye may be also*, John 14:1-3. The new Jerusalem is His Father's house of many mansions. It is the place that the Saviour has prepared for His people. The new Jerusalem, like all that the Lord has prepared for His redeemed people, is of such beauty and splendour that it is beyond the imagination of unregenerate men. *But as it is written, Eye hath not seen, nor ear heard, neither have entered into the heart of man, the things which God hath prepared for them that love him. But God hath revealed them unto us by his Spirit*, 1 Corinthians 2:9-10.

3. Its description. *Behold, the tabernacle of God is with men, and he will dwell with them, and they shall be his people, and God himself shall be with them, and be their God*, verse 3. All pining after God will cease. We shall know utter satisfaction as we abide in His presence. Was it not for this that the psalmist longed? *As the hart panteth after the water brooks, so panteth my soul after thee, O God. My soul thirsteth for God, for the living God: when shall I come and appear before God?* Psalm 42:1-2. That thirst shall be forever quenched in the new Jerusalem.

Prepared as a bride adorned for her husband, verse 2. What care, what love, what labour! What radiance of beauty will adorn the new Jerusalem and all for His people!

4. Those who will never gain entrance. As if to emphasise the loss the Christ-rejecter will suffer, we have the blessings of salvation reiterated. *And he said unto me, It is done. I am Alpha and Omega, the beginning and the end. I will give unto him that is athirst of the fountain of the water of life freely. He that overcometh shall inherit all things; and I will be his God, and he shall be my son,* verses 6-7. The water of life is freely offered to those who are athirst. The one, who by the grace of God comes to Christ and believes in Him, and so overcomes all that would keep him from salvation, shall inherit all things and enter into an intimate relationship with God, even that of Father and son.

And then in contrast we have the lot of the wicked set forth. Note how it begins with the word BUT. *But the fearful, and unbelieving, and the abominable, and murderers, and whoremongers, and sorcerers, and idolaters, and all liars, shall have their part in the lake which burneth with fire and brimstone: which is the second death,* verse 8. Heading the list are the fearful. Fearful of men, they rejected Christ. *The fear of man bringeth a snare: but whoso putteth his trust in the LORD shall be safe,* Proverbs 29:25. Now they are found amongst the most fearsome of beings and cast out of God's presence forever to dwell with the everlasting burnings in the lake of fire.

My dear unsaved reader, whose salvation has been long prayed for, will you not cease from your folly and hasten away to Christ lest this be your eternal fate? Against the backcloth of this terrible declaration, consider your latter end and call upon the Lord today for salvation.

The new Jerusalem

A s we have already observed, chronological order is not observed from vision to vision. Here in this vision we go back to the time of the old earth and the millennial reign of Christ, when the new Jerusalem first descended out of heaven, to that time referred to in the early verses of chapter 20. In the section that we are studying, there are clear references to the old order of nations on the earth. *And the nations of them which are saved shall walk in the light of it: and the kings of the earth do bring their glory and honour into it*, verse 24. Furthermore, verse 27 clearly implies that sin still has its presence upon the earth. *And there shall in no wise enter into it any thing that defileth, neither whatsoever worketh abomination, or maketh a lie: but they which are written in the Lamb's book of life*. And again, in 22:2 . . . *and the leaves of the tree were for the healing of the nations*. In the new heaven and the new earth such healing would not be required. This then is a view of the new Jerusalem in its relationship to the millennial earth.

The view John is given of the new Jerusalem is, at first, a distant one, an external one. It is as if he viewed it from below, looking up towards it. It is not until the new earth has been formed that the new Jerusalem will descend to the earth and be permanently sited. In the view given us in this section, the new Jerusalem descends *toward* the earth but does not descend *to* the earth. The tabernacle of God is not yet with men as is stated in verse 3. The new Jerusalem during the millennial period will be as the holy place in the tabernacle and temple of old. It stood between the outer court and the holy of holies where God's presence was. Worshipping God on the earth, in the outer court as it were, will be converted Israel and those converted amongst the nations to which Israel will then be sent. Permitted to enter into the holy place will be the glorified saints, ministering to God Who dwells in heaven, the holy of holies, and also to the needs of the nations of the earth from *the tree of life, which bare twelve manner of fruits, and yielded her fruit every month: and the leaves of the tree were for the healing of the nations*, 22:2.

There is a reference to such a responsibility and authority being undertaken by the glorified saints in the parable of the pounds. *And he said unto him, Well, thou good servant: because thou hast been faithful in a very little, have thou authority over ten cities*, Luke 19:17. The reward for Christian faithfulness will be the exercising of authority over ten cities on the millennial earth. It is interesting to recall that in the dividing of the inheritance of Canaan amongst the tribes, cities were given to the Levites from the territories allotted to the other tribes, the tribe of Levi, the priestly tribe, having no allocation of land as such. In one instance, the families of Kohath were given ten cities. *All the cities were ten with their suburbs for the families of the children of Kohath that remained*, Joshua 21:26. There is here, in type, a picture of the labours of the glorified saints during the millennium.

Consider then the portion before us.

And there came unto me one of the seven angels which had the seven vials full of the seven last plagues, and talked with me, saying, Come hither, I will shew thee the bride, the Lamb's wife, verse 9. Let me underline again that the messenger of damnation and judgment for the sinner is also the messenger of grace and mercy for the child of God. *To the one we are the savour of death unto death; and to the other the savour of life unto life*, 2 Corinthians 2:16. How do you stand in relation to the Word of God? Does it save you or condemn you? Do you believe and receive it, or refuse and reject it?

As in chapter 17:1, there is here an invitation to see a city. The first was in order to warn against the wickedness of the city that it might, at all costs, be avoided. The second was to gladden and encourage the pilgrims' hearts as they travelled toward it. The evil city was viewed from a position in the wilderness, for it was of the wilderness of this world. The new Jerusalem was viewed from a mountain top, which denotes communion with God. The city that your eyes are focused upon depends upon where you dwell. The dweller in sin will seek after the city of sin, while the dweller on the mountain top will have eyes and desires only for the new Jerusalem.

I.   THE DESCENT OF THE CITY.

And he carried me away in the spirit to a great and high mountain, and shewed me that great city, the holy Jerusalem, descending out of heaven from God, verse 10. It is a city built in heaven by God.

Cities contain all that man can assemble for his delight according to all his depravities. The cities of this earth at present are notorious for their wickedness. They have rightly been known for some decades as the urban jungles. The first city was built by the first murderer. *And Cain knew his wife; and she conceived, and bare Enoch: and he builded a city, and called the name of the city, after the name of his son, Enoch,* Genesis 4:17. The Hebrew word translated *city* is closely allied to that which means *terror or anguish.* It is not an insignificant association when we consider life in today's cities.

This earth will be influenced one day by a city of an entirely different character. A holy, heavenly city, a city *having the glory of God,* verse 11.

II.   THE DESCRIPTION OF THE CITY.

1. Its light. *Her light was like unto a stone most precious, even like a jasper stone, clear as crystal,* verse 11. The city bears the image of its maker. *Behold, a throne was set in heaven, and one sat on the throne. And he that sat was to look upon like a jasper,* 4:2-3. As the earth and the heaven today declare the glory of God and His handiwork, even so, but more gloriously, the new Jerusalem will manifest the glory of the Almighty. The jasper stone was Benjamin's stone on the breastplate of the high priest. Benjamin means *son of my right hand.* The glory of the new Jerusalem will be the glory of the One on God's right hand, Jesus the Son of God.

2. Its walls. *And had a wall great and high, and the building of the wall of it was of jasper: and the city was pure gold, like unto clear glass,* verses 12, 18. It was a city of unassailable purity. Its inhabitants were safe from attack and danger, surrounded by walls of jasper, a bright, clear stone, most likely the diamond, the hardest natural material known to man. It was an impregnable place. How secure are those who commit their ways unto the Lord! *Thou wilt keep him in perfect peace, whose mind is stayed on thee: because he trusteth in thee,* Isaiah 26:3.

3. Its foundations. *And the wall of the city had twelve foundations, and in them the names of the twelve apostles of the Lamb. . . . And the foundations of the wall of the city were garnished with all manner of precious stones. The first foundation was jasper; the second, sapphire; the third, a chalcedony; the fourth, an emerald; the fifth, sardonyx; the sixth, sardius; the seventh, chrysolite; the eighth, beryl; the ninth, a topaz; the tenth, a chrysoprasus; the eleventh, a jacinth; the twelfth, an amethyst,* verses 14, 19-20. How precious, how enduring, how glorious are these foundations! If such precious material is used to adorn the foundations, what riches must be employed in the rest of the structure?

These stones correspond largely with the stones that were inserted in the breastplate of the high priest. When we see the twelve tribes of Israel and the twelve apostles linked in the foundations of this city, we are thereby reminded of the foundation upon which our faith is built. *Now therefore ye are no more strangers and foreigners, but fellowcitizens with the saints, and of the household of God; and are built upon the foundation of the apostles and prophets, Jesus Christ himself being the chief corner stone; in whom all the building fitly framed together groweth unto an holy temple in the Lord: in whom ye also are builded together for an habitation of God through the Spirit,* Ephesians 2:19-22. There will be no division between the Old Testament saints and those of the New Testament. They are all members of the church of the firstborn.

4. Its gates. *And had twelve gates, and at the gates twelve angels, and names written thereon, which are the names of the twelve tribes of the children of Israel: on the east three gates; on the north three gates; on the south three gates; and on the west three gates,* verses 12-13. An abundant entrance is afforded to the city as it could be approached from any direction. What a gospel lesson is here presented! No matter where we dwell, we may come in repentance and gain an entrance to the city of salvation. An old evangelist once remarked that as the eagle made its way from the high peaks and the antelope made its way from the plains and the tiger from the shades of the forest, and all were drawn by the power of God to the safety of Noah's ark, so it is with sinners. We all come from different backgrounds and have travelled different paths as, drawn by the Spirit of God, we have made our way to the feet of Christ.

III. THE DIMENSIONS OF THE CITY.

And the city lieth foursquare, and the length is as large as the breadth: and he measured the city with the reed, twelve thousand furlongs. The length and the breadth and the height of it are equal, verse 16. Twelve thousand furlongs equal fifteen hundred miles. This means that the capacity of the city is 1500 miles x 1500 miles x 1500 miles. That amounts to 3,375,000,000 cubic miles. Multiply that figure by 64 and you have the number of allotments equalling one quarter of a cubic mile the city could provide. That gives a total of 216,000,000,000 or two hundred and sixteen billion segments. These calculations are merely for the purpose of showing just how capacious the new Jerusalem will be.

IV. THE DELIGHTS OF THE CITY.

In verse 22, we are given an inside view of the city. Having looked at the foundations, the walls and the gates, we now progress to see something of its interior delightfulness. How many are acquainted only with the exteriors of religious matters! They know nothing of what it means to press into the kingdom. We must never be content with an external acquaintance with the things of God. Let us enter in and be saved.

1. The presence of God. *And I saw no temple therein: for the Lord God Almighty and the Lamb are the temple of it. And the city had no need of the sun, neither of the moon, to shine in it: for the glory of God did lighten it, and the Lamb is the light thereof. And there shall be no night there; and they need no candle, neither light of the sun; for the Lord God giveth them light: and they shall reign for ever and ever,* 21:22-23, 22:5. No temple, no sun.

The symbols are gone and that symbolised is realised. Since the dawn of time, the people of God have received a clearer and clearer revelation of God and His purpose during the different dispensations of His grace. The patriarchal times, the Mosaic period, the New Testament all had their symbols, but in the new Jerusalem we are face to face with the Lord. *For now we see through a glass, darkly; but then face to face: now I know in part; but then shall I know even as also I am known,* 1 Corinthians 13:12.

Such knowledge has been the desire and longing of the church throughout the ages. Job experienced this desire. *For I know that my redeemer liveth, and that he shall stand at the latter day upon the earth: and though after my skin worms destroy this body, yet in my flesh shall I see God: whom I shall see for myself, and mine eyes shall behold, and not another; though my reins be consumed within me,* Job 19:25-27.

Moses likewise longed for the company of God. *And he said, I beseech thee, shew me thy glory,* Exodus 33:18. Philip experienced a like desire. *Philip saith unto him, Lord, shew us the Father, and it sufficeth us,* John 14:8. To see God is the essence of the spiritual desires of the true child of God. Sin shut us out from God. It hid His face from us. The purpose of redemption is to bring us into a living fellowship and communion with God again. That shall prove to be our utter satisfaction. *As for me, I will behold thy face in righteousness: I shall be satisfied, when I awake, with thy likeness,* Psalm 17:15.

The mark of God will be upon the saints. *And they shall see his face; and his name shall be in their foreheads,* 22:4. Your religion leaves its mark upon you. The rebel Cain was marked. Antichrist's followers are marked. So are the people of God. *Now when they saw the boldness of Peter and John, and perceived that they were unlearned and ignorant men, they marvelled; and they took knowledge of them, that they had been with Jesus,* Acts 4:13. All who come before God are marked by that experience. *And when Aaron and all the children of Israel saw Moses, behold, the skin of his face shone; and they were afraid to come nigh him,* Exodus 34:30.

The curse is ended. *And there shall be no more curse: but the throne of God and of the Lamb shall be in it; and his servants shall serve him,* 22:3. There will be no curse within the city. At this time, the curse will still be upon the earth, though greatly curtailed by the workings of God's grace and power through the gospel in an unprecedented way.

But there will be no influence or power of the curse within the city of God. Under the curse the sinner served sin. But in the new Jerusalem God's servants serve Him.

2. The crystal river. *And he shewed me a pure river of water of life, clear as crystal, proceeding out of the throne of God and of the Lamb,* 22:1.

It springs from God's throne. Life has only one fount. It runs in only one channel. The Word, the decrees, the judgments of that throne are the channel in which the water of life is to be found. *It is the spirit that quickeneth; the flesh profiteth nothing: the words that I speak unto you, they are spirit, and they are life. Then Simon Peter answered him, Lord, to whom shall we go? thou hast the words of eternal life,* John 6:63, 68. Stay close to God's throne and drink often of the water that springs up there by kneeling in prayer.

Its waters are pure and clean. They are waters that purify and purge. They are life-giving. In this age, we are used to hearing complaints about pollution in the rivers, lakes and seas. Pure water is an essential for life. There will be no pollution in the new Jerusalem. It will be as Ezekiel the prophet saw in his vision. *Afterward he brought me again unto the door of the house; and, behold, waters issued out from under the threshold of the house eastward: for the forefront of the house stood toward the east, and the waters came down from under from the right side of the house, at the south side of the altar. Then brought he me out of the way of the gate northward, and led me about the way without unto the utter gate by the way that looketh eastward; and, behold, there ran out waters on the right side. . . . Now when I had returned, behold, at the bank of the river were very many trees on the one side and on the other. Then said he unto me, These waters issue out toward the east country, and go down into the desert, and go into the sea: which being brought forth into the sea, the waters shall be healed. And it shall come to pass, that every thing that liveth, which moveth, whithersoever the rivers shall come, shall live: and there shall be a very great multitude of fish, because these waters shall come thither: for they shall be healed; and every thing shall live whither the river cometh,* Ezekiel 47:1-2, 7-9.

There will be abundance of life supplied. It shall supply all the needs of all in the city for it will flow from the eternal fullness of God's throne. Who can exhaust that supply?

3. The tree of life. *In the midst of the street of it, and on either side of the river, was there the tree of life, which bare twelve manner of fruits, and yielded her fruit every month: and the leaves of the tree were for the healing of the nations,* verse 2. Here is the fullness of God's grace ever available to the citizens of this city. Twelve is composed of seven plus five. The number of fullness plus the number of grace. What a variety of fruit is available! The delights of God's glory are beyond our reckoning. It is ever available. There never will be a shortage. Each month is harvest time in the new Jerusalem. Even the leaves provide blessing. The nations of the millennial earth will be ministered to from their healing virtues. Leaves provide shade and shelter. They also oxygenate the air and thus refresh. What refreshment the tree will provide!

There is a tree planted here on earth today that refreshes those who repose under its shade. It too may be called the tree of life. I refer to the cross of Calvary. What fruit is there for the picking! What healing may be enjoyed by those who apply its leaves to the wounds caused by sin! Have you availed yourself of this tree? None will ever see the tree of life in the new Jerusalem but those who have partaken of the fruit of the cross here.

The closing scenes

What wonderful things we have seen and witnessed as we have perused the pages of this wonderful book! We have travelled from the lonely shores of tiny Patmos, the solitary abode of the banished apostle John to the realms of eternal day in the new heavens and the new earth. We have mingled with the angels and the elders around the throne. We have gazed upon the glory of Him Who sits upon the throne.

We have watched the emergence, the dominance for a time, and then the ignominious demise of the false bride of Christ, of the Antichrist and his co-conspirators. We have been amazed and trembled at the terrible things that shall yet come upon this earth. We have rejoiced with all creation at the victory of the Lamb over all His enemies.

We come now to the conclusion of the matter in these verses 6 to 21 of chapter 22, the final chapter.

I.   THE CHARACTER OF THE BOOK OF THE REVELATION.

And he said unto me, These sayings are faithful and true: and the Lord God of the holy prophets sent his angel to shew unto his servants the things which must shortly be done, verse 6.

1. Its veracity affirmed. *These sayings are faithful and true.* What else could they be, since they are the sayings of *Jesus Christ, who is the* *faithful witness?* 1:5. We have been studying *the Revelation of Jesus Christ, which God gave unto him, to shew unto his servants,* 1:1. What else could these sayings be, only faithful and true?

2. Its parity with other Scripture. This book has issued forth from the same source as all other Scripture: *the Lord God of the holy prophets.* If anything, it stands in eminence above other Scripture, since it is the closing word of the canon of Holy Scripture. What is deemed to be a loved one's final words are accorded all the more regard for this very reason. Ought we not to treasure this book in a special way as it is God's final word to His people? How is it then that it is neglected, its study often treated with barely concealed mockery? Brethren, it ought not so to be.

3. The power of its writings. *Blessed is he that keepeth the sayings of the prophecy of this book,* verse 7. The one who keeps the sayings of this book will find himself amongst the angels in heaven. *I am thy fellowservant, and of thy brethren the prophets, and of them which keep the sayings of this book,* verse 9. Obeying this book will not only place you among the angels, but it will give you access to the new Jerusalem and the tree of life which is denied to the wicked, the rejecters of the Word of God. *Blessed are they that do his commandments, that they may have right to the tree of life, and may enter in through the gates into the city. For without are dogs, and sorcerers, and whoremongers, and murderers, and idolaters, and whosoever loveth and maketh a lie,* verses 14-15.

4. The relevance of the book. *And he saith unto me, Seal not the sayings of the prophecy of this book: for the time is at hand,* verse 10. Unlike the book of Daniel, which was sealed up, for it was not for that age, the prophecy of the book of the Revelation is for today, for the time is at hand, that is the time of the fulfilling of these prophecies and also of those other prophecies which refer to the last days. *But thou, O Daniel, shut up the words, and seal the book, even to the time of the end: many shall run to and fro, and knowledge shall be increased. And he said, Go thy way, Daniel: for the words are closed up and sealed till the time of the end,* Daniel 12:4, 9. Let us remember that we are those *upon whom the ends of the world are come,* 1 Corinthians 10:11. This book should be allowed to speak more and more to us all, for *the coming of the Lord draweth nigh,* James 5:8.

5. The sacredness of the book. *And if any man shall take away from the words of the book of this prophecy, God shall take away his part out of the book of life, and out of the holy city, and from the things which are written in this book*, verse 19. God never issues a warning against a non-existent danger. That this book should close with this warning indicates that it is a book that would come under the attack of the denier and discreditor. That in itself is an indication of the value of the book when the enemy directs such fire upon it. Historically, many battles have been fought over the text of this book. Many would dismiss the translation that we have in our Bibles as the concoction of men. They would deride its trustworthiness. In the light of this dire threat, let us be careful not to heed the detractors.

While we may not doubt the inspiration and preservation of this last book of the Bible, we nevertheless may *take away from the words of this prophecy* by disregarding it or declaring it as too difficult to understand and therefore best left alone. This is to *cut off* (the meaning of the words *take away*) or cut out of our considerations the words of this book. Let us not be guilty of such an negligent attitude.

In what high esteem this book is held in heaven that such a threat should be made against any who would deride it! Let us observe the spirit of this verse then, and give to this book the reverent study which is due to it.

II. THE COMMENTS OF THE REDEEMER.

The Saviour speaks directly to John in this closing chapter. That is significant and especially worthy of note.

1. He speaks of His near return. Three times in this closing chapter the Saviour reiterates this truth. *Behold, I come quickly,* verse 7. *And, behold, I come quickly,* verse 12. *Surely I come quickly,* verse 20. The Saviour not only assures us of His return but of His quick return. The word *quickly* means *without delay.* The Saviour will be on time, on schedule. Nothing will cause any delay to His eternal plan.

That this promise should be repeated in such a fashion indicates the awareness the Saviour has of the temptation to listen to the tempter, and doubt His return or allow the second advent to slip to the back of our minds with the resulting carelessness and worldliness that such a thing would promote. There is a danger then. We would be wise to ask ourselves, 'Just how aware and how conscious am I of the Saviour's return?' Do we live and labour in its light? Such a consciousness will save us from the slumbering of which the church generally will be guilty, as depicted in the parable of the wise and foolish virgins, Matthew 25:1-14.

But of the times and the seasons, brethren, ye have no need that I write unto you. For yourselves know perfectly that the day of the Lord so cometh as a thief in the night. For when they shall say, Peace and safety; then sudden destruction cometh upon them, as travail upon a woman with child; and they shall not escape. But ye, brethren, are not in darkness, that that day should overtake you as a thief. Ye are all the children of light, and the children of the day: we are not of the night, nor of darkness. Therefore let us not sleep, as do others; but let us watch and be sober. For they that sleep sleep in the night; and they that be drunken are drunken in the night. But let us, who are of the day, be sober, putting on the breastplate of faith and love; and for an helmet, the hope of salvation. For God hath not appointed us to wrath, but to obtain salvation by our Lord Jesus Christ, who died for us, that, whether we wake or sleep, we should live together with him, 1 Thessalonians 5:1-10.

2. He speaks of His individual rewards. *And, behold, I come quickly; and my reward is with me, to give every man according as his work shall be,* verse 12. Here is incentive to obedience and watchfulness indeed!

Before our work can be rewarded it must be recorded. An assessment of our labours will be undertaken and then an appropriate reward given. The evaluation of our labours will not be based upon volume or quantity but rather on quality. Quality in Christ's eyes means only one thing - faithfulness. *His lord said unto him, Well done, thou good and faithful servant: thou hast been faithful over a few things, I will make thee ruler over many things: enter thou into the joy of thy lord,* Matthew 25:21. The word faithfulness means *trustworthiness* and *reliability*. That is what the Lord is looking for in us and what He will reward.

Have we been faithful to the trust given us? Are we found today still toiling at the task He gave us to do? Will He find us so doing when He comes or calls?

3. He speaks of His glorious titles. *I am Alpha and Omega, the beginning and the end, the first and the last. I am the root and the offspring of David, and the bright and morning star*, verses 13 and 16. He is the Eternal God, the Incarnate God and the only Hope of this dark world, the harbinger of a glorious day to come. Is He known to you, reader, under these titles? Is He the beginning and the end of all your hopes and aspirations?

4. He reiterates gracious invitations. *And the Spirit and the bride say, Come. And let him that heareth say, Come. And let him that is athirst come. And whosoever will, let him take the water of life freely*, verse 17. Could anything be more broad or wide than this invitation to partake of the water of life? Here is a chorus of invitations. It ends in the widest of all invitations. *And whosoever will, let him take the water of life freely*. The water of life may be freely partaken of by any who are willing. The words *whosoever will* refer to those who have a mind to, who are resolved upon coming and drinking. The meaning is summed up in the word *athirst*. That word means simply he that has a thirst, a desire after that which will quench his inner need. A spiritual thirst is a desire for Christ the Saviour, a desire for the cleansing that His blood alone can impart. Where there is that thirst, then let the thirsty one come freely, come without fear or hesitation, and drink of the water of life offered in the gospel. O, happy is the one who feels such a desire after Christ! *Blessed are they which do hunger and thirst after righteousness: for they shall be filled*, Matthew 5:6.

When once we have partaken of the water of life then let us join this chorus of invitations, for does not the Bride, the Lamb's wife, join with the Spirit in issuing the call to come and drink? He that *heareth,* that is obeys the gospel, must take up the cry and say, *Come.*

5. He issues a final promise. *Surely I come quickly*, verse 20. His return is very much on the mind of our Saviour. He spoke of it in His last words to the disciples before His ascension. Now again, He closes the canon of Holy Writ with words of His return. Let our minds reflect that same priority and let us contemplate His return and labour in its light. Holiness, faithfulness and zeal will stamp the people who live in the spirit of this promise.

Remember again the words of Peter: *But the day of the Lord will come as a thief in the night; in the which the heavens shall pass away with a great noise, and the elements shall melt with fervent heat, the earth also and the works that are therein shall be burned up. Seeing then that all these things shall be dissolved, what manner of persons ought ye to be in all holy conversation and godliness, looking for and hasting unto the coming of the day of God, wherein the heavens being on fire shall be dissolved, and the elements shall melt with fervent heat? Nevertheless we, according to his promise, look for new heavens and a new earth, wherein dwelleth righteousness. Wherefore, beloved, seeing that ye look for such things, be diligent that ye may be found of him in peace, without spot, and blameless,* 2 Peter 3:10-14.

There is no doctrine better suited to promote holiness than that which keeps the return of Christ as Judge and King before the eyes of the people. The ever-increasing level of wickedness in society today is a direct result of the decline in preaching such truths. Where the Saviour's return is neglected then there is a breaking out of the spirit of that evil servant whose portrait is given in Matthew 24:44-51. *Therefore be ye also ready: for in such an hour as ye think not the Son of man cometh. Who then is a faithful and wise servant, whom his lord hath made ruler over his household, to give them meat in due season? Blessed is that servant, whom his lord when he cometh shall find so doing. Verily I say unto you, That he shall make him ruler over all his goods. But and if that evil servant shall say in his heart, My lord delayeth his coming; and shall begin to smite his fellowservants, and to eat and drink with the drunken; the lord of that servant shall come in a day when he looketh not for him, and in an hour that he is not aware of, and shall cut him asunder, and appoint him his portion with the hypocrites: there shall be weeping and gnashing of teeth.* Such are the consequences of letting slip these vital truths.

III. THE CRY OF THE RIGHTEOUS.

Even so, come, Lord Jesus, verse 20. Even so, assuredly, quickly, come, Lord Jesus.

Here is the spirit and desire that ought to abide within our hearts. As the father viewed the road down which he hoped his prodigal son would return, so let us view the road down which our beloved Lord shall return.

Here is a reverence we ought ever to show toward the Lord. Seeing what he saw did not make John more familiar with Christ. No! He still speaks in reverence and awe. He addresses Him as *Lord Jesus.* A knowledge of Christ will promote only reverence and respect. Today's language of familiarity, when speaking of the things of God and of God Himself, is alien to those who have seen something of His glory and experienced something of His power and grace.

Here is the prayerfulness that ought to be manifest in our lives. Is this not the prayer that the Saviour gave His disciples to pray? *And he said unto them, When ye pray, say, Our Father which art in heaven, Hallowed be thy name. Thy kingdom come* . . . Luke 11:2.

Here is the embodiment of the spirit wrought within the true believer. *For the grace of God that bringeth salvation hath appeared to all men, teaching us that, denying ungodliness and worldly lusts, we should live soberly, righteously, and godly, in this present world; looking for that blessed hope, and the glorious appearing of the great God and our Saviour Jesus Christ; who gave himself for us, that he might redeem us from all iniquity, and purify unto himself a peculiar people, zealous of good works,* Titus 2:12-14. We are looking for the glorious appearing of the great God and our Saviour Jesus Christ.

It is my prayer that this publication does something to promote just such a spirit amongst His people in these final hours of this age.

We close with the words of benediction which form the final verse of this great book.

The grace of our Lord Jesus Christ be with you all. Amen.

Appendix

Attention to the detail of prophetic description is needful, not only for enabling us to form a correct estimate of the future, but also for guarding against that error which has for ages been the bane of truth, viz., the application of prophecy to wrong objects, and thereby the assertion of its accomplishment long before the real subjects of description have arisen. This error will always be fallen into when the specific facts of Scripture are neglected, and we satisfy ourselves with general resemblances merely, and remote analogies. The modern habit of referring this chapter to the head of the Papal system is a memorable example of this culpable carelessness of interpretation. I say, *modern* habit, because during all the darkness of the first thirteen centuries, and even later, we find a series of writers concurrently asserting that this dispensation at its close is to be marked by the development of a *secular*, despotic, and (as regards the Roman world) universal, system of blasphemous infidelity, and that its head is described in the chapter before us. But in the Protestant conflicts with Popery all this has been forgotten, and prophetic Scripture has been throughout interpreted as if Popery were the one sole subject of its denunciations. That an influential worldly system, like Popery, will have many principles of evil in common with another influential system like Antichristianism, is certain especially when the first has been for ages acting on, and morally forming, some of the leading countries out of which Antichristianism is to arise. Popery is no doubt a chief channel towards Antichrist. But this is no more than can be said of many other worldly systems that are cast in a different mould from Popery, and are in many things antagonistic to it, such as Mahomedanism; the Greek Churches of the East; Socinion, Neologian, and other forms of nominal Protestantism; and Judaism.

Attention to one simple fact is sufficient to prove the futurity of this chapter. It describes the whole Roman world, throughout all its extent, as brought completely under one resistless despotism. Now inasmuch as neither the whole, nor a half, nor a third, nor a tenth of the Roman world is at present under the *sole* control of any one individual, or any one system, (for it is emphatically an hour of the division of power,) it follows that this tyrannic system of successful despotism must yet be future. That it cannot *have* appeared and waned, or passed away, is manifest from this that the power of the beast and of the ten kingdoms who are to be with him, never wane; but, when once they have appeared, will continue in the full vigour and plenitude of power, until they shall suddenly be swept into destruction by the glory of the coming of the King of kings, and Lord of lords.

Again, one of the most remarkable and characteristic features of this chapter is, that it marks the SECULAR as *taking precedence of* the ECCLESIASTICAL power. The second beast, who is to direct the worship of all over whom Antichrist will rule, takes the *secondary* place in the presence of the mighty secular monarch on whom the ten diadems rest. Subordination to the crown, which Popery hates, will be the very principle in which the false prophet who ministers in the presence of Antichrist will glory.

Indeed if we examine the specific descriptions of chapter 13 we shall find that Popery answers to none.

I. The beast with ten horns is distinctively a *secular* power : Popery is distinctively *ecclesiastical*.

II. The beast from the moment of his appearance in this chapter on to the end of his course has his ten horns crowned with *diadems* but Popery has never worn the *diadems* of the Roman world. Even ecclesiastically it has never reigned continuously over the *Western* division of the Roman empire, much less over the East and West together.

III. The beast had seven heads. When did all the ruling systems, commercial, educational, religious, military, political, &c., throughout the whole prophetic earth, fall under the exclusive control of Popery, or of any other system or individual, that yet has been?

IV. The beast when it *first* is seen in this chapter, has all its horns crowned. How could this be said of Popery?

V. The beast when it first appeared had one of its heads *already* wounded. How could this be interpreted of Popery?

VI. The beast was like a leopard. The leopard was the Grecian beast. Has not Popery been distinctively *Latin*, and not *Greek*, both in origin, territory, character, and everything else that can, under this head, be mentioned as a point of contrast? The influence of Popery has been remarkably *obstructed* in the Eastern part of the Roman empire, where Antichrist will be chiefly dominant.

VII. The *whole* prophetic earth is not only subject to, but wonders after and worships the beast. When has the Pope been thus worshipped?

VIII. The beast continues forty and two months. Is this the limit of the duration of Popery?

IX. Another, and he distinctly a minister of *religious* power, exercises the power of the ten-horned beast in his presence. When has the Pope ever had such a minister?

X. All, except those whose names are written in the Lamb's book of life, consent to worship the beast. In other words, every servant of Satan throughout the whole Roman world will unite himself to Antichrist. Have there never been any wicked men who have stood aloof from Popery?

XI. An image of the beast is made, endued with life, caused to speak, and to command that whosoever would not worship it, should neither buy, nor sell, but be put to death, and this throughout the whole extent of the Roman world. Where do we find anything in the history of Popery answering even remotely to this?

- Taken from 'Thoughts on the Apocalypse' by B. W. Newton.

BIOGRAPHICAL INFORMATION ON
BENJAMIN WILLS NEWTON

Benjamin Wills Newton was born in Plymouth on December 12th 1807 and died in Tunbridge Wells on June 26th 1899. He graduated from Oxford University with a First Class in Classics in 1828.

Upon returning to Plymouth, he became one of the early leaders of the Assembly of Brethren and persuaded J. N. Darby to join them. It was from this Assembly that the name 'Plymouth Brethren' is derived.

He pastored the Assembly from 1831 until 1845 when he left after a dispute with Darby over his 'Higher Dispensationalism' and his views on the Second Coming of Christ which included the teaching of an 'any minute rapture' of the Church.

The writings of B. W. Newton contain predictions regarding political and spiritual developments in Europe at the end of the age, based upon his studies of the prophetic Scriptures. He lived in a time of great disunity in Europe following the upheavals of the Napoleonic Wars and the national bitterness that followed in their wake. Humanly speaking, there were no grounds for seeing any future union between nations that had spilled the blood of hundreds of thousands of men in the pursuit of national ambitions. Yet in his writings, particularly in *Prospects of the Ten Kingdoms of the Roman Empire Considered*, he depicted with amazing accuracy the union that we all see developing before our eyes. Such accuracy lends great credibility to his expositions of Holy Scripture regarding the Antichrist. After the passage of some 150 years, his expositions are still very relevant today.

His writings were not innovative. Rather, they were a continuation of the witness that may be found in the writings of some of the early Church Fathers. Among those who shared his views were such men of God as Horatio and Andrew Bonar, Robert Murray McCheyne, C. H. Spurgeon, David Baron, George Muller and S. P. Tregelles.

About the author

IVAN FOSTER is a native of Lisnaskea in Co. Fermanagh, Northern Ireland. Following his conversion in 1964, when he was twenty, he left Ulster Television where he was employed as a news film editor and entered the Theological Hall of the Free Presbyterian Church of Ulster.

He was ordained in April 1968 and installed in Lisbellaw Free Presbyterian Church in his native county. He had been pioneering the work there since its inception in 1967. The congregation later moved to a new church building in nearby Enniskillen.

Under his ministry the congregation became the centre of a number of outreaches. New churches were commenced in Clogher Valley in Co. Tyrone, Coragarry in Co. Monaghan in the Irish Republic, Kesh in Co. Fermanagh and Kilskeery in Co. Tyrone where he is now the minister.

He is Convenor of the Education Board of the General Presbytery of the Free Presbyterian Church of Ulster. He has been involved in the Free Presbyterian Christian Schools movement since its inception with the establishing of the first school in Kilskeery in 1979. His wife, Ann, was the first teacher and principal of the school. It presently has a staff of 4 full-time teachers and 3 part-time teachers and provides a primary to university entrance education.

Ivan Foster edits a widely read monthly Protestant newsheet called *The Burning Bush* and a gospel bulletin, *The Day Star*. He has also authored many pamphlets and leaflets on such topics as abortion, the political situation in Northern Ireland, ecumenism, Christian education and various historical booklets. Amongst the publications he has penned is a brief account of the life of Patrick and the Gospel work in Ireland during the last 1500 years and an examination of the conflicts in Ireland in 1688-1691 entitled, *The Ulster Protestant & the Williamite Wars*.

He has preached on numerous occasions in Canada and the United States of America. He helped pioneer a church in Newtown Square, Pennsylvania - which Rev. John Greer presently pastors - one of the first Free Presbyterian congregations on the American continent.

He and his wife Ann have six children, three boys and three girls, and five grandchildren.